Mathematics
for Key Stage Three

Hundreds of practice questions and worked examples
covering the Key Stage Three Maths curriculum.

Book Two

Contents

Number

Ratio, Proportion and Rates of Change

Section 6 — Ratio and Proportion

Section 7 — Units and Scales

Algebra

Section 8 — Algebraic Expressions

Section 9 — Equations

Section 10 — Formulas

Section 11 — Sequences

Section 12 — Graphs and Equations

Geometry and Measures

Section 13 — Angles and Shapes

Section 14 — Constructions

Section 15 — Perimeter, Area, Volume and Pythagoras

Section 16 — Transformations

Probability

Section 17 — Probability

Statistics

Section 18 — Statistics

Throughout the book, the more challenging questions are marked like this:

Editors:

Katherine Craig, Shaun Harrogate, David Ryan, Sophie Scott, Caley Simpson, Dawn Wright

Contributors:

Alastair Duncombe, Helen Greaves, Simon Greaves, Stephen Green, Philip Hale,
Phil Harvey, Judith Hornigold, Mark Moody, Rosemary Rogers, Jan Walker, Kieran Wardell,
Jeanette Whiteman

Reviewers:

Mona Allen and Alastair Duncombe

Proofreaders:

Alison Palin and Ben Train

Published by CGP

ISBN: 978 1 78294 161 3

www.cgpbooks.co.uk

Clipart from Corel®

Printed by Elanders Ltd, Newcastle upon Tyne.

Based on the classic CGP style created by Richard Parsons.

Section 1 — Numbers and Arithmetic

1.1 Place Value and Ordering Decimals

Place Value in Decimals

Decimal numbers can be split up into columns just like whole numbers.
The columns after the decimal point are called decimal places.

units   tenths   hundredths

4 . 5 9 2   thousandths

Example 1 | **Write down the value of each digit in 4.592 as words and as a number.**

1. Start with the digits before the decimal point: Four units   4.000
2. Then the first column after the decimal point: Five tenths   0.500
3. Then the second column after the decimal point: Nine hundredths   0.090
4. Finally the third column after the decimal point: Two thousandths   0.002

The separate parts should add up to 4.592

Exercise 1

1 For each of the following decimal numbers, write down in words the value of the digit in:

i) the units column   ii) the tenths column   iii) the hundredths column

a) 2.11   b) 4.25   c) 6.94   d) 3.32   e) 16.247

f) 0.78   g) 9.02   h) 92.274   i) 0.053   j) 18.403

2 Write down the value of each digit in the following decimals as a number.

a) 2.3   b) 5.23   c) 1.132   d) 7.62   e) 0.26

f) 8.27   g) 2.810   h) 8.552   i) 4.02   j) 3.389

3 Write down the value of the highlighted digit in the following decimals:

i) as a number   ii) in words

a) 1.02<u>6</u>   b) 1.<u>4</u>2   c) 12.<u>2</u>2   d) 10.1<u>3</u>3   e) 11.49<u>7</u>

f) 0.09<u>7</u>   g) 9<u>1</u>.293   h) 72.2<u>0</u>9   i) 2.<u>9</u>72   j) 102.93<u>1</u>

**A penny (1p) is one hundredth of a pound (£1).
Use this fact to:**

a) write 7p in pounds.

7p is 7 hundredths of a pound,
so put 7 in the hundredths column   7p = **£0.07**

b) write £1.44 in pence.

The whole number of pence is the string
of digits up to the hundredths column.   £1.4<u>4</u> = **144p**

Exercise 2

1 Write each of these amounts in pounds (£).

   a) 9p   **b)** 12p   **c)** 60p   **d)** 199p   **e)** 240p

2 Write each of these amounts in pence (p).

   a) £0.08   **b)** £0.20   **c)** £1.11   **d)** £4.03   **e)** £16.20

3 A gram (g) is one thousandth of a kilogram (kg). Use this fact to write:

   a) 3 g in kg   **b)** 12 g in kg   **c)** 135 g in kg   **d)** 520 g in kg   **e)** 1345 g in kg

   f) 0.007 kg in g   **g)** 0.255 kg in g   **h)** 0.14 kg in g   **i)** 1.772 kg in g   **j)** 0.5 kg in g

4 A centimetre (cm) is one hundredth of a metre (m).
A millimetre (mm) is one tenth of a centimetre.
Use these facts to write 1.635 m in millimetres.

> ### Investigate — Multiplying and Dividing Decimals
>
> Use a calculator to find the answers when you:
>
>   **a)** multiply 1.234 by 10, 100 and 1000.
>
>   **b)** divide 1.234 by 10, 100 and 1000.
>
> What do you notice about the answers? Can you write a rule that would help
> you multiply and divide decimals by 10, 100 and 1000 without a calculator?
>
> Test out your rule on some different decimals.

Ordering Decimals

Example 3 Which decimal is larger, 0.21 or 0.201?

Compare the digits in each number column by column,
moving left to right, until one has a larger digit than the other.

1. Start by comparing the number
   in the units column: 0.21 and 0.201 both have 0 units

2. Compare the digits in the
   tenths column: 0.21 and 0.201 both have 2 tenths

3. Compare the digits in the   0.21 has a 1 in this column.
   hundredths column: 0.201 has a 0 in this column, so is smaller.

4. You can use the < or > signs to
   show which number is bigger.
   The wide end of the symbol
   goes next to the larger number.   **0.21 > 0.201**

Exercise 3

1 Which sign, < or >, should go between the numbers in these pairs?

    a) 0.01, 0.1   **b)** 0.7, 0.75   **c)** 0.8, 0.69   **d)** 0.27, 0.2

    e) 1.9, 1.82   **f)** 2.3, 2.39   **g)** 1.29, 1.09   **h)** 7.6, 7.652

    i) 8.289, 8.28   **j)** 7.19, 7.019   **k)** 1.9, 1.899   **l)** 6.39, 6.4

    m) 6.972, 5.972   **n)** 2.09, 2.1   **o)** 0.294, 0.2939   **p)** 20.92, 20.922

2 Which sign, < or >, should go between the amounts in these pairs?

    a) 21.6 kg, 12.6 kg   **b)** 7 s, 6.98 s   **c)** 1.5 g, 14.7 g   **d)** 0.99 cm, 0.9 cm

    e) 15.42 m, 15.4 m   **f)** 6.01 ml, 6.1 ml   **g)** 0.287 kg, 0.827 kg   **h)** 7.6 mm, 7.59 mm

    i) 11.391 g, 11.39 g   **j)** 14.405 m, 14.5 m   **k)** 2.831 kg, 2.83 kg   **l)** 6.52 cl, 6.6 cl

3 Write down the smaller amount from each of these pairs.

    a) 0.105 m, 0.15 m   **b)** 15.6 g, 15.07 g   **c)** 14.199 cm, 14.99 cm

    d) 11.21 kg, 11.201 kg   **e)** 0.98 ms, 0.975 ms   **f)** 9.774 ml, 9.78 ml

Example 4 Put the following numbers in order from smallest to largest:
0.055, 0.4, 0.0045, 0.04, 0.45, 0.0043

They all have 0 units, so you'll
need to look at the decimal places.

	thousandths	hundredths	tenths
1. Sort the numbers into groups based on where their first non-zero digit starts.	0.00<u>4</u>5	0.0<u>5</u>5	0.<u>4</u>
	0.00<u>4</u>3	0.04	0.<u>4</u>5

2. Then put each group in order by comparing the digits in the columns, going from left to right.

Increasing size ———→

0.0043	0.04	0.40
0.0045	0.055	0.45

3. Write out the full list in order.   **0.0043 0.0045 0.04 0.055 0.4 0.45**

4 Sort these lists of numbers into the correct order from smallest to largest.

a) 0.11, 0.2, 0.1
b) 0.33, 0.143, 0.276
c) 0.067, 0.002, 0.001

d) 1.28, 1.001, 1.281
e) 2.7813, 2.699, 2.785
f) 0.832, 1.554, 1.5641

g) 0.009, 0.0082, 0.02
h) 12.24, 12.279, 12.287
i) 0.023, 0.003, 1.01

j) 18.3931, 17.999, 18.39
k) 3.92, 3.9, 3.9211
l) 6, 6.016, 6.0822, 6.081

5 Sort these lists of numbers into size order, starting with the smallest.

a) 7.04, 6.04, 7.14, 6.004, 7.19
b) 0.102, 0.149, 0.092, 0.028, 0.0961

c) 0.901, 0.905, 0.912, 0.9, 0.9023
d) 1.276, 1.0276, 1.4726, 1.467, 1.4276

e) 3.0009, 3.09, 3.001, 3.002, 3.9
f) 2.119, 2.089, 3.01, 3.119, 2.09

6 By arranging these decimals in size order,
match each one to a position A-F on the number line.

0.5, 0.15, 0.525, 0.955, 0.05, 0.905

7 Copy out the number lines and label them with the decimals in each list.

a) 0.95, 0.59, 0.09, 0.45, 0.9

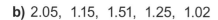

b) 2.05, 1.15, 1.51, 1.25, 1.02

c) 0.875, 0.125, 0.25, 0.6, 0.45

d) 1.035, 1.019, 1.0075, 1.0205, 1.015

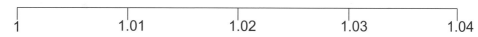

8 **a)** Arrange these positive and negative decimals in size order, from smallest to largest.

−0.1	0.95	0.05	−1.05
−0.5	1.1	−0.05	

b) Use your answer to **a)** to help position each number on a copy of this number line:

9 Write down a decimal that is between:

a) 0.6 and 0.61   **b)** 0.784 and 0.785

c) 0.99 and 1   **d)** 0.08 and 0.081

e) 0.0049 and 0.005   **f)** −0.001 and −0.0011

1.2 Multiplication and Division

Multiplying and Dividing by 10, 100 and 1000

When you're multiplying a number by 10, 100 or 1000, you move each digit a number of places to the left.

× 10	each digit moves one place to the left.
× 100	each digit moves two places to the left.
× 1000	each digit moves three places to the left.

When you're dividing by 10, 100 or 1000, you move each digit a number of places right.

÷ 10	each digit moves one place to the right.
÷ 100	each digit moves two places to the right.
÷ 1000	each digit moves three places to the right.

Always leave the decimal point in place and move the digits around it.

Example 1

a) Multiply 0.89 by 1000.

1. To multiply by **1000**, move each digit **three** places to the **left**, leaving the decimal point where it is.

2. Fill up the places to the left of the decimal point with zeros, and get rid of the zero at the start.

0.89 × 1000 = **890**

---

b) Divide 7.2 by 100.

1. To divide by **100**, move each digit **two** places to the **right**, leaving the decimal point where it is.

2. Fill in the gaps with zeros.

7.2 ÷ 100 = **0.072**

Exercise 1

Don't use a calculator for this exercise.

1 Work out the answers to these multiplications.

    a) 18 × 10   **b)** 26 × 10   **c)** 23 × 10   **d)** 90 × 100

    e) 139 × 100   **f)** 732 × 100   **g)** 27 × 1000   **h)** 931 × 1000

2 Work out the answers to these divisions.

    a) 14 ÷ 10   **b)** 12 ÷ 10   **c)** 164 ÷ 10   **d)** 48 ÷ 100

    e) 2011 ÷ 100   **f)** 9201 ÷ 100   **g)** 1921 ÷ 1000   **h)** 47 ÷ 1000

3 Answer these multiplication questions.

    a) 6.6 × 10   **b)** 28.55 × 10   **c)** 152.8 × 10   **d)** 21.02 × 100

    e) 3.381 × 100   **f)** 0.732 × 100   **g)** 56.21 × 1000   **h)** 0.106 × 1000

4 Work out the answers to these divisions.

    a) 220.2 ÷ 10   **b)** 16.3 ÷ 10   **c)** 10.02 ÷ 10   **d)** 1828.9 ÷ 100

    e) 53.89 ÷ 100   **f)** 0.823 ÷ 100   **g)** 110.03 ÷ 1000   **h)** 12.487 ÷ 1000

5 Work out the missing numbers in each of these calculations.

    a) 424.012 × ..... = 4240.12   **b)** 244.2 ÷ ..... = 2.442   **c)** ..... ÷ 1000 = 0.0013

    d) ..... × 100 = 46 6970   **e)** 8.013 ÷ ..... = 0.08013   **f)** ..... × 1000 = 125 900

6 There are 100 rows of seats in a concert hall.
In each row there are 28 seats. How many seats are there altogether?

7 A box contains 1000 packets of sweets, each weighing 12.5 g.
What do the sweets weigh in total?

8 A 1.4 litre bottle of water is shared equally between 10 cups.
How many litres of water are in each cup?

Section 1 — Numbers and Arithmetic

Written Multiplication

Example 2   Calculate 137 × 18 using the column method.

1. Write one number above the other and make sure the columns line up.
   It's best to put the larger number at the top.

```
    1 3 7
  ×   1 8
```

2. Start by working out 137 × 8.
   Multiply each digit in 137 by 8, working from right to left.
   If the answer is 10 or more, carry the tens digit.

```
    1 3 7
  ×   1 8
  1 0 9 6
     2 5
```

   E.g. 7 × 8 = 56, so write the 6 in the units column and carry the 5. Then 3 × 8 = 24, plus the carried 5 gives 29...

3. Work out 137 × 10 on the next row.
   You can do this by putting a 0 in the right hand column and multiplying each digit in 137 by 1.
   Work from right to left.

```
    1 3 7
  ×   1 8
  1 0 9 6
     2 5
  1 3 7 0
```

4. Add the two rows together to get your final answer.

```
    1 3 7
  ×   1 8
  1 0 9 6
     2 5
+ 1 3 7 0
  2 4 6 6
     1
```

Exercise 2

Do not use a calculator for this exercise.

1   Use the column method of multiplication to do the following questions.

a) 17 × 3   b) 43 × 6   c) 29 × 3   d) 93 × 7

e) 36 × 5   f) 94 × 8   g) 22 × 6   h) 48 × 4

i) 32 × 8   j) 98 × 3   k) 871 × 5   l) 992 × 9

2   Work out the following multiplications.

a) 116 × 30   b) 231 × 70   c) 147 × 23   d) 203 × 86

e) 235 × 32   f) 438 × 23   g) 357 × 21   h) 132 × 52

i) 512 × 21   j) 308 × 27   k) 2624 × 17   l) 7947 × 78

Calculate 2.83 × 61 using the grid method.

1. It's easiest if you ignore the decimal point at first and work out 283 × 61.

	200	80	3
60			
1			

2. Split the numbers up and write them around a grid.

3. Multiply each separate part together in the grid.

	200	80	3
60	200 × 60 = 12000	80 × 60 = 4800	3 × 60 = 180
1	200 × 1 = 200	80 × 1 = 80	3 × 1 = 3

4. Add together the numbers in the grid.

$$\begin{array}{r} 1\,2\,0\,0\,0 \\ 4\,8\,0\,0 \\ 1\,2\,0 \\ 2\,0\,0 \\ 8\,0 \\ +\quad 3 \\ \hline 283 \times 61 = \quad 1\,7_1\,2_1\,0\,3 \end{array}$$

5. Count the number of decimal places from the right in the actual question.

2.<u>83</u> × 61 ← Two decimal places

6. Position the decimal point in the answer to give the same number of decimal places.

2.83 × 61 = **172.03**

---

3 Find the square of the following numbers by multiplying each number by itself.

a) 15   b) 26   c) 78   d) 44

e) 32   f) 81   g) 53   h) 99

4 A school has hired 18 mini buses for a school trip.
Each mini bus can hold 15 children.
How many children can fit in the mini buses altogether?

5 There are 88 keys on a piano. How many keys are there altogether on 12 pianos?

6 Mark plays 16 games of cricket. In each of the first 12 games he scores 56 runs.
In each of the last 4 games he scores 116 runs. How many runs does Mark score in total?

7   Fiona has these 4 number cards:

She arranges them to form two 2 digit numbers.
She multiplies the numbers together. Work out the largest possible answer.

8   Fatima is buying bags of sweets for a party. Each bag contains 296 individual sweets.
If Fatima buys 121 bags of sweets, how many individual sweets does she have?

9   Work out the answers to these questions:

    a) 8.3 × 7   **b)** 9.4 × 9   **c)** 2.2 × 2   **d)** 1.7 × 8

    e) 0.2 × 8   **f)** 3.5 × 3   **g)** 5.8 × 4   **h)** 9.5 × 9

    i) 7.9 × 3   **j)** 2.7 × 5   **k)** 7.2 × 8   **l)** 9.9 × 5

10   Work out the answers to these multiplication questions.

    a) 0.91 × 9   **b)** 3.21 × 8   **c)** 2 × 86.6   **d)** 14.3 × 6

    e) 63.1 × 5   **f)** 4 × 3.21   **g)** 14.9 × 5   **h)** 7.94 × 8

    i) 4.82 × 3   **j)** 8.72 × 9   **k)** 8 × 76.6   **l)** 94.9 × 9

11   Answer the following questions. Show your working.

    a) 1.2 × 31   **b)** 7.6 × 15   **c)** 5.5 × 24   **d)** 6.1 × 86

    e) 1.5 × 74   **f)** 4.8 × 41   **g)** 21 × 3.2   **h)** 6.4 × 39

    i) 7.5 × 33   **j)** 22 × 6.7   **k)** 9.2 × 77   **l)** 78 × 4.8

    m) 38 × 3.3   **n)** 9.4 × 44   **o)** 52 × 9.7   **p)** 7.9 × 93

12   Answer the following questions.

    a) 24.7 × 24   **b)** 83.2 × 20   **c)** 17.4 × 15   **d)** 29 × 24.1

    e) 42.8 × 52   **f)** 15.6 × 42   **g)** 53 × 5.32   **h)** 15.2 × 48

    i) 40.8 × 17   **j)** 66 × 2.73   **k)** 7.29 × 72   **l)** 8.28 × 35

13 Work out the answers to the following questions.

    a) 0.9 × 0.3   **b)** 0.8 × 0.6   **c)** 0.75 × 0.4   **d)** 0.6 × 0.23

    e) 4.2 × 8.9   **f)** 2.8 × 1.4   **g)** 6.6 × 7.9   **h)** 1.9 × 9.1

14 Work out the answers to the following questions.

    a) 11.2 × 4.1   **b)** 2.52 × 5.2   **c)** 4.21 × 1.5   **d)** 2.5 × 1.52

    e) 2.4 × 5.87   **f)** 1.2 × 5.28   **g)** 0.16 × 6.2   **h)** 2.63 × 1.3

15 It costs £4 for 1 kg of cheese. Work out how much it will cost to buy cheese that weighs...

    a) ...1.21 kg   **b)** ...9.72 kg   **c)** ...12.83 kg   **d)** ...16.01 kg

    e) ...8.07 kg   **f)** ...0.08 kg   **g)** ...60.01 kg   **h)** ...28.91 kg

16 Patrick spends £375.83 on his water bill.
If the bill is the same each year, how much will his water bill cost him over 5 years?

17 Samuel is putting bags of flour onto his lorry. He can fit 206 bags of flour on his lorry.
If each bag of flour weighs 20.75 kg, how many kilograms of flour can he fit on his lorry?

18 Caley works 7.5 hours a day, 5 days a week.
How many hours will she work for over the course of 52 weeks?

19 Helen's house is 2.28 miles away from the post office.
In one day, Helen drives to and from the post office 6 times.
How many miles does she drive on that day?

20 Chris is training for a race. He runs 12.33 km every day for 4 weeks.
How far does Chris run altogether?

21 Here are 8 numbers: 0.1   0.3   0.4   0.8   4   6   7   9
Fill in the gaps using these numbers to make the calculations correct.

    a) ..... × ..... = 2.4   **b)** ..... × ..... = 0.9   **c)** ..... × ..... = 1.2   **d)** ..... × ..... = 5.6

Written Division

Example 4   **Work out 897 ÷ 26 using long division.**

1. Set out the division with the number you're dividing inside the 'box', and the number you're dividing by outside.

$$26\overline{)8\ 9\ 7}$$

2. Start by dividing 89 by 26. 26 goes into 89 three times.

    Then subtract 78 from 89 to find your remainder.

$26 \times 3 = 78$

```
        3
26 | 8 9 7
     7 8
     1 1
```

3. Bring down the 7 from above.

```
        3
26 | 8 9 7
     7 8 ↓
     1 1 7
```

4. Divide 117 by 26. 26 goes into 117 four times.

    Then subtract 104 from 117 to find your remainder.

$26 \times 4 = 104$

```
      3 4
26 | 8 9 7
     7 8
     1 1 7
     1 0 4
       1 3
```

5. 26 doesn't go into 13. You could either give your answer as 34 remainder 13, or carry on dividing to give a decimal. To do this, start by putting a decimal point in both the question and the answer.
897 is the same as 897.0, so you can bring down a 0 from above.

```
      3 4.
26 | 8 9 7.0
     7 8
     1 1 7
     1 0 4 ↓
       1 3 0
```

6. 26 goes into 130 exactly five times.

$26 \times 5 = 130$

```
      3 4.5
26 | 8 9 7.0
     7 8
     1 1 7
     1 0 4
       1 3 0
       1 3 0
           0
```

Exercise 3

Don't use a calculator in this exercise.

1 Work out the answers to these divisions.

    a) 338 ÷ 13   **b)** 252 ÷ 21   **c)** 408 ÷ 12   **d)** 615 ÷ 15

    e) 506 ÷ 23   **f)** 756 ÷ 63   **g)** 704 ÷ 16   **h)** 759 ÷ 11

    i) 925 ÷ 25   **j)** 855 ÷ 19   **k)** 896 ÷ 14   **l)** 988 ÷ 13

2 6248 children are divided equally into 4 houses. How many children are in each house?

3 Work out the answers to these divisions. Give your answers as decimals.

    a) 366 ÷ 30   **b)** 558 ÷ 15   **c)** 576 ÷ 40   **d)** 505 ÷ 25

    e) 888 ÷ 20   **f)** 536 ÷ 16   **g)** 901 ÷ 34   **h)** 657 ÷ 18

    i) 637 ÷ 26   **j)** 948 ÷ 40   **k)** 871 ÷ 26   **l)** 737 ÷ 22

4 A circus does 16 performances. It sells 2240 tickets in total.
How many people attend each performance if it's the same each time?

5 Give answers to the following divisions as whole numbers with remainders.

    a) 6720 ÷ 17   **b)** 7732 ÷ 31   **c)** 6612 ÷ 47   **d)** 4191 ÷ 22

    e) 6631 ÷ 18   **f)** 1046 ÷ 11   **g)** 7843 ÷ 36   **h)** 6464 ÷ 29

6 For each of these annual salaries, work out the salary per week.

    a) £22 620   **b)** £28 678   **c)** £15 444   **d)** £42 770

7 Large boxes can hold 56 books, and small boxes can hold 32 books.
Carol packs 2296 books into large boxes and 1760 books into small boxes.
If she completely fills every box, how many boxes does she fill altogether?

8 Jeff has 26 flower beds in his garden and 39 bags of compost.
Each bag of compost weighs 69 kg. If Jeff shares all of the compost equally between all
of the flower beds, how many kilograms of compost will go on each flower bed?

Example 5 Work out 95.62 ÷ 7 without a calculator.

1. Set out the division as usual. Include the decimal
   point in both the question and the answer.

   $7\overline{)9\ 5.6\ 2}$

2. Carry the division out exactly like you would with a
   whole number, using either short or long division.

   $\dfrac{1\ \ .\ \ }{7\overline{)9\,^25.6\ 2}}$

   $\dfrac{1\ 3.\ \ }{7\overline{)9\,^25.^46\ 2}}$

   $\dfrac{1\ 3.6}{7\overline{)9\,^25.^46\,^42}}$

   $\dfrac{\mathbf{1\ 3.6\ 6}}{7\overline{)9\,^25.^46\,^42}}$

Exercise 4

Don't use a calculator for this exercise.

1   Complete the following divisions.

   a) 7.8 ÷ 6   **b)** 27.3 ÷ 7   **c)** 44.8 ÷ 7   **d)** 80.1 ÷ 9

   e) 97.5 ÷ 5   **f)** 76.8 ÷ 8   **g)** 60.8 ÷ 4   **h)** 44.8 ÷ 8

2   Work out the answers to the following divisions.

   a) 72.16 ÷ 8   **b)** 56.52 ÷ 9   **c)** 39.45 ÷ 5   **d)** 85.32 ÷ 6

   e) 79.31 ÷ 7   **f)** 97.28 ÷ 4   **g)** 96.16 ÷ 8   **h)** 77.44 ÷ 4

3   **a)** Work out 680 ÷ 170   **b)** Work out 680 ÷ 17

   c) Use your answers to **a)** and **b)** to work out: **i)** 680 ÷ 1.7   **ii)** 680 ÷ 0.17

> ## Investigate — Remainders
>
> *12 ÷ 10 has a remainder of 2. So does 22 ÷ 10.*
> *Both 12 and 22 can be written as 2(mod10).*
>
>   **a)** Find more numbers that have a remainder of **2** when you divide them by **10**.
>   Can you spot any patterns in them?
>
>   **b)** Now find numbers that have a remainder of **2** when you divide them by **11**.
>   These can all be written as 2(mod11).
>   Are the patterns the same as before? Are there any new patterns?
>
>   **c)** Try finding some 2(mod12) numbers, or 3(mod11) numbers.

1.3 Calculations with Negative Numbers

Negative Numbers on the Number Line

Example 1 Use the number line to work out:

a) −5 + 6

1. Start at −5.
2. Count 6 places up (right).
3. You finish at 1, so: −5 + 6 = **1**

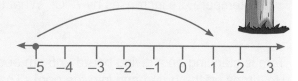

b) 3 − 7

1. Start at 3.
2. Count 7 places down (left).
3. You finish at −4, so: 3 − 7 = **−4**

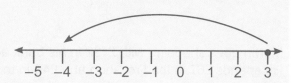

Exercise 1

Don't use a calculator for this exercise.

1 Work out the following, using a number line if you need to.

a) −4 + 7	**b)** −2 + 11	**c)** −3 + 14	**d)** −17 + 11
e) −12 + 8	**f)** −7 + 25	**g)** −16 + 23	**h)** −28 + 17
i) −51 + 60	**j)** −43 + 24	**k)** −72 + 14	**l)** −44 + 75

2 Work out the answers to these subtraction questions.

a) 4 − 7	**b)** 2 − 9	**c)** 5 − 17	**d)** 16 − 20
e) 10 − 12	**f)** 13 − 28	**g)** 15 − 31	**h)** 49 − 56

3 Work out the answers to these subtraction questions.

a) −4 − 7	**b)** −5 − 10	**c)** −7 − 3	**d)** −11 − 9
e) −3 − 12	**f)** −16 − 11	**g)** −25 − 12	**h)** −32 − 16

4 Find the missing numbers in each of these calculations.

a) −15 + ... = −7   **b)** −2 − ..... = −15   **c)** ..... − 9 = −11   **d)** ..... + 14 = 3

5 Use a number line to help you to answer this question.

a) It was –8 °C on Monday. It was 11 °C warmer on Friday.
What was the temperature on Friday?

b) In Ulverly it is 12 °C. In Trentown it is –2 °C.
How much warmer is it in Ulverly than Trentown?

c) The temperature in Rutforth is –10 °C in January. Each month, until June,
the temperature increases by 7 °C. What is the temperature in June?

6 Tom is standing on a diving board 205 cm above the surface of a swimming pool.
He jumps off the board and into the pool. The total distance that he falls is 317 cm.
How many centimetres under the water was Tom at the deepest point?

7 Martin goes shopping with £132 in his bank account. He goes to three different shops.
He spends £67 in the first shop and £44 in the second shop. He ends up £12 overdrawn.
How much did he spend in the third shop?

8 Frank goes on a walk. He starts at 6 metres below sea level.
He then climbs 52 metres, before dropping 77 metres.
How many metres above or below sea level does Frank end up?

9 During June, the temperature at the South Pole is –81 °F.
The temperature in Jamaica is 97 °F.

a) How much hotter is Jamaica than the South Pole in June?

b) The temperature at the South Pole is 63 °F hotter in January than in June.
The temperature in Jamaica is 15 °F colder in January than in June.
How much hotter is Jamaica than the South Pole in January?

Adding and Subtracting Negative Numbers

Adding a <u>negative</u> number is the same as subtracting a <u>positive</u> number.

Subtracting a negative number is the same as adding a positive number.

Look at the signs next to each other in a calculation to work out what you need to do:

+ next to –	means subtract
– next to –	means add

Example 2   Work out the answers to the following calculations.

a) 7 + (−4)   1. There is a + and a − sign next to each other.   7 + (−4)

2. So replace them with one − sign.   7 − 4

3. Work out the answer.   7 − 4 = **3**

b) 2 − (−7)   1. There are two − signs next to each other.   2 − (−7)

2. So replace them with one + sign.   2 + 7

3. Work out the answer.   2 + 7 = **9**

Exercise 2

Don't use a calculator for this exercise.

1   Answer these questions.

    a) 6 + (−3)   **b)** 14 + (−10)   **c)** 8 + (−9)   **d)** 13 + (−7)

    e) 16 + (−21)   **f)** 29 + (−14)   **g)** 44 + (−11)   **h)** 18 + (−35)

    i) 66 + (−20)   **j)** 43 + (−51)   **k)** 78 + (−43)   **l)** 20 + (−58)

2   Answer these questions.

    a) 5 − (−7)   **b)** (−6) − (−4)   **c)** 3 − (−14)   **d)** (−13) − (−9)

    e) 22 − (−17)   **f)** 8 − (−31)   **g)** (−37) − (−21)   **h)** 64 − (−33)

    i) (−35) − (−18)   **j)** 19 − (−77)   **k)** (−50) − (−27)   **l)** 15 − (−83)

3   Answer these questions.

    a) 13 − (−22)   **b)** 7 + (−36)   **c)** (−11) − (−49)   **d)** 63 + (−15)

    e) (−51) − (−17)   **f)** (−11) − (−33)   **g)** 38 + (−19)   **h)** (−22) + (−43)

    i) (−25) − (−68)   **j)** (−89) − (−17)   **k)** (−40) + (−27)   **l)** 29 − (−72)

4   Work out the answers to the following questions.

    a) (−19) − (−12) + (−5)   **b)** 21 + (−12) − (−39)   **c)** (−8) − (−35) − (−54)

    d) 45 + (−23) − (−11)   **e)** 54 − (−12) + (−39)   **f)** (−52) + (−33) − (−80)

    g) 11 + (−58) − (−23)   **h)** 47 − (−18) + (−82)   **i)** (−11) + (−71) + (−14)

Multiplying and Dividing Negatives

A <u>multiplication</u> or <u>division</u> with one <u>positive</u> and one <u>negative</u> number will have a negative (–ve) answer.

If both numbers are negative, the answer will be positive (+ve).

> \+ and – means a negative answer
>
> – and – means a positive answer

Example 3 **Work out the answers to the following calculations.**

a) 4 × (–6)

   1. Ignore the signs and work out the answer to the number bit.   4 × 6 = 24

   2. Work out the sign. A positive and a negative number give a negative answer.   4 × (–6) = **–24**

b) (–49) ÷ (–7)

   1. Ignore the signs and work out the answer to the number bit.   49 ÷ 7 = 7

   2. Work out the sign. Two negative numbers give a positive answer.   (–49) ÷ (–7) = **7**

Exercise 3

Don't use a calculator for this exercise.

1 Answer these multiplication questions.

   a) 3 × (–2)   **b)** (–4) × (–11)   **c)** (–5) × 3   **d)** (–2) × (–11)

   e) (–6) × 5   **f)** (–12) × 2   **g)** (–11) × 6   **h)** (–7) × (–8)

   i) 20 × (–10)   **j)** (–12) × (–12)   **k)** (–3) × 33   **l)** (–10) × (–24)

2 Answer these division questions.

   a) 16 ÷ (–8)   **b)** 49 ÷ (–7)   **c)** 80 ÷ (–8)   **d)** (–72) ÷ 9

   e) (–54) ÷ (–6)   **f)** (–55) ÷ (–11)   **g)** (–132) ÷ 11   **h)** 32 ÷ (–8)

   i) 60 ÷ (–12)   **j)** (–180) ÷ (–20)   **k)** 76 ÷ (–4)   **l)** (–96) ÷ 24

3 Answer these questions.

a) $10 \times (-4)$ b) $(-72) \div (-8)$ c) $(-15) \times 7$ d) $(-12) \times (-14)$

e) $(-22) \times 3$ f) $168 \div (-8)$ g) $(-98) \div 14$ h) $32 \div (-4)$

i) $(-189) \div (-9)$ j) $(-8) \times (-13)$ k) $(-50) \div 2$ l) $(-11) \times 14$

m) $333 \div (-3)$ n) $(-112) \div (-7)$ o) $88 \div (-4)$ p) $110 \div (-11)$

4 For each of these calculations, replace the star with the correct number.

a) $12 \times \bigstar = -12$ b) $\bigstar \times 11 = -99$ c) $(-15) \times -8 = \bigstar$

d) $(-14) \times \bigstar = -56$ e) $(-9) \times \bigstar = 81$ f) $\bigstar \times (-40) = -2800$

5 For each of these calculations, replace the star with the correct number.

a) $\bigstar \div 6 = -6$ b) $\bigstar \div -7 = 11$ c) $(-40) \div (-5) = \bigstar$

d) $(-90) \div \bigstar = 3$ e) $(-65) \div \bigstar = -5$ f) $\bigstar \div 14 = -2$

6 Answer these questions.

a) $9 \times (-8) \div 2$ b) $(-11) \times (-8) \div 4$ c) $(-8) \times 9 \div (-3)$

d) $(-144) \div (-12) \times (-7)$ e) $81 \div (-3) \times (-7)$ f) $96 \div (-6) \times 5$

Investigate — Negative Square Numbers

A square number is a number multiplied by itself.
E.g. $1 = 1 \times 1 = 1^2$, $4 = 2 \times 2 = 2^2$, $9 = 3 \times 3 = 3^2$.

a) Write down the squares of the numbers from 1 to 5.

b) What happens when you square a negative number?
Start by working out: $(-1)^2 = (-1) \times (-1)$, $(-2)^2 = (-2) \times (-2)$
and so on from (-1) to (-5).

c) Experiment by finding the squares of bigger positive and negative numbers.

d) Can you find any numbers that give negative squares?
Use your findings to explain why.

e) Investigate whether the same applies to cubes (e.g. $8 = 2 \times 2 \times 2 = 2^3$).

1.4 Calculators, BODMAS and Checking

BODMAS

Operations in a calculation are things like addition, subtraction, multiplication and division. The order you do these things in is really important.

BODMAS tells you the order you should do things in a calculation:

BRACKETS ⟵————————— Work out things in **brackets** first.

OTHER ⟵————————— Then do other things like **squaring** and **powers**.

DIVISION
MULTIPLICATION ⟵————————— **Divide/Multiply** groups of numbers working from left to right.

ADDITION
SUBTRACTION ⟵————————— **Add/Subtract** groups of numbers working from left to right.

Example 1 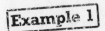 **Work out the answers to these questions.**

a) 6 + 7 × 12 – 11

1. This calculation involves addition, multiplication and subtraction.

2. BODMAS tells us that the **multiplication** needs to be done first.

    $7 × 12 = 84$
    $6 + 84 – 11$

3. Working from left to right, the **addition** needs to be done next.

    $6 + 84 = 90$

4. Then finally the **subtraction**.

    $90 – 11 = \mathbf{79}$

b) 2 × (11 + 15) – 7

1. This calculation involves multiplication, brackets, addition and subtraction.

2. BODMAS tells us that the things inside the **brackets** need to be done first.

    $(11 + 15) = 26$
    $2 × 26 – 7$

3. The two operations left are multiplication and subtraction. The **multiplication** needs to be done next.

    $2 × 26 = 52$

4. Then finally the **subtraction**.

    $52 – 7 = \mathbf{45}$

Exercise 1

Don't use a calculator for this exercise.

1 Use BODMAS to answer these questions.

a) $6 + 3 \times 11$ **b)** $8 \div 4 + 12$ **c)** $10 \times 8 + 12$ **d)** $13 - 9 + 17$

e) $14 + 12 \div 3$ **f)** $20 \times 8 \div 5$ **g)** $11 \times 6 + 12$ **h)** $49 \div 7 + 31$

i) $100 - 7 \times 11$ **j)** $22 + 60 \div 5$ **k)** $16 \div 4 \times 11$ **l)** $17 + 81 \div 9$

2 Use BODMAS to answer these questions.

a) $2 \times (8 - 7)$ **b)** $16 \div (8 - 4)$ **c)** $10 \times (36 - 3)$ **d)** $(27 - 13) \times 6$

e) $(8 + 15) \times 3$ **f)** $121 \div (32 - 21)$ **g)** $(15 + 6) \div 3$ **h)** $(9 + 11) \times 4$

i) $10 \times (18 - 6)$ **j)** $88 \div (3 + 1)$ **k)** $(70 - 18) \div 4$ **l)** $100 \div (99 - 74)$

3 Use BODMAS to answer these questions.

a) $8 + 11 \times 12 - 9$ **b)** $15 \times 4 - 18 \div 9$ **c)** $32 + 19 - 2 \times 8$

d) $50 - 14 \times 3 + 9$ **e)** $8 \times 12 \div 3 + 6$ **f)** $90 \div 5 + 6 \times 3$

g) $12 + 10 \times 9 \div 6$ **h)** $8 \times 6 + 7 \times 3$ **i)** $66 \div 6 - 10 + 29$

4 Use BODMAS to answer these questions.

a) $12 \times (11 - 8) \div 9$ **b)** $16 - 39 \div (10 + 3)$ **c)** $15 \div 3 \times (11 - 4)$

d) $(10 + 21) + 9 \times 4$ **e)** $(22 - 8) \times 4 + 17$ **f)** $9 \times (16 - 8) \div 3$

g) $15 \times 9 - (22 + 17)$ **h)** $7 \times (3 + 4) - 6$ **i)** $(27 + 33) - 92 \div 4$

5 Use BODMAS to answer these questions.

a) $(12 - 8) \times (16 + 9)$ **b)** $(44 + 12) \div (23 - 15)$ **c)** $(12 \div 6) + (45 - 21)$

d) $(30 + 4) \div (21 - 19)$ **e)** $(24 + 11) - (16 - 8)$ **f)** $(62 + 8) + (25 - 17)$

g) 4×9^2 **h)** $10^2 \div 5$ **i)** $(5 + 6)^2$

j) $(30 - 24)^2$ **k)** $(8 + 2 \times 4)^2$ **l)** $(12 - 5)^2 + 11^2$

m) $15 - (20 \div 10)^2$ **n)** $(9 \times 2 - 10)^2$ **o)** $(3^2 + 2^2) + (3 + 2)^2$

Using Calculators

When doing calculations with multiple operations, you'll need to use these buttons on your calculator:

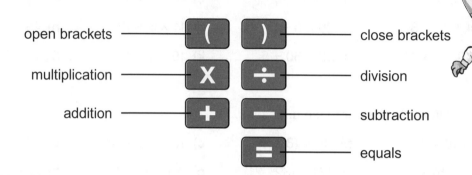

open brackets ———— ( ) ———— close brackets

multiplication ———— X ÷ ———— division

addition ———— + — ———— subtraction

= ———— equals

You can tell the calculator what order to do the operations in by putting brackets into the calculation. Calculators will work out the things in brackets first.

Calculations expressed as fractions can be written as: (top line) ÷ (bottom line).

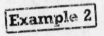 **Example 2** **Add brackets to the following calculation so it is correct when worked out on a calculator: 7 + 8 × 3 = 45**

1. There are two possible places for the brackets to go.

   $7 + (8 \times 3)$ or $(7 + 8) \times 3$

2. Enter each option in on your calculator to see which gives you the right answer.

   $7 + (8 \times 3) = 31$

   $(7 + 8) \times 3 = 45$

Example 3 **Work out** $\dfrac{12 \times 4 - 3}{25 \div 5}$ **using your calculator.**

1. You need to divide the top line by the bottom line.

2. The top line needs to be worked out separately from the bottom line, so put brackets around each part when you enter it into your calculator.

   $(12 \times 4 - 3) \div (25 \div 5)$

   $= 9$

Exercise 2

1 Add brackets to these calculations so they're correct.
Check your answers on a calculator.

a) $32 \div 4 \times 2 = 4$

b) $120 \div 4 + 16 = 6$

c) $13 \times 15 - 12 = 39$

d) $8 - 5 \times 20 = 60$

e) $10 + 5 \times 9 = 135$

f) $12 + 6 \times 3 = 54$

g) $7 + 132 \div 11 = 19$

h) $52 \div 2 + 2 = 13$

i) $44 + 10 \div 6 = 9$

j) $2 + 7 \times 9 = 81$

k) $60 \times 3 + 11 = 840$

l) $15 - 9 \times 22 = 132$

m) $16 + 2 \times 3 = 54$

n) $133 - 5 \div 4 = 32$

o) $18 + 5 \times 6 = 138$

2 Write each fraction as a division with brackets as you would enter them on a calculator.
Then use your calculator to work out the answer.

a) $\dfrac{12 + 13}{7 - 2}$

b) $\dfrac{2 \times 8 + 2}{3 \times 3}$

c) $\dfrac{12 \times 11 - 2}{76 - 66}$

d) $\dfrac{17 - 3 + 22}{3 \times 2}$

e) $\dfrac{5 \times 3 + 17}{16 \div 2}$

f) $\dfrac{8 \times 2 + 64}{43 - 38}$

g) $\dfrac{51 + 9 + 100}{88 \div 11}$

h) $\dfrac{11 \times 2 \times 5}{27 - 16}$

i) $\dfrac{240 \div 8 \div 5}{96 \div 48}$

3 Add one pair of brackets to each of these calculations so
they're correct. Use your calculator to check each one.

a) $1 + 6 \times 2 \times 8 = 112$

b) $18 \div 2 \times 7 + 3 = 90$

c) $21 - 8 + 3 \times 12 = 120$

d) $8 \times 5 + 6 - 20 = 68$

e) $11 + 14 \div 5 \times 2 = 10$

f) $2 \times 6 \times 17 - 11 = 72$

g) $9 \times 12 \div 4 + 14 = 6$

h) $88 \div 4 + 4 - 3 = 8$

i) $15 + 10 \times 7 \div 5 = 35$

j) $12 \times 8 + 90 \div 3 = 126$

4 Write these calculations out as a division with brackets.
Then work out the answer by entering this into your calculator.

a) $\dfrac{18 + (7 \times 2)}{56 \div (3 + 4)}$

b) $\dfrac{(12 + 12) \times 4}{(8 \times 6) \div 24}$

c) $\dfrac{36 \div (13 - 4)}{10 - (18 \div 3)}$

d) $\dfrac{8 \times (11 + 1)}{(6 \times 9) \div 18}$

e) $\dfrac{(5 + 7) \times 10}{(9 + 1) \times 2}$

f) $\dfrac{(9 + 12) \times 10}{(6 \times 5) \div 15}$

5 Write the following word problems in numbers, as you would enter them into a calculator. Then use a calculator to work out the answer.
Remember to include brackets.

a) Divide the product of 8 and 3 by the difference between 16 and 14.

b) Add the difference between 29 and 10 to the result of dividing 86 by 2.

c) Multiply together the result of adding 9 and 6, to the difference between 14 and 7.

d) Subtract the result of adding together 2 and 18 from the product of 6, 10 and 3.

Investigate — Using Calculators

Simple calculators work through calculations moving from left to right.
Scientific calculators are a bit smarter and work things out using BODMAS.

a) Get a scientific calculator and a non-scientific calculator.
Enter the following on both: 9 + 11 × 16.
Do you get the same answer on both calculators? If not, why not?

b) Now enter 8 × 7 + 11. Do you get the same answer on both calculators?
Can you explain why you get the answers you do?

c) Think of a rule to explain when the calculators will give the same answer, and when they'll give different answers.

d) Investigate with more calculations containing different operations and numbers. For each one, predict if the calculators will give the same answer.

Checking Answers using Inverses

One way to check your answers is to do the inverse calculation.
Inverse is just another word for opposite.

Addition and **subtraction** are opposites.

If you start off with a number, add any number to it and then subtract the same number from the answer, you'll end up with your original number.

Multiplying and **dividing** are opposites.

If you start off with a number, multiply it by a number that isn't zero, and then divide the answer by the same number, you'll end up with your original number.

Example 4	What inverse calculation could you do to check that 322 ÷ 14 = 23?

1. First identify what sort of calculation the question is.
   This is a **division**.

   $322 ⊕ 14 = 23$

2. **Multiplication** is the opposite of **division**.
   If you multiply your answer by the number you divided
   by, you should get the number you started with.

   23 × 14 = 322

   (You could also check that 322 ÷ 23 = 14.)

Exercise 3

1 Write an inverse calculation to check the following.

   a) 56 + 88 = 144   **b)** 14 + 77 = 91   **c)** 97 – 61 = 36

   d) 66 – 13 = 53   **e)** 119 – 54 = 65   **f)** 24 + 94 = 118

   g) 152 – 65 = 87   **h)** 27 + 94 = 121   **i)** 188 – 99 = 89

2 Write an inverse calculation for each of the following.

   a) 5 × 4 = 20   **b)** 19 × 4 = 76   **c)** 144 ÷ 6 = 24

   d) 3 × 55 = 165   **e)** 180 ÷ 5 = 36   **f)** 19 × 11 = 209

   g) 12 × 43 = 516   **h)** 252 ÷ 18 = 14   **i)** 612 ÷ 12 = 51

3 Write down the answers to these calculations by simplifying the questions.

   a) 8 × 7 ÷ 8   **b)** 346 + 324 – 346   **c)** 18 + 67 – 67

   d) 90 ÷ 18 × 18   **e)** 46 ÷ 9 × 9 × 2   **f)** 17 + 63 + 12 – 63

   g) 100 ÷ 4 × 4 + 3   **h)** 121 – 18 + 44 + 18   **i)** 99 ÷ 3 × 3 × 6

4 Use an inverse calculation to check these calculations.
   Put a tick by the ones that are correct, and a cross by the ones that are incorrect.

   a) 167 + 774 = 930   **b)** 528 ÷ 22 = 24   **c)** 32 × 31 = 922

   d) 693 ÷ 11 = 69   **e)** 972 – 555 = 427   **f)** 664 + 285 = 949

   g) 663 ÷ 17 = 39   **h)** 19 × 46 = 874   **i)** 537 – 493 = 45

Section 2 — Approximations

2.1 Rounding

Decimal Places

Numbers are sometimes <u>approximated</u> or <u>rounded</u> to make them easier to work with.

You can round to different numbers of <u>decimal places</u> (d.p.).

For example, a number like 4.728 could be rounded: to one decimal place (= 4.7)

to two decimal places (= 4.73)

Example 1 Round 6.8357 to...

a) ... one decimal place.

1. Look at the digit in the second decimal place.

2. It's less than 5, so round down.

a) 6.8**3**57
round down to **6.8**

b) ... two decimal places.

1. Look at the digit in the third decimal place.

2. It's 5, so round up.

b) 6.83**5**7
round up to **6.84**

c) ... three decimal places.

1. Look at the digit in the fourth decimal place.

2. It's more than 5, so round up.

c) 6.835**7**
round up to **6.836**

Exercise 1

1 Round each of these numbers to one decimal place:

a) 3.42   b) 6.83   c) 5.26   d) 8.91   e) 7.59

f) 0.62   g) 0.08   h) 0.04   i) 0.37   j) 0.078

k) 21.25   l) 12.38   m) 2.869   n) 14.217   o) 0.99

2 Write down all the numbers from the box that round to 2.8 to the nearest tenth.

2.87	2.83	2.91	2.78	2.75
2.765	2.699	2.827	2.748	2.772

3 Write down four numbers that round to 9.3 to one decimal place.

4 Round the following numbers to 2 decimal places.

a) 2.784

b) 4.628

c) 9.292

d) 0.247

e) 0.006

f) 1.065

g) 12.3605

h) 2.0345

i) 4.92862

j) 0.9949

k) 6.495

l) 7.999

5 Write down all the numbers from the box that round to 1.38 to the nearest hundredth.

1.369	1.378	1.384	1.338	1.388
1.395	1.3658	1.3862	1.3821	1.3846

6 Round the following numbers to 3 decimal places.

a) 7.2184

b) 5.0436

c) 2.6648

d) 8.5045

e) 0.0465

f) 1.04078

g) 2.7005

h) 0.1025

i) 4.32946

j) 7.980621

k) 1.0098

l) 3.999898

7 Round the following numbers to the number of decimal places specified.

a) 2.818 — to 1 d.p.

b) 6.293 — to 2 d.p.

c) 11.92945 — to 3 d.p.

d) 0.6023 — to 2 d.p.

e) 5.27652 — to 3 d.p.

f) 123.465 — to 1 d.p.

g) 27.6254 — to 2 d.p.

h) 0.04078 — to 3 d.p.

i) 29.994 — to 1 d.p.

8 Tom is 1.682 m tall. Round his height to two decimal places.

9 The mass of a walrus is 1.458 tonnes.
Round this mass to one decimal place.

10 The nearest recycling centre is 2.9998 km from Rob's house.
Round this distance to three decimal places.

11 A number, when rounded to one decimal place, equals 2.4.
What is the smallest possible value of this number?

Significant Figures

You can also round to different numbers of <u>significant figures</u> (s.f.).

For example, 126 409 could be rounded: to one significant figure (= 100 000)

to two significant figures (= 130 000)

to three significant figures (= 126 000)

Zeros at the start of a decimal do not count as significant figures.
The first significant figure is the first non-zero digit — so 0.00152 to 1 s.f. is 0.002.

Example 2   **Round 40.621 to the number of significant figures specified.**

a) Round 40.621 to one significant figure.

1. Look at the second digit.

2. It's less than 5, so round down.

a) 40.621
round down to **40**

b) Round 40.621 to two significant figures.

1. Look at the third digit.

2. It's greater than 5, so round up.

b) 40.621
round up to **41**

c) Round 40.621 to three significant figures.

1. Look at the fourth digit.

2. It's less than 5, so round down.

c) 40.621
round down to **40.6**

Exercise 2

1   Round the following numbers to one significant figure.

a) 523	**b)** 27	**c)** 345	**d)** 0.684
e) 32	**f)** 1024	**g)** 0.00257	**h)** 9399
i) 11 459	**j)** 2.077	**k)** 156 092	**l)** 330 763

2   Round the following numbers to two significant figures.

a) 568	**b)** 932	**c)** 0.0629	**d)** 6566
e) 3478	**f)** 0.2149	**g)** 25 693	**h)** 12 371
i) 78 452	**j)** 130.89	**k)** 5.672	**l)** 0.002059

3 Round the following numbers to three significant figures.

    a) 9281   **b)** 3736   **c)** 123.59   **d)** 13.892

    e) 0.005078   **f)** 75 614   **g)** 67 839   **h)** 0.03826

    i) 176 378   **j)** 576 514   **k)** 738.094   **l)** 2.0076

4 Round the following numbers to the number of significant figures (s.f.) indicated.

    a) 0.0829 — to 1 s.f.   **b)** 37.62 — to 2 s.f.   **c)** 85.729 — to 3 s.f.

    d) 4782 — to 2 s.f.   **e)** 3929 — to 1 s.f.   **f)** 274.65 — to 3 s.f.

    g) 0.00715 — to 2 s.f.   **h)** 438 967 — to 3 s.f.   **i)** 96 849 — to 1 s.f.

5 A racing snail has a top speed of 28 mm/s.
Round this speed to one significant figure.

6 In one year, 164 578 people visited a theme park.
Round this number to two significant figures.

7 The mass of a rock is 22.784 kg. Round this mass to three significant figures.

8 The area of a pond is 0.0004999 km². Round this area to two significant figures.

Investigate — Significant Figures

The number of people at a concert has been rounded to 20 000. What are the smallest and largest numbers of people if this has been rounded to:

a) 1 significant figure,   **b)** 2 significant figures,   **c)** 3 significant figures?

What do you notice about your answers?

d) Different levels of accuracy are needed for different things.
Suggest what level of accuracy you would round these to:

    i) Olympic 100 m race times   **ii)** distances travelled to school

    iii) measurements at a building site   **iv)** the heights of people in your class.

2.2 Estimating

Estimating Answers by Rounding

You can <u>estimate</u> the answer to a calculation by <u>rounding</u> numbers in the calculation to numbers that are easier to use — usually by rounding to one <u>significant figure</u>.

Even though the answer isn't exactly right, it can still be useful.

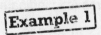 **1** Use rounding to estimate the answers to:
  a) 37 × 11   b) 516 ÷ 46

1. Round both numbers in the calculation to one significant figure.

   a) To 1 s.f. 37 rounds to **40** and 11 rounds to **10**.

2. Rewrite the calculation using the rounded numbers.

   So estimate 37 × 11 using 40 × 10 = **400**

3. Estimate the answer using the rounded numbers.

   b) To 1 s.f. 516 rounds to **500** and 46 rounds to **50**.

   So estimate 516 ÷ 46 using 500 ÷ 50 = **10**

Example 2 Use rounding to estimate the answer to 22 ÷ 1.7.

1. Rewrite the calculation using the rounded numbers.

   To 1 s.f. 22 rounds to **20** and 1.7 rounds to **2**.

2. Estimate the answer using the rounded numbers.

   So estimate 22 ÷ 1.7 using 20 ÷ 2 = **10**

Exercise 1

Answer questions 1-18 **without using your calculator**.

1   a) Round 286 and 121 to one significant figure.

   b) Use your answer to part **a)** to estimate 286 + 121.

2   a) Round 686 and 243 to one significant figure.

   b) Use your answer to part **a)** to estimate 686 − 243.

3 **a)** Round 777 and 188 to one significant figure.

    b) Use your answer to part **a)** to estimate 777 − 188.

4 **a)** Round 34 and 8 to one significant figure.

    b) Use your answer to part **a)** to estimate 34 × 8.

5 **a)** Round 57 and 26 to one significant figure.

    b) Use your answer to part **a)** to estimate 57 ÷ 26.

6 By rounding to one significant figure, estimate 475 + 241.

7 By rounding to one significant figure, estimate 583 − 312.

8 By rounding to one significant figure, estimate 22 × 13.

9 By rounding to one significant figure, estimate 332 ÷ 64.

10 Use rounding to estimate the answer to each of these calculations.

    a) 425 + 873   **b)** 185 + 37   **c)** 629 − 172

    d) 834 − 206   **e)** 37 × 12   **f)** 67 × 13

    g) 243 × 9   **h)** 97 ÷ 12   **i)** 62 ÷ 23

    j) 826 ÷ 43   **k)** 705 ÷ 98   **l)** 1049 ÷ 123

11 **a)** Round 68 and 7.1 to one significant figure.

    b) Use your answer to part **a)** to estimate 68 ÷ 7.1.

12 **a)** Round 723 and 4.5 to one significant figure.

    b) Use your answer to part **a)** to estimate 723 × 4.5.

13 Use rounding to estimate the answer to each of these calculations.

    a) 44 × 2.8   **b)** 19 × 7.2   **c)** 97 × 3.6

    d) 78 ÷ 3.9   **e)** 62 ÷ 3.2   **f)** 89.2 ÷ 8.8

14 A bag of 12 doughnuts costs 92p.
Use rounding to estimate the cost in pence of one doughnut.

15 A bag of crisps weighs 27 g. Louise needs 22 bags of crisps for a party.
Use rounding to estimate the weight of crisps needed for the party.

16 Amir buys 18 m of fabric for £57.82. Use rounding to estimate the cost of 1 m of fabric.

17 Jake's sunflower measures 17.8 cm. It grows by 42.3 cm.
Estimate the new height of the sunflower in cm.

18 Use rounding to estimate the answer to the following calculations.

    a) 756 ÷ (19.2 + 23.8)   **b)** (1826 ÷ 537) × 18

    c) 52 × (198 ÷ 97)   **d)** (4276 ÷ 38.9) − (3.2 × 13)

Using Estimates

You can use <u>estimates</u> to check that your answer is right. Compare the estimate with the actual answer — they should be reasonably close together.

So if you'd done 29.6 × 18.3 and got an answer of 5416.8, a quick estimate (30 × 20 = 600) would show that you're way off, and probably made a mistake. The correct answer is 541.68 — much closer to the estimate.

Exercise 2

1 Abigail says "I worked out 313.6 ÷ 32 and got the answer 98".

    a) By rounding to one significant figure, estimate 313.6 ÷ 32.

    b) Use your answer to part **a)** to decide whether Abigail is correct. Explain your answer.

2 Luna has done the calculation 14.2 × 27.9 on her calculator. She got the answer 3961.8. Her friend Milo has done the same calculation and got the answer 396.18.

a) By rounding to one significant figure, estimate 14.2 × 27.9.

b) Use your answer to part **a)** to decide who was correct, Luna or Milo. Explain your answer.

3 Use rounding to choose the correct answer (A, B or C) to the following calculations.

a) 2.72 × 18.68	A: 50.8096	B: 25.7862	C: 108.96
b) 48.5 × 23.1	A: 146.15	B: 530.35	C: 1120.35
c) 577.1 ÷ 29	A: 19.9	B: 12.2	C: 32.1
d) 2272.86 ÷ 36.6	A: 621.12	B: 62.1	C: 6.21
e) (12.7 + 23.6) × 3.1	A: 942.42	B: 350.04	C: 112.53

4 The decimal points have been missed out from each of the answers to these calculations. Use rounding to find an approximate answer in each case, and then decide where the decimal point should be.

a) 11.8 × 52.3 = 61714

b) 2062.72 ÷ 58.6 = 352

c) 92.7 × 1.8 = 16686

d) 38.08 ÷ 28 = 136

e) (22.6 + 76.3) × 18.2 = 179998

f) (433.84 ÷ 13.6) + 271 = 3029

Investigate — Using Estimates

a) Estimate the number of footballs it would take to fill up your classroom. Think about what information you need to know before you can start estimating.

b) Compare your estimate to other people's estimates. How different are your answers? How accurate do you think your estimates are?

c) Which estimate do you think is the best, and why?

Section 3 — Powers

3.1 Powers and Roots

Powers

Powers show something that is being multiplied by itself.

They are usually written using a 'base' and a 'power'
— the power tells you how many lots of the base to multiply together.

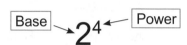

For example, $2^4 = 2 \times 2 \times 2 \times 2$ — this is four 2's multiplied together.
It is read as "2 to the power of 4".

You can work out powers on your calculator using the button that looks like this: x^n

So press 3 x^n 5 and the calculator works out $3^5 = 3 \times 3 \times 3 \times 3 \times 3 = 243$.

Example 1 a) **Write $7 \times 7 \times 7 \times 7 \times 7$ as a power.**

The base number is 7. There are 5 lots of the base multiplied together, so the power is 5.

$7 \times 7 \times 7 \times 7 \times 7 = 7^5$

b) **Write 9^6 as a multiplication, then use your calculator to find its value.**

1. The base number is 9. The power is 6. So rewrite the power as 6 lots of 9 multiplied together.

$9^6 = 9 \times 9 \times 9 \times 9 \times 9 \times 9$

2. Either work out the multiplication on your calculator, or use the power button.

$9^6 = $ 9 x^n 6 $= 531\ 441$

Exercise 1

1 Which number is the base and the power in each of these?

a) 4^6

b) 9^7

c) 11^5

d) 6^4

e) 8^{11}

f) 100^{13}

g) $9 \times 9 \times 9 \times 9$

h) 8×8

i) $5 \times 5 \times 5$

j) $6 \times 6 \times 6 \times 6 \times 6$

k) $14 \times 14 \times 14 \times 14 \times 14 \times 14$

2 Write each of these as a power.

a) $6 \times 6 \times 6$

b) 9×9

c) $4 \times 4 \times 4 \times 4$

d) $7 \times 7 \times 7$

e) $5 \times 5 \times 5 \times 5 \times 5$

f) $8 \times 8 \times 8 \times 8 \times 8 \times 8$

g) $13 \times 13 \times 13$

h) $15 \times 15 \times 15 \times 15$

i) $27 \times 27 \times 27 \times 27 \times 27$

3 Write each of these powers as a multiplication, then use a calculator to find its value.

a) 2^5

b) 3^6

c) 4^5

d) 6^7

e) 9^4

f) 12^3

4 Find the value of each of these.

a) four to the power of two

b) two to the power of three

c) six to the power of three

d) twelve to the power of four

e) nine to the power of five

f) one hundred to the power of four

Squares and cubes are types of powers.
"Squared" just means to the power of 2, and "cubed" means to the power of 3.

The square of any number is positive. The cube of a positive number is positive,
but the cube of a negative number is also negative.

Example 2   Which is greater, 3^3 or $(-6)^2$?

1. First work out the value of each power.
   Remember that a negative number squared
   is always a positive number.

   $3^3 = 3 \times 3 \times 3 = 27$
   $(-6)^2 = -6 \times -6 = 36$

2. Then see which number is greater.

   $(-6)^2$ is greater than 3^3

---

5 Find the value of each of these without using your calculator.

a) five squared

b) two cubed

c) six squared

d) nine squared

e) three cubed

f) minus-two squared

6 Copy and complete the table to find the first 10 square numbers.
Don't use your calculator.

a	1	2	3	4	5	6	7	8	9	10
a^2						36				

7 Copy and complete the table to find some common cube numbers.

a	1	2	3	4	5	10
a^3			27			

8 Work out these squares and cubes, using a calculator if you need to.

a) 11^2 　　　　**b)** 12^2 　　　　**c)** 13^2 　　　　**d)** 15^2 　　　　**e)** 20^2

f) 6^3 　　　　**g)** 8^3 　　　　**h)** 10^3 　　　　**i)** 15^3 　　　　**j)** 20^3

9 Find the value of these squares and cubes, using your calculator where necessary.

a) $(-2)^2$ 　　**b)** 0.3^2 　　**c)** $(-12)^2$ 　　**d)** 0.6^2 　　**e)** 0.4^3

f) $(-3)^3$ 　　**g)** $(-5)^3$ 　　**h)** 0.8^3 　　**i)** 3.6^2 　　**j)** $(-30)^2$

k) $(-1.1)^3$ 　　**l)** $(-2.5)^2$ 　　**m)** $(-11)^3$ 　　**n)** $(-0.7)^3$ 　　**o)** 10.2^2

10 Without using a calculator, work out which is greater out of these pairs of numbers.

a) three squared and two cubed 　　　**b)** 12^2 and 6^3 　　　**c)** 2^7 and 7^2

11 Use the power button on your calculator to find the value of:

a) 5^4 　　　　**b)** 6^5 　　　　**c)** 4^7 　　　　**d)** 8^5

e) 11^4 　　　　**f)** 12^6 　　　　**g)** 3^9 　　　　**h)** 7^4

i) 6^6 　　　　**j)** 2^{10} 　　　　**k)** 7^8 　　　　**l)** 100^4

12 Find the value of each of these powers, using the power button on your calculator.
Write down all the numbers on your calculator's screen.

a) 0.5^4 　　　**b)** $(-3)^6$ 　　　**c)** $(-2)^7$ 　　　**d)** 2.5^5

e) 1.1^4 　　　**f)** $(-14)^5$ 　　　**g)** $(-1.8)^6$ 　　　**h)** $(-2.1)^5$

13 Use a calculator to work out these calculations.
(Hint: Work out powers **before** carrying out any addition or subtraction.)

a) $2^3 + 4^2$ b) $5^2 + 3^3$ c) $3^4 - 6^2$ d) $4^3 + 6^3$

e) $3^5 - 5^3$ f) $4^5 - 5^4$ g) $5^2 - 2^3$ h) $3^6 - 11^2$

i) $8 + 2^5$ j) $350 - 3^5$ k) $50 + 10^3$ l) $10^6 - 10$

14 Which of the numbers in the box are:

a) square numbers?   b) cube numbers?

256	3	400	343	55
169	101	8000	144	72

15 Find the value of these powers, using a calculator if you need to.
Remember to work out the calculations in brackets first.

a) $(6 - 4)^2$ b) $(5 - 2)^3$ c) $(10 - 8)^4$

d) $(11 + 2)^5$ e) $(3^2)^2$ f) $(5^2)^3$

g) 4×2^3 h) $(50 - 6 \times 8)^4$ i) $\dfrac{3^4}{9}$

16 Find the number that should replace the ◊ in each of these:

a) $4^2 = 2^◊$ b) $3^4 = ◊^2$ c) $2^6 = 4^◊$

Investigate — Powers

a) Write 2^3 and 2^6 as multiplications.

b) Now combine those two multiplications to write $2^3 \times 2^6$ as one multiplication.

c) Turn your single multiplication into a power, with 2 as the base number.
Do you notice anything special about the two powers you start with,
and the one power you finish up with?

d) Try doing this with other pairs of powers with the same base, e.g. $3^5 \times 3^7$.
Do you always get the same results? Write your findings as a general rule.

Roots

Roots are the inverse of powers.

So 3^4 ("3 to the power of 4") is 81. And $\sqrt[4]{81}$ ("the fourth root of 81") is 3.

The most common roots you'll come across are square roots and cube roots.

Finding the square root of a number is the opposite of squaring it.

Every positive number has two square roots — one positive ($\sqrt{x}$) and one negative ($-\sqrt{x}$). Negative numbers don't have square roots.

Finding the cube root of a number is the opposite of cubing it. Every number has exactly one cube root. The symbol $\sqrt[3]{}$ is used for cube roots.

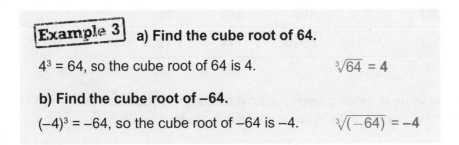

Example 3   **a) Find the cube root of 64.**

$4^3 = 64$, so the cube root of 64 is 4. $\sqrt[3]{64} = 4$

b) Find the cube root of −64.

$(-4)^3 = -64$, so the cube root of −64 is −4. $\sqrt[3]{(-64)} = -4$

To find roots on your calculator, just use one of the three root buttons:

  $\boxed{\sqrt{}}$ to find square roots $\boxed{\sqrt[3]{}}$ to find cube roots $\boxed{\sqrt[x]{}}$ to find any other roots

So press $\boxed{4}\,\boxed{\sqrt[x]{}}\,\boxed{2}\,\boxed{5}\,\boxed{6}$ and the calculator works out $\sqrt[4]{256} = 4$.

Watch out though — a calculator will only give you the **positive** square root.

Exercise 2

1   Match each number to its positive square root. One has been done for you.

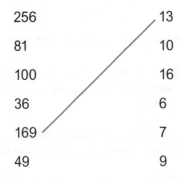

256   13

81   10

100   16

36   6

169   7

49   9

2 Without using a calculator, find:

a) $\sqrt{4}$ b) $-\sqrt{4}$ c) $\sqrt{9}$ d) $-\sqrt{9}$

e) $\sqrt{25}$ f) $-\sqrt{25}$ g) $\sqrt{64}$ h) $-\sqrt{64}$

i) $\sqrt{121}$ j) $-\sqrt{121}$ k) $\sqrt{144}$ l) $-\sqrt{144}$

3 Copy and complete this table of cube roots, without using your calculator.

x	8	27	64	1000
$\sqrt[3]{x}$			4	

4 Find these cube roots without using your calculator.

a) $\sqrt[3]{125}$ b) $\sqrt[3]{-8}$ c) $\sqrt[3]{-1}$

d) $\sqrt[3]{-125}$ e) $\sqrt[3]{216}$ f) $\sqrt[3]{-1000}$

5 a) Without using a calculator, work out 2^5.

b) Use your answer to part a) to find $\sqrt[5]{32}$ without a calculator.

6 Find these roots, without using your calculator.

a) $\sqrt[4]{(2^4)}$ b) $\sqrt[3]{(-2)^3}$ c) $\sqrt[5]{12^5}$

d) $\sqrt[10]{(6^{10})}$ e) $\sqrt[9]{(5^9)}$ f) $\sqrt[6]{(100^6)}$

7 Find both square roots of these numbers. You may use a calculator if you need to.

a) 256   b) 361   c) 400   d) 10 000

e) 225   f) 625   g) 324   h) 196

8 Use your calculator to find the cube root of each of these numbers:

a) 1331   b) 729   c) −343   d) −1728

e) 8000   f) 3375   g) −1331   h) 512

9 Find these square and cube roots using your calculator.

a) $\sqrt{0.25}$

b) $-\sqrt{2.25}$

c) $\sqrt[3]{15.625}$

d) $\sqrt{0.81}$

e) $\sqrt{1.44}$

f) $\sqrt[3]{0.008}$

g) $\sqrt[3]{-0.027}$

h) $\sqrt[3]{0.343}$

i) $-\sqrt{4.84}$

j) $\sqrt[3]{0.729}$

k) $-\sqrt{0.0625}$

l) $\sqrt[3]{-0.015625}$

10 Use your calculator to find these roots.

a) $\sqrt[4]{16}$

b) $\sqrt[5]{243}$

c) $\sqrt[4]{625}$

d) $\sqrt[6]{1\,000\,000}$

e) $\sqrt[4]{4096}$

f) $\sqrt[6]{64}$

g) $\sqrt[5]{1024}$

h) $\sqrt[5]{-32}$

i) $\sqrt[6]{15\,625}$

j) $\sqrt[7]{2187}$

k) $\sqrt[10]{1024}$

l) $\sqrt[7]{-78\,125}$

m) $\sqrt[4]{5.0625}$

n) $\sqrt[5]{0.03125}$

o) $\sqrt[8]{1\,679\,616}$

p) $\sqrt[9]{19\,683}$

11 a) Use your calculator to work out these roots, and write down what the display says.

i) $\sqrt[4]{1296}$

ii) $\sqrt[4]{-1296}$

b) Explain your answer to part **a) ii)**.

12 Give an example to show that this statement is **not** always true:

"When you square root a positive number, the answer is always a smaller number."

> ## Investigate — Powers and Roots
>
> **a)** Find the value of these powers of 2:
>
> 2^2, 2^3, 2^4, 2^5, 2^6, 2^7, 2^8
>
> **b)** Now find the value of these powers of –2:
>
> $(-2)^2$, $(-2)^3$, $(-2)^4$, $(-2)^5$, $(-2)^6$, $(-2)^7$, $(-2)^8$
>
> **c)** Which powers give the same answer for parts **a)** and **b)**? What do you notice about these powers?
>
> **d)** Repeat parts **a)-c)** with 3 and –3, or 4 and –4. Keep going with pairs of numbers until you notice something about the powers.
>
> **e)** Can you write a rule which type of roots will have both a positive and a negative answer?

3.2 Standard Form

Powers of 10

Numbers that can be written as a power with 10 as the base are called <u>powers of 10</u>.

Exercise 1

1 Find the value of these powers of 10.

a) 10^3 **b)** 10^4 **c)** 10^2 **d)** 10^5

e) 10^6 **f)** 10^7 **g)** 10^8 **h)** 10^9

2 Copy and complete the following sentences.

a) "10^2 can be written as a '1' followed by .... zeros."

b) "10^3 can be written as a '1' followed by .... zeros."

c) "10^5 can be written as a '1' followed by .... zeros."

d) "10^7 can be written as a '1' followed by .... zeros."

3 Rewrite each of these numbers as a power of 10.

a) 100   **b)** 1000   **c)** 10 000

d) 100 000   **e)** 1 000 000   **f)** 10 000 000

g) 1 000 000 000   **h)** 1 000 000 000 000   **i)** 10

4 Rewrite each of these numbers as a power of 10.

a) one thousand   **b)** ten thousand   **c)** one hundred

d) one million   **e)** one hundred thousand   **f)** ten million

g) one hundred million   **h)** one billion

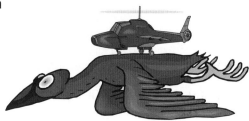

Standard Form

Standard form is used to make it easier to write very large or very small numbers, like 2 670 000 000 000 and 0.0000000000014. In standard form, numbers are written as a multiple of a power of 10. Like this:

A can be any number between 1 and 10 $\longrightarrow$ (but not 10 itself)

$$A \times 10^{n}$$

$\longleftarrow$ n can be any whole number

Example 1 **Write 300 000 in standard form.**

1. First, write 300 000 as a number between 1 and 10 multiplied by a power of ten.

   $300\ 000 = 3 \times 100\ 000$

2. Rewrite the power of 10 as a power.

   $3 \times 100\ 000 = \mathbf{3 \times 10^{5}}$

Exercise 2

1 Which of these numbers are **not** written in standard form?

5.2×10^{9} 3.5×12^{2} 55×10^{6}

3×10^{8} $1.25 \times 10^{1.5}$

6.5×100^{2} 2.5×10^{11} 0.5×10^{7}

2 Fill in the gaps to show how these numbers can be written in standard form.

   a) $200\ 000 = \ldots\ldots \times 100\ 000 = \ldots\ldots \times 10^{5}$

   b) $3\ 000\ 000 = 3 \times \ldots\ldots\ldots\ldots = 3 \times \ldots\ldots$

3 Write these numbers in standard form.

   a) 200   **b)** 2000   **c)** 40 000   **d)** 600 000

   e) 8000   **f)** 900   **g)** 5 000 000   **h)** 70 000 000

   i) 450 000   **j)** 4100   **k)** 625 000   **l)** 54 000

Example 2 Write 3.5×10^3 as an ordinary number.

1. First, rewrite the power of 10 in full as an ordinary number.

   $3.5 \times 10^3 = 3.5 \times 1000$

2. Then do the multiplication to find the value of the standard form number.

   $3.5 \times 1000 = \mathbf{3500}$

4   Fill in the gaps to show how these can be written as ordinary numbers.

a) $8 \times 10^3 =$ .... $\times 1000 =$ ....

b) $5 \times 10^6 = 5 \times$ .... $=$ ....

5   Write each of these as an ordinary number.

a) 4×10^3 b) 5×10^2 c) 8×10^6 d) 7×10^9

e) 6.2×10^3 f) 1.4×10^5 g) 6.9×10^7 h) 7.2×10^8

i) 6.05×10^4 j) 7.27×10^5 k) 3.65×10^9 l) 5.201×10^4

6   Put each of these groups of numbers in order, from smallest to largest.

a) 4×10^5, 2×10^3, 3×10^2, 6×10^4, 7×10^3, 2×10^2

b) 2.5×10^3, 4.6×10^6, 1.5×10^4, 9.8×10^2, 1.1×10^6, 6.8×10^4

c) $410\ 100$, 4.105×10^6, 4.11×10^6, $4\ 100\ 000$, 4.105×10^5, $4\ 101\ 000$

7   By writing each of the numbers as an ordinary number first, work out these calculations. Give your answers in standard form.

a) $(2 \times 10^3) + (5 \times 10^2)$ b) $(3 \times 10^4) + (6 \times 10^4)$

c) $(8.5 \times 10^6) + (7.7 \times 10^5)$ d) $(2.05 \times 10^5) + (6.02 \times 10^4)$

e) $(8 \times 10^4) - (2 \times 10^4)$ f) $(5 \times 10^7) - (9 \times 10^6)$

8   The population of country A is 5.3×10^7 and the population of country B is 3.1×10^6. How many more people live in country A than in country B?

Section 4 — Multiples, Factors and Primes

4.1 Multiples

Multiples

The <u>multiples</u> of a number are just the numbers that are in its <u>times table</u>.

So the multiples of 3 are 3, 6, 9, 12, 15, ... and the multiples of 10 are 10, 20, 30, 40, 50, ...

> **Example 1**
>
> **a) List the first five multiples of 6.**
>
> Just write down the first five numbers in the 6 times table:
>
> **6, 12, 18, 24, 30**
>
> **b) Which of the numbers in the box are:**
> **(i) multiples of 4?**
> **(ii) multiples of 7?**
>
> | 14 | 16 | 2 | 24 | 28 | 8 |
> |----|----|---|----|----|---|
>
> 4 divides into 16, 24, 28 and 8 exactly —
> so these numbers are multiples of 4.
> But 4 doesn't divide into 14 or 2 exactly —
> so these aren't multiples of 4.
>
> (i) **16, 24, 28, and 8**
>
> 7 divides into 14 and 28 exactly,
> but not into 16, 2, 24 or 8.
>
> (ii) **14 and 28**

Exercise 1

1 List the first five multiples of:

    a) 2   **b)** 5   **c)** 7

    d) 9   **e)** 8   **f)** 11

2 Write down the numbers in the box that are:

    a) multiples of 6

    b) multiples of 8

36	25	7	15	18	24	16
19	12	30	32	22	28	40

3 Write down all the multiples of 12 that are less than 50.

4 Write down all the multiples of 9 between 30 and 60.

5　**a)** Find the only multiple of 11 between 30 and 40.

　　b) List the multiples of 7 between 20 and 50.

　　c) Find the only multiple of 8 between 50 and 60.

6　**a)** List all the multiples of 2 between 11 and 25.

　　b) List all the multiples of 3 between 11 and 25.

　　c) List all the numbers between 11 and 25 that are multiples of both 2 and 3.

7　Write down all the numbers from the box that aren't multiples of 9.

22	27	54	17	18	23	45
9	90	63	65	77	49	36

Investigate — Multiples　*"Multiples of 2 always end in an even number."*

　a) Can you find rules for saying whether a number is definitely a multiple of
　　3, 4, 5, 6, 7, 8, 9, or 10?
　　Make sure any rules you find work for numbers up to 100.

　b) Now see if you can extend any of your rules
　　to make them work for numbers over 100.

　c) Try and find rules for multiples of bigger numbers — such as 11, 12, 15, 20...
　　Can you predict which numbers might have rules?

Lowest Common Multiples

A <u>common multiple</u> is a number that's in the times table of two or more different numbers.

The <u>lowest common multiple</u> (<u>LCM</u>) of a group of numbers is the smallest common multiple of those numbers. It's the lowest number they all divide into exactly.

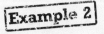　**Find the lowest common multiple of 4 and 5.**

1. Write down the multiples of 4 and 5:

　multiples of 4:
　4, 8, 12, 16, ⟨20⟩ 24, ...
　multiples of 5:
　5, 10, 15, ⟨20⟩ 25, ...

2. The lowest common multiple is the smallest number that's in both lists.

　LCM of 4 and 5 is **20**.

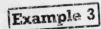 Example 3

Example 3 Chris weeds his garden every 6 days. His next-door neighbour Kim weeds her garden every 8 days. If they both weeded today, how many days will it be before they weed on the same day again?

You need to find the lowest common multiple of 6 and 8:

Chris weeds his garden on day 6, 12, 18, (24), 30, ...
Kim weeds her garden on day 8, 16, (24), 32, ...

So they will next weed on the same day on **day 24**.

Exercise 2

1 a) Write down the first ten multiples of 2.

   b) Write down the first ten multiples of 3.

   c) Write down the common multiples of 2 and 3 from your lists.

   d) Find the lowest common multiple of 2 and 3 — the smallest number in your list from **c)**.

2 a) Write down the first eight multiples of 4.

   b) Write down the first eight multiples of 7.

   c) Find the lowest common multiple of 4 and 7.

3 a) Write down the first five multiples of 6.

   b) Write down the first five multiples of 9.

   c) Find the lowest common multiple of 6 and 9.

4 Find the lowest common multiple (LCM) of each of the following pairs of numbers.

   a) 3 and 5   **b)** 2 and 7   **c)** 3 and 4

   d) 5 and 9   **e)** 3 and 7   **f)** 8 and 9

5 Find the LCM of each of the following pairs of numbers.

   a) 4 and 6   **b)** 8 and 10   **c)** 9 and 12

6 **a)** Write down the first five multiples of 3.

   b) Write down the first five multiples of 4.

   c) Write down the first five multiples of 6.

   d) Find the lowest common multiple of 3, 4 and 6 —
     the smallest number that's in all three lists.

7 **a)** Write down the first eight multiples of 4, 6 and 8.

   b) Find the lowest common multiple of 4, 6 and 8.

8 **a)** Write down the first eight multiples of 3, 6 and 9.

   b) Find the lowest common multiple of 3, 6 and 9.

9 Find the LCM of each of the sets of numbers below.

   a) 2, 3 and 4   **b)** 3, 5 and 6   **c)** 5, 10 and 15

   d) 5, 6 and 10   **e)** 5, 8 and 10   **f)** 4, 9 and 12

10 Coralie visits the hairdresser every 8 weeks. Victor visits the same hairdresser
    every 12 weeks. They go for the first time in Week 0, and keep going for a year.

   a) In which weeks does Coralie visit the hairdresser?
     Write down all possible answers.

   b) In which weeks does Victor visit the hairdresser?
     Write down all possible answers.

   c) In which week will they next visit the hairdresser at the same time?

11 Tabitha empties her bins every 5 days and Peter empties his bins every 7 days.
    If they both emptied their bins today, how many days will it be before they both
    empty them on the same day again?

12 Miss Norfolk splits a class of children into 10 equal groups.
    Mr Wales splits the same class into 15 equal groups.
    What is the smallest possible number of children in the class?

4.2 Factors

Factors

The <u>factors</u> of a number are all the numbers that divide into it ('go into it') exactly.

So the factors of 6 are 1, 2, 3 and 6 — all these numbers go into 6 exactly.

Example 1   **Find all the factors of 18.**

1. Start by writing 1 × 18.

2. Then try 2 × something to make 18.
   2 × 9 = 18, so write this on the next row.

3. Carry on trying to make 18 by multiplying pairs of numbers: 3 × something, 4 × something etc.

4. Write each pair of numbers in a new row. Put a dash if a number doesn't divide exactly.

5. Stop when you get a repeated number (6).

6. Write down all the numbers in the multiplications.

Increasing by 1 each time →

1 × 18
2 × 9
3 × 6
4 × —
5 × —
6 × 3

So the factors of 18 are
1, 2, 3, 6, 9 and 18

Exercise 1

1   Copy and complete the boxes to find all the factors of:

a) 15

| 1 × 15 |
| 2 × — |
| 3 × .... |
| 4 × .... |
| 5 × 3 |

b) 24

| 1 × 24 |
| 2 × 12 |
| 3 × .... |
| 4 × .... |
| 5 × .... |
| 6 × 4 |

2   Write down the numbers from the box that are factors of:

a) 10   **b)** 13   **c)** 30

d) 28   **e)** 22   **f)** 32

| 2 | 7 | 1 | 4 | 5 | 8 |

3 Find all the factors of each of these numbers.

a) 7   **b)** 25   **c)** 16

d) 45   **e)** 64   **f)** 48

4 Write down the numbers from the box that are factors of both:

a) 8 and 28

b) 15 and 21

> 3 5 4 7 2 8

5 A number is called **perfect** if the sum of all its factors is exactly double the number itself. So 6 is a perfect number because $1 + 2 + 3 + 6 = 12$, and $12 = 2 \times 6$.

a) Show that 20 is not a perfect number.

b) Show that 28 is a perfect number.

> ## Investigate — Factors
>
> Find the factors of all the numbers from 1-50. Then answer these questions:
>
> **a)** Which numbers have the most factors? Which have the least?
>
> **b)** Which numbers have an odd number of factors? Can you spot any patterns? Try and make some conclusions from your work.

Highest Common Factors

A <u>common factor</u> is a number that divides exactly into two or more different numbers.

The <u>highest common factor</u> (<u>HCF</u>) of a group of numbers is the largest common factor of those numbers. It's the biggest number that divides into all of them exactly.

> **Example 2**   **Find the highest common factor of 18 and 27.**
>
> 1. Write down the factors of 18 and 27:   factors of 18:
>   1, 2, 3, 6, ⑨ 18
>   factors of 27:
>
> 2. The highest common factor is the   1, 3, ⑨ 27
>   biggest number that's in both lists.
>   HCF of 18 and 27 is **9**.

Exercise 2

1 a) Write down all the factors of 6.

b) Write down all the factors of 24.

c) Write down the common factors of 6 and 24 from your lists.

d) Find the highest common factor of 6 and 24 — the biggest number in your list from **c)**.

2 a) Write down all the factors of 10.

b) Write down all the factors of 15.

c) Find the highest common factor of 10 and 15.

3 a) Write down all the factors of 12.

b) Write down all the factors of 25.

c) Find the highest common factor of 12 and 25.

4 Find the highest common factor (HCF) of each of the following pairs of numbers.

   a) 4 and 16   **b)** 8 and 32

   c) 7 and 28   **d)** 5 and 35

   e) 6 and 24   **f)** 10 and 40

5 Find the HCF of each of the following pairs of numbers.

   a) 3 and 8   **b)** 4 and 15

   c) 8 and 21   **d)** 10 and 27

   e) 13 and 28   **f)** 9 and 32

6 Find the HCF of each of the following pairs of numbers.

   a) 8 and 12   **b)** 6 and 8

   c) 20 and 30   **d)** 14 and 35

   e) 9 and 24   **f)** 16 and 40

7 **a)** Write down all the factors of 8.

    b) Write down all the factors of 28.

    c) Write down all the factors of 36.

    d) Write down the common factors of 8, 28 and 36 from your lists.

    e) Find the highest common factor of 8, 28 and 36 —
        the biggest number in your list from **d)**.

8 **a)** Write down all the factors of 20.

    b) Write down all the factors of 25.

    c) Write down all the factors of 40.

    d) Find the highest common factor of 20, 25 and 40.

9 **a)** Write down all the factors of 6, 18 and 36.

    b) Find the highest common factor of 6, 18 and 36.

10 Find the HCF of each of the following sets of numbers.

    a) 4, 7 and 13   **b)** 4, 16 and 20

    c) 12, 19 and 25   **d)** 15, 30 and 60

    e) 3, 5 and 14   **f)** 6, 12 and 24

    g) 15, 21 and 33   **h)** 9, 27 and 36

    i) 12, 20 and 28   **j)** 9, 16 and 23

    k) 14, 35 and 49   **l)** 18, 36 and 48

11 Geoff and Barbara have the same number of grandchildren.
Geoff shares 60 sweets equally between his grandchildren (with no sweets left over).
Barbara shares 72 sweets equally between her grandchildren (with no sweets left over).
What is the largest number of grandchildren they could each have?

4.3 Prime Numbers

Prime Numbers

A prime number is a number that has no factors except itself and 1.

In other words, the only numbers that divide exactly into a prime number are itself and 1.

But remember... 1 is not a prime number.

Here are the first few prime numbers: 2, 3, 5, 7, 11, 13, 17, 19, 23, 29, ...

Example 1 **Which of the numbers in the box are primes?**

$$37 \quad 38 \quad 39 \quad 40 \quad 41$$

1. Look for factors of each of the numbers.

2. If you can find factors, then the number isn't prime.

3. If there are no factors other than itself and 1, the number is prime.

$38 = 2 \times 19$, so 38 isn't prime
$39 = 3 \times 13$, so 39 isn't prime
$40 = 4 \times 10$, so 40 isn't prime

37 has no factors other than 1 and 37.
41 has no factors other than 1 and 41.

So the prime numbers are **37** and **41**.

Exercise 1

1 a) Find all the factors of the three numbers in the box.

$$30 \quad 31 \quad 32$$

b) Which of the three numbers is a prime number? Explain your answer.

2 Look at the list of numbers.

$$41 \quad 43 \quad 45 \quad 47$$

a) Which number in the list is not prime?

b) Explain how you know that this number is not prime.

3 a) Which three numbers in the box are not prime?

$$21 \quad 23 \quad 25 \quad 27 \quad 29$$

b) Explain how you know that these numbers are not prime.

4   Write down the prime numbers from this list:

7,   15,   23,   28,   35,   49,   53,   59.

5   **a)** Write down the four prime numbers between 10 and 20.

b) Find the two prime numbers between 30 and 40.

6   **a)** Find the largest prime number that is less than 70.

b) Find all the prime numbers between 40 and 50.

7   Explain why 42 is not a prime number.

8   Explain why 41 is a prime number.

9   Is 51 a prime number? Explain your answer.

10 Look at the numbers in the box.

| 71 | 72 | 73 | 74 | 75 | 76 | 77 | 78 | 79 |

Write down all the prime numbers in the box.

11 Without doing any calculations, explain how you can tell
that none of the numbers in the box are prime.

| 102 | 104 | 106 | 108 | 110 | 55 | 60 | 65 | 70 | 75 |

12 **a)** Find two prime numbers that add to make 16.

b) Find two prime numbers that add to make 36.

c) Find an example to show that this statement is **false**:

"The sum of two prime numbers is always even".

Prime Factors

Whole numbers which are not prime can be broken down into <u>prime factors</u>. The <u>product</u> of these factors is the original number. (Remember, 'product' means the result of multiplying things).

You can write the prime factors using <u>powers</u> — so $12 = 2 \times 2 \times 3 = 2^2 \times 3$.

Example 2   **Write 18 as a product of prime factors.**

Make a factor tree.

1. First find any two factors whose product is 18 (here, $3 \times 6 = 18$). Circle any of these factors that are prime.

2. Repeat step 1 for any factors you didn't circle (here, $6 = 2 \times 3$).

3. Stop when all the branches end in a circle. The product of all the circled primes is the number you started with.

4. You can rewrite the prime factors using powers to simplify.

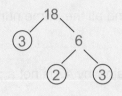

$18 = 2 \times 3 \times 3$

$18 = \mathbf{2 \times 3^2}$

Exercise 2

In the following questions, write any repeated factors as powers.

1   a) Copy and complete the following factor trees.

    i) 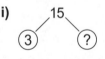   **ii)** 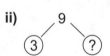   **iii)** 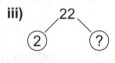   **iv)**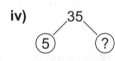

    b) Use your factor trees to write the following as products of prime factors.

    i) 15   **ii)** 9   **iii)** 22   **iv)** 35

2   Write the following numbers as the product of two prime factors.

    a) 4   **b)** 10   **c)** 26

    d) 34   **e)** 55   **f)** 65

3 a) Copy and complete the following factor trees.

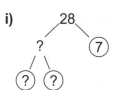 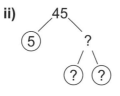 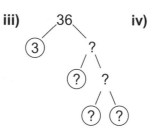 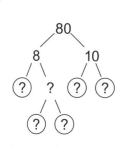

b) Use your factor trees to write the following as products of prime factors.

i) 28   **ii)** 45   **iii)** 36   **iv)** 80

4 a) Copy and complete these three factor trees.

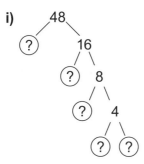 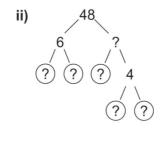 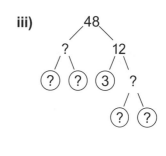

b) Use each of your factor trees to write 48 as the product of prime factors. What do you notice?

5 Use factor trees to write the following numbers as the product of prime factors.

a) 27   **b)** 30   **c)** 63

d) 75   **e)** 99   **f)** 110

6 Write the following numbers as the product of prime factors.

a) 40   **b)** 56

c) 64   **d)** 81

e) 108   **f)** 120

7 Write the following as the product of prime factors.

a) 20

b) 32

c) 44

d) 54

e) 72

f) 88

g) 124

h) 144

i) 225

8 a) Write 96 as the product of prime factors.

b) Use your answer to part a) to write 1440 (= 96 × 15) as the product of prime factors.

9 a) Write 210 as the product of prime factors.

b) Use your answer to part a) to write 70 (= 210 ÷ 3) as the product of prime factors.

10 a) Copy and complete this factor tree.

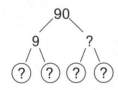

b) Use your factor tree to write 90 as the product of prime factors.

c) Use your answer to part b) to write 90^2 as the product of prime factors.

Investigate — Prime Factors

a) Write each of the square numbers from 2^2 to 15^2 as the product of prime factors.

b) What do you notice about these prime factorisations?

c) Pick any number (except a square number) between 1 and 225 and write it as the product of prime factors.
Using the prime factorisation, work out the smallest number you need to multiply your original number by to form a square number.

Section 5 — Fractions and Percentages

5.1 Adding and Subtracting Fractions

Adding and Subtracting Fractions

Fractions with different denominators can be added and subtracted. You need to rewrite them with a common denominator first, before adding or subtracting the numerators.

Example 1 Work out $\frac{3}{8} + \frac{1}{4}$.

1. Rewrite $\frac{1}{4}$ with a denominator of 8 by multiplying top and bottom by 2.

$$\overset{\times 2}{\frown}$$
$$\frac{1}{4} = \frac{2}{8}$$
$$\underset{\times 2}{\smile}$$

2. Now the fractions have a common denominator, so add the numerators.

$$\frac{3}{8} + \frac{2}{8} = \frac{3+2}{8} = \frac{5}{8}$$

Example 2 Work out $\frac{5}{6} - \frac{2}{9}$.

1. Use the lowest common multiple of 6 and 9 as a common denominator.

LCM of 6 and 9 = 18

2. Rewrite the fractions with a common denominator of 18.

$$\overset{\times 3}{\frown} \qquad \overset{\times 2}{\frown}$$
$$\frac{5}{6} = \frac{15}{18} \qquad \frac{2}{9} = \frac{4}{18}$$
$$\underset{\times 3}{\smile} \qquad \underset{\times 2}{\smile}$$

3. Now you can subtract the numerators.

$$\frac{15}{18} - \frac{4}{18} = \frac{15-4}{18} = \frac{11}{18}$$

Exercise 1

1 Alice eats $\frac{3}{9}$ of a cake. Tariq eats $\frac{4}{9}$ of the cake.

What fraction of the cake has been eaten?

2 A box contains biscuits. Chris eats $\frac{9}{16}$ of the biscuits.

Paul eats $\frac{3}{16}$ of the biscuits. What fraction of the biscuits have been eaten?

Give your answer in its simplest terms.

3 Copy and complete these calculations.

a) $\dfrac{1}{6} + \dfrac{1}{3} = \dfrac{1}{6} + \dfrac{}{6} = \dfrac{}{6}$

b) $\dfrac{5}{9} + \dfrac{1}{3} = \dfrac{5}{9} + \dfrac{}{9} = \dfrac{}{9}$

c) $\dfrac{5}{6} - \dfrac{3}{12} = \dfrac{}{12} - \dfrac{3}{12} = \dfrac{}{12}$

d) $\dfrac{11}{12} - \dfrac{1}{3} = \dfrac{11}{12} - \dfrac{}{12} = \dfrac{}{12}$

e) $\dfrac{1}{2} + \dfrac{1}{5} = \dfrac{5}{10} + \dfrac{}{10} = \dfrac{}{10}$

f) $\dfrac{2}{3} - \dfrac{1}{7} = \dfrac{}{21} - \dfrac{}{21} = \dfrac{}{21}$

4 **a)** Rewrite the fractions $\dfrac{2}{3}$ and $\dfrac{3}{15}$ so they have a common denominator.

b) Use your answer to **a)** to work out $\dfrac{2}{3} + \dfrac{3}{15}$.

5 **a)** Rewrite the fractions $\dfrac{3}{5}$ and $\dfrac{1}{4}$ so they have a common denominator.

b) Use your answer to **a)** to work out $\dfrac{3}{5} - \dfrac{1}{4}$.

6 Add or subtract these fractions by first rewriting them so they have a common denominator. Give your answers in their simplest terms.

a) $\dfrac{1}{6} + \dfrac{4}{12}$

b) $\dfrac{3}{5} + \dfrac{2}{10}$

c) $\dfrac{3}{4} - \dfrac{5}{12}$

d) $\dfrac{8}{16} - \dfrac{1}{4}$

e) $\dfrac{1}{6} + \dfrac{3}{24}$

f) $\dfrac{17}{20} - \dfrac{3}{4}$

g) $\dfrac{3}{5} + \dfrac{9}{25}$

h) $\dfrac{10}{22} + \dfrac{3}{11}$

i) $\dfrac{2}{6} + \dfrac{4}{18}$

j) $\dfrac{8}{10} - \dfrac{6}{30}$

k) $\dfrac{24}{28} - \dfrac{3}{7}$

l) $\dfrac{4}{5} - \dfrac{7}{15}$

7 Add or subtract these fractions by first rewriting them so they have a common denominator. Give your answers in their simplest terms.

a) $\dfrac{3}{4} + \dfrac{1}{6}$

b) $\dfrac{7}{8} - \dfrac{1}{6}$

c) $\dfrac{1}{2} + \dfrac{1}{5}$

d) $\dfrac{3}{5} - \dfrac{2}{6}$

e) $\dfrac{1}{7} + \dfrac{4}{6}$

f) $\dfrac{4}{5} - \dfrac{2}{8}$

g) $\dfrac{6}{7} - \dfrac{2}{5}$

h) $\dfrac{3}{4} - \dfrac{3}{7}$

8 In a shop, $\frac{4}{15}$ of the kites are red and $\frac{2}{5}$ are blue.

What is the total fraction, in its simplest form, of kites that are either red or blue?

9 Josie has a ribbon that is $\frac{4}{5}$ m long. She cuts off $\frac{2}{7}$ m of the ribbon.

How long is the ribbon now? Give your answer as a fraction.

10 Jack is baking. He puts $\frac{7}{8}$ kg of sugar in a bowl.

He removes $\frac{3}{6}$ kg of the sugar and replaces it with butter.

How much sugar is left in the bowl?
Give your answer as a fraction in its simplest form.

11 Look at the following fractions:

$$\frac{3}{8} \qquad \frac{1}{3} \qquad \frac{3}{4} \qquad \frac{1}{6} \qquad \frac{7}{12} \qquad \frac{11}{24}$$

a) Which two of these fractions add up to $\frac{5}{8}$?

b) Which two of these fractions have a difference of $\frac{1}{4}$?

Investigate — Fractions of Shapes

$\frac{1}{2}$	$\frac{1}{2}$

a) The rectangle is split to show the sum $\frac{1}{2} + \frac{1}{2} = 1$.

Copy the rectangle, and add a line to show the sum $\frac{1}{2} + \frac{1}{4} + \frac{1}{4} = 1$.

b) Draw another line to split one of the quarters into half.
Write out the fraction sum that the rectangle now shows.

c) Keep dividing parts of the rectangle up, and each time write out the sum
that it shows. How far can you go?

Dealing With Mixed Numbers

A <u>mixed number</u> is a whole number combined with a fraction, such as $1\frac{2}{5}$.

A fraction where the <u>numerator</u> is bigger than the <u>denominator</u>, such as $\frac{7}{5}$, is a top-heavy or <u>improper fraction</u>.

Example 3 **Write the mixed number $3\frac{2}{7}$ as an improper fraction.**

1. Find the fraction which is equivalent
    to 3 and which has 7 as the denominator.
    3 is the same as $\frac{3}{1}$.

2. Add the two fractions to give
    one improper fraction.

$$\overset{\times 7}{\frac{3}{1} = \frac{21}{7}}$$
$$\underset{\times 7}{}$$

$$3\frac{2}{7} = \frac{21}{7} + \frac{2}{7} = \frac{23}{7}$$

Exercise 2

1 Use the diagrams to help you write improper fractions equivalent to the whole numbers.

a)
$$2 = \frac{\bigstar}{4}$$

Clue: How many quarters are there in 2?

b)
$$3 = \frac{\bigstar}{5}$$

Clue: How many fifths are there in 3?

2 Find the values of the letters to write the following whole numbers as improper fractions.

a) $3 = \frac{a}{4}$ **b)** $4 = \frac{b}{3}$ **c)** $7 = \frac{35}{c}$ **d)** $11 = \frac{66}{d}$

3 **a)** Find the value of a if $5 = \frac{a}{4}$.

b) Use your answer to **a)** to write the mixed number $5\frac{3}{4}$ as an improper fraction.

4 **a)** Find the value of b if $4 = \frac{b}{7}$.

b) Use your answer to **a)** to write the mixed number $4\frac{3}{7}$ as an improper fraction.

5 Find the values of the letters to write the following mixed numbers as improper fractions.

a) $2\frac{1}{4} = \frac{a}{4}$ **b)** $1\frac{3}{8} = \frac{b}{8}$ **c)** $5\frac{2}{3} = \frac{c}{3}$ **d)** $2\frac{5}{9} = \frac{d}{9}$

6 Write the following mixed numbers as improper fractions.

a) $1\frac{3}{7}$ b) $1\frac{3}{5}$ c) $3\frac{7}{8}$ d) $3\frac{9}{10}$ e) $4\frac{4}{5}$ f) $8\frac{5}{9}$

g) $12\frac{4}{5}$ h) $13\frac{3}{4}$ i) $12\frac{1}{3}$ j) $3\frac{5}{6}$ k) $9\frac{7}{12}$ l) $5\frac{7}{11}$

Example 4   Write the improper fraction $\frac{15}{4}$ as a mixed number in its simplest terms.

1. Split the numerator into:
   (i) a multiple of the denominator, plus
   (ii) a 'remainder' (since 15 ÷ 4 = 3, with remainder 3).

2. Separate the fraction to write it as a mixed number.
   The first part will always simplify to a whole number.

$$\frac{15}{4} = \frac{12+3}{4}$$
$$= \frac{12}{4} + \frac{3}{4}$$
$$= 3 + \frac{3}{4} = 3\frac{3}{4}$$

Exercise 3

1 Write the whole number that is equivalent to these improper fractions.

a) $\frac{12}{6}$ b) $\frac{27}{9}$ c) $\frac{54}{6}$ d) $\frac{81}{9}$

2 a) Write down the value of c if $\frac{16}{3} = \frac{c+1}{3}$.

   b) Use your answer to write $\frac{16}{3}$ as a mixed number in its simplest terms.

3 a) Write down the value of a if $\frac{15}{9} = \frac{9+a}{9}$.

   b) Use your answer to write $\frac{15}{9}$ as a mixed number in its simplest terms.

4 Write the following improper fractions as mixed numbers in their simplest terms.

a) $\frac{7}{4}$ b) $\frac{12}{9}$ c) $\frac{11}{8}$ d) $\frac{11}{10}$ e) $\frac{9}{5}$

f) $\frac{15}{6}$ g) $\frac{20}{11}$ h) $\frac{16}{9}$ i) $\frac{6}{5}$ j) $\frac{13}{7}$

5 a) Cancel down the improper fraction $\frac{30}{4}$ so that it is in its simplest terms.

   b) Use your answer to **a)** to write $\frac{30}{4}$ as a mixed number.

6 Write the following improper fractions as mixed numbers in their simplest terms.

a) $\dfrac{14}{8}$ b) $\dfrac{10}{6}$ c) $\dfrac{40}{12}$ d) $\dfrac{36}{8}$ e) $\dfrac{21}{9}$

f) $\dfrac{70}{20}$ g) $\dfrac{28}{6}$ h) $\dfrac{57}{11}$ i) $\dfrac{52}{8}$ j) $\dfrac{50}{15}$

7 a) Write the mixed number $2\dfrac{3}{5}$ as an improper fraction.

b) Use your answer to **a)** to work out $2\dfrac{3}{5} + \dfrac{4}{5}$ as an improper fraction.

c) Write your answer to **b)** as a mixed number.

8 Work out the following. Give your answers as mixed numbers in their simplest form.

a) $2\dfrac{3}{4} + \dfrac{3}{4}$ b) $3\dfrac{5}{7} - \dfrac{4}{7}$ c) $1\dfrac{4}{5} + \dfrac{3}{5}$

d) $6\dfrac{5}{7} - \dfrac{6}{7}$ e) $3\dfrac{7}{8} + 3\dfrac{7}{8}$ f) $4\dfrac{4}{9} - 2\dfrac{8}{9}$

9 a) Write the following as improper fractions:

i) $3\dfrac{1}{4}$ ii) $1\dfrac{5}{6}$

b) Use your answers to **a)** to work out $3\dfrac{1}{4} - 1\dfrac{5}{6}$ as a mixed number in its simplest form.

10 Work out the following. Give your answers as mixed numbers in their simplest form.

a) $2\dfrac{2}{7} + 1\dfrac{3}{14}$ b) $3\dfrac{5}{8} - 1\dfrac{2}{5}$ c) $3\dfrac{2}{6} - 1\dfrac{1}{4}$

d) $4\dfrac{1}{9} + 3\dfrac{1}{2}$ e) $2\dfrac{5}{6} + 2\dfrac{4}{9}$ f) $4\dfrac{3}{9} - 2\dfrac{1}{4}$

11 Find the missing number in these calculations:

a) $2\dfrac{5}{6} + \text{..........} = 4\dfrac{1}{2}$ b) $\text{..........} - 1\dfrac{1}{3} = 3\dfrac{5}{12}$

5.2 Multiplying and Dividing Fractions

Multiplying Fractions

To find a <u>fraction</u> of an amount, multiply the amount by the fraction.

> **Example 1** What is $\dfrac{4}{5}$ of 180 g?
>
> 1. Multiply by the numerator... $180 \times 4 = 720$
> 2. ...and divide by the denominator. $720 \div 5 = \mathbf{144\ g}$

Exercise 1

1 What is:

    a) $\dfrac{5}{6}$ of 48 kg?
    b) $\dfrac{3}{8}$ of 88 miles?
    c) $\dfrac{7}{12}$ of 96 cm?

2 **a)** Work out $\dfrac{3}{4}$ of $\dfrac{2}{3}$ of 36.
    b) Work out $\dfrac{2}{5}$ of $\dfrac{5}{7}$ of 56.

3 A school has 840 pupils. $\dfrac{3}{7}$ of the pupils are learning to play an instrument.

Work out how many pupils are learning to play an instrument.

4 **a)** One third of a number is 15. What is the number?

    b) Three quarters of a number is 18. What is the number?

5 A swimming pool has 480 members.

$\dfrac{2}{5}$ of the members are women. $\dfrac{1}{3}$ of the members are men.

The rest of the members are children. How many of the members are children?

6 A jar contains red, yellow and orange sweets. $\dfrac{1}{4}$ of the sweets are red.

There are equal numbers of yellow and orange sweets.
Work out how many red sweets there are if there are 18 yellow sweets.

To multiply one fraction by another fraction, multiply the <u>numerators</u> together and the <u>denominators</u> together separately.

> **Example 2**   Work out $\frac{3}{8} \times \frac{2}{3}$.
>
> 1. Multiply the numerators.
> 2. Multiply the denominators.
>
> $$\frac{3}{8} \times \frac{2}{3} = \frac{3 \times 2}{8 \times 3} = \frac{6}{24}$$
>
> 3. Simplify the fraction by dividing the top and bottom number by 6.
>
> $$\frac{6}{24} \xrightarrow{\div 6} \frac{1}{4} \quad \div 6$$

Exercise 2

Answer these questions **without using a calculator**.

1   Copy and complete these calculations.

a) $\frac{1}{3} \times \frac{1}{4} = \frac{1 \times 1}{3 \times 4} = ---$

b) $\frac{1}{3} \times \frac{1}{5} = \frac{1 \times 1}{3 \times 5} = ---$

c) $\frac{3}{4} \times \frac{1}{7} = \frac{3 \times}{4 \times} = ---$

d) $\frac{2}{5} \times \frac{3}{5} = \frac{\times 3}{\times 5} = ---$

e) $\frac{2}{9} \times \frac{3}{4} = \frac{\times 3}{9 \times} = ---$

f) $\frac{1}{9} \times \frac{1}{8} = \frac{1 \times}{\times} = ---$

g) $\frac{1}{7} \times \frac{4}{5} = \frac{1 \times}{\times} = ---$

h) $\frac{3}{7} \times \frac{4}{5} = \frac{\times}{\times} = ---$

2   Work out these multiplications.

a) $\frac{1}{3} \times \frac{5}{7}$

b) $\frac{1}{4} \times \frac{1}{4}$

c) $\frac{1}{3} \times \frac{2}{9}$

d) $\frac{3}{4} \times \frac{1}{8}$

e) $\frac{3}{5} \times \frac{1}{8}$

f) $\frac{1}{6} \times \frac{1}{3}$

g) $\frac{1}{5} \times \frac{4}{7}$

h) $\frac{2}{3} \times \frac{2}{5}$

i) $\frac{1}{4} \times \frac{1}{9}$

j) $\frac{2}{5} \times \frac{1}{7}$

3   Work out these multiplications.

a) $\frac{4}{7} \times \frac{2}{3}$

b) $\frac{3}{5} \times \frac{4}{9}$

c) $\frac{5}{7} \times \frac{6}{7}$

d) $\frac{5}{7} \times \frac{5}{6}$

4 Work out these multiplications. Give your answers in their simplest terms.

a) $\dfrac{2}{5} \times \dfrac{3}{4}$ b) $\dfrac{1}{4} \times \dfrac{4}{6}$ c) $\dfrac{2}{4} \times \dfrac{3}{12}$ d) $\dfrac{1}{2} \times \dfrac{8}{9}$ e) $\dfrac{3}{3} \times \dfrac{2}{6}$

f) $\dfrac{1}{4} \times \dfrac{4}{7}$ g) $\dfrac{5}{7} \times \dfrac{1}{5}$ h) $\dfrac{2}{3} \times \dfrac{2}{10}$ i) $\dfrac{5}{9} \times \dfrac{3}{5}$ j) $\dfrac{4}{5} \times \dfrac{5}{10}$

5   a) Write the following as improper fractions: i) $2\dfrac{1}{3}$ ii) $1\dfrac{1}{4}$

   b) Use your answers to **a)** to work out $2\dfrac{1}{3} \times 1\dfrac{1}{4}$. Give the answer as a mixed number.

6 Work out these multiplications.
Give your answers as mixed numbers in their simplest terms.

a) $2\dfrac{1}{3} \times 2\dfrac{3}{4}$ b) $2\dfrac{2}{5} \times 1\dfrac{4}{5}$ c) $1\dfrac{4}{5} \times 2\dfrac{1}{3}$ d) $1\dfrac{3}{5} \times 2\dfrac{1}{4}$ e) $1\dfrac{1}{6} \times 2\dfrac{1}{2}$

7 Jen made $12\dfrac{3}{4}$ metres of bunting on Saturday. On Sunday, she made $2\dfrac{2}{5}$ times more.
Work out the length of bunting that Jen made on Sunday.

8 On Monday Liam cycles $2\dfrac{3}{5}$ miles. He cycles $1\dfrac{1}{2}$ times further on Tuesday.
Work out the total distance he travels on Monday and Tuesday.

Investigate — Multiplying by a Fraction

a) Copy this grid and shade in $\dfrac{3}{8}$ of it.

    Then multiply $\dfrac{3}{8}$ by $\dfrac{1}{2}$. Shade your answer on another copy of the grid.
    Does the fraction get bigger or smaller?

b) Try multiplying $\dfrac{3}{8}$ by smaller fractions, such as $\dfrac{1}{3}$ and $\dfrac{1}{6}$,

    and shade in your answers on copies of the grid.
    What do you notice about the size of the answers?

c) Repeat, but this time choose a different starting fraction and make
    your own grids. Can you write a rule about how a fraction changes
    when it's multiplied by another fraction?

Dividing Fractions

To divide by a fraction, you multiply by its reciprocal.
You get the reciprocal by swapping around the numerator and the denominator.

Example 3 **Work out:**

a) $\frac{1}{3} \div \frac{2}{5}$ Multiply $\frac{1}{3}$ by the reciprocal of $\frac{2}{5}$. $\frac{1}{3} \times \frac{5}{2} = \frac{1 \times 5}{3 \times 2} = \frac{5}{6}$

b) $\frac{2}{7} \div 3$ Multiply $\frac{2}{7}$ by the reciprocal of 3.

3 is the same as $\frac{3}{1}$, so its reciprocal is $\frac{1}{3}$. $\frac{2}{7} \times \frac{1}{3} = \frac{2 \times 1}{7 \times 3} = \frac{2}{21}$

Exercise 3

Answer these questions **without using a calculator**.

1 Copy and complete these calculations.

a) $\frac{1}{8} \div \frac{1}{4} = \frac{1}{8} \times \frac{4}{1} = \frac{1 \times 4}{8 \times 1} = \text{—}$

b) $\frac{2}{5} \div \frac{1}{2} = \frac{2}{5} \times \frac{2}{1} = \frac{2 \times 2}{5 \times 1} = \text{—}$

c) $\frac{1}{4} \div \frac{5}{6} = \frac{1}{4} \times \frac{}{5} = \frac{1 \times}{4 \times 5} = \text{—}$

d) $\frac{4}{7} \div \frac{2}{3} = \frac{4}{7} \times \frac{3}{} = \frac{4 \times 3}{7 \times} = \text{—}$

e) $\frac{3}{8} \div \frac{1}{2} = \frac{3}{8} \times \frac{}{\text{—}} = \frac{3 \times}{8 \times} = \text{—}$

f) $\frac{1}{9} \div \frac{3}{8} = \frac{1}{9} \times \frac{}{\text{—}} = \frac{1 \times}{9 \times} = \text{—}$

2 Work out these calculations. Give your answers in their simplest terms.

a) $\frac{1}{3} \div \frac{3}{8}$ b) $\frac{2}{5} \div \frac{1}{2}$ c) $\frac{1}{4} \div \frac{4}{5}$ d) $\frac{3}{11} \div \frac{11}{12}$ e) $\frac{4}{15} \div \frac{2}{3}$ f) $\frac{3}{30} \div \frac{3}{20}$

3 Copy and complete these calculations.

a) $3 \div \frac{3}{5} = 3 \times \frac{5}{3} = \frac{3 \times 5}{3} = \frac{}{3} = \text{......}$

b) $4 \div \frac{2}{6} = 4 \times \frac{6}{} = \frac{4 \times 6}{} = \frac{}{} = \text{......}$

4 Work out these calculations. Give your answers in their simplest terms.

a) $11 \div \frac{3}{9}$ b) $7 \div \frac{2}{6}$ c) $5 \div \frac{5}{6}$ d) $3 \div \frac{4}{12}$ e) $12 \div \frac{3}{5}$

5 Copy and complete these calculations.

a) $\dfrac{5}{6} \div 4 = \dfrac{5}{6} \times \underline{\quad} = \dfrac{5 \times}{6 \times} = \underline{\quad}$ **b)** $\dfrac{7}{8} \div 6 = \dfrac{7}{8} \times \underline{\quad} = \dfrac{7 \times}{8 \times} = \underline{\quad}$

6 Work out these calculations. Give your answers in their simplest terms.

a) $\dfrac{5}{6} \div 5$ **b)** $\dfrac{6}{9} \div 4$ **c)** $\dfrac{10}{12} \div 5$ **d)** $\dfrac{5}{8} \div 5$ **e)** $\dfrac{3}{11} \div 3$

7 Change the mixed numbers to improper fractions to work out these calculations. Give your answers in their simplest terms.

a) $2\dfrac{3}{4} \div 3$ **b)** $1\dfrac{5}{6} \div 4$ **c)** $4\dfrac{2}{7} \div 5$ **d)** $3\dfrac{5}{8} \div 5$ **e)** $2\dfrac{8}{9} \div 5$

8 Work out these calculations. Give your answers as mixed numbers in their simplest terms.

a) $2\dfrac{1}{5} \div \dfrac{1}{3}$ **b)** $4\dfrac{2}{7} \div \dfrac{1}{2}$ **c)** $2\dfrac{3}{7} \div \dfrac{2}{3}$ **d)** $1\dfrac{2}{5} \div \dfrac{3}{5}$ **e)** $2\dfrac{2}{3} \div \dfrac{2}{5}$

9 $\dfrac{5}{7}$ of a cake is left over after a party. It is divided out equally between 5 people.

Work out what fraction of the cake each person gets, in its simplest form.

10 Adi buys a piece of rope which is $\dfrac{4}{5}$ m long. He cuts the rope into 8 equal parts.

Work out the length of each piece of rope as a fraction in its simplest form.

11 Faye wins some money. She wants to give $\dfrac{8}{9}$ of it to charity.

She chooses 4 charities and splits the money equally between them.
Work out what fraction of the money each charity gets.

12 James shares out $2\dfrac{6}{8}$ bars of chocolate equally between his 3 brothers.

Work out what fraction of a bar each of his brothers gets.

13 A hard drive has enough storage space left for $7\dfrac{1}{2}$ hours of TV programmes.

How many programmes each lasting $\dfrac{5}{6}$ of an hour can be recorded on the hard drive?

5.3 Changing Fractions to Decimals and Percentages

Fractions and Decimals

Any fraction can be written as a decimal.
You can do this by dividing the numerator by the denominator.

Example 1 Write $\frac{3}{8}$ as a decimal using:

a) a calculator

Divide 3 by 8 on the calculator. $\boxed{3} \div \boxed{8} = 0.375$

b) short division

1. Set out your short division, leaving space for decimal places.

   $8\,|\,\overline{3.000}$

2. Carry out the short division.

   $$\frac{0.375}{8\,|\,3.{}^30{}^60{}^40}$$

Exercise 1

1 Use your calculator to write these fractions as decimals.

a) $\frac{5}{8}$ b) $\frac{5}{32}$ c) $\frac{11}{25}$ d) $\frac{9}{40}$ e) $\frac{9}{16}$ f) $\frac{1}{16}$

g) $\frac{7}{16}$ h) $\frac{9}{50}$ i) $\frac{7}{125}$ j) $\frac{9}{375}$ k) $\frac{11}{250}$ l) $\frac{93}{625}$

2 Use your calculator to write these improper fractions as decimals.

a) $\frac{27}{20}$ b) $\frac{33}{24}$ c) $\frac{15}{4}$ d) $\frac{127}{80}$ e) $\frac{33}{8}$ f) $\frac{171}{125}$

3 Write these fractions as decimals using short division.

a) $\frac{1}{8}$ b) $\frac{7}{8}$ e) $\frac{17}{8}$

d) $\frac{7}{20}$ e) $\frac{11}{40}$ f) $\frac{19}{16}$

It's easier to write fractions as decimals when the denominator is 10, 100 or 1000.

Remember: $\dfrac{1}{10} = 0.1$ $\quad$ $\dfrac{1}{100} = 0.01$ $\quad$ $\dfrac{1}{1000} = 0.001$

Just put the numerator digits in the right decimal places.

$$\dfrac{135}{1000} \;=\; 0.1\,3\,5$$

tenths $\qquad$ hundredths $\qquad$ thousandths

If the fraction has a denominator which is a factor or multiple of 10, 100 or 1000, find the equivalent fraction with a denominator of 10, 100 or 1000 first. Then it's easy to change it into a decimal.

Example 2   **Write the following fractions as decimals:**

a) $\dfrac{6}{10}$

This is the same as 6 tenths, so write 6 in the tenths column.

$\dfrac{6}{10} = \mathbf{0.6}$

b) $\dfrac{3}{100}$

This is the same as 3 hundredths, so write 3 in the hundredths column.

$\dfrac{3}{100} = \mathbf{0.03}$

c) $\dfrac{67}{1000}$

This is 67 thousandths, so line up the digits so that the 7 is in the thousandths column.

$\dfrac{67}{1000} = \mathbf{0.067}$

Exercise 2

Answer these questions **without using a calculator**.

1 Copy and complete these conversions:

a) $\dfrac{9}{10}$ = ... tenths = 0.9

b) $\dfrac{5}{100}$ = 5 .... = 0.05

c) $\dfrac{16}{1000}$ = ... thousandths = ...

d) $\dfrac{98}{100}$ = 98 .... = ...

2 Write these fractions as decimals.

a) $\dfrac{4}{10}$ b) $\dfrac{8}{10}$ c) $\dfrac{2}{10}$ d) $\dfrac{3}{10}$ e) $\dfrac{4}{100}$ f) $\dfrac{6}{100}$ g) $\dfrac{81}{100}$

h) $\dfrac{14}{100}$ i) $\dfrac{26}{100}$ j) $\dfrac{2}{1000}$ k) $\dfrac{5}{1000}$ l) $\dfrac{57}{1000}$ m) $\dfrac{39}{1000}$ n) $\dfrac{391}{1000}$

Example 3   Write $\dfrac{20}{50}$ as a decimal.

1. First, find a fraction equivalent to $\dfrac{20}{50}$ which has 10, 100 or 1000 as the denominator.

2. Multiply the numerator and denominator by 2 to rewrite the fraction with denominator 100.

$$\dfrac{20}{50} = \dfrac{40}{100}$$

3. Change the fraction to a decimal. You don't need the extra zero on the end.

$$\dfrac{40}{100} = 40 \text{ hundredths}$$

$$= 0.40 = \mathbf{0.4}$$

---

3   a) Find the value of a if $\dfrac{4}{20} = \dfrac{a}{10}$.

    b) Use your answer to a) to write the fraction $\dfrac{4}{20}$ as a decimal.

4   a) Find a fraction equivalent to $\dfrac{12}{20}$ which has a denominator of 10.

    b) Use your answer to write $\dfrac{12}{20}$ as a decimal.

5   For each of these fractions:

    i) rewrite the fraction so that it has a denominator of 10, and

    ii) write the fraction as a decimal.

    a) $\dfrac{4}{5}$ b) $\dfrac{1}{5}$ c) $\dfrac{2}{5}$

6 For each of these fractions:

i) rewrite the fraction so that it has a denominator of 100, and

ii) write the fraction as a decimal.

a) $\dfrac{3}{20}$ b) $\dfrac{22}{50}$ c) $\dfrac{4}{25}$ d) $\dfrac{9}{20}$ e) $\dfrac{48}{50}$ f) $\dfrac{15}{25}$

7 For each of these fractions:

i) rewrite the fraction so that it has a denominator of 1000, and

ii) write the fraction as a decimal.

a) $\dfrac{9}{500}$ b) $\dfrac{31}{500}$ c) $\dfrac{40}{500}$ d) $\dfrac{25}{200}$ e) $\dfrac{37}{200}$ f) $\dfrac{11}{250}$

g) $\dfrac{7}{500}$ h) $\dfrac{39}{500}$ i) $\dfrac{47}{500}$ j) $\dfrac{9}{200}$ k) $\dfrac{41}{200}$ l) $\dfrac{13}{250}$

8 Write these fractions as decimals.

a) $\dfrac{8}{25}$ b) $\dfrac{7}{25}$ c) $\dfrac{3}{5}$ d) $\dfrac{21}{50}$ e) $\dfrac{12}{25}$ f) $\dfrac{11}{25}$

g) $\dfrac{19}{20}$ h) $\dfrac{17}{20}$ i) $\dfrac{37}{50}$ j) $\dfrac{16}{25}$ k) $\dfrac{11}{20}$ l) $\dfrac{9}{25}$

9 Write these fractions as decimals.

a) $\dfrac{11}{50}$ b) $\dfrac{13}{25}$ c) $\dfrac{91}{500}$ d) $\dfrac{187}{200}$ e) $\dfrac{201}{500}$ f) $\dfrac{103}{250}$

g) $\dfrac{127}{200}$ h) $\dfrac{99}{200}$ i) $\dfrac{245}{500}$ j) $\dfrac{3}{200}$ k) $\dfrac{9}{250}$ l) $\dfrac{17}{500}$

10 Damian won some money in a lottery.

He spends $\dfrac{70}{200}$ of the money and wants to give the rest to charity.

What fraction of the money will he give to charity? Give your answer as a decimal.

11 Write the digits 2, 4 and 6 in the gaps to make a correct conversion:

$$\frac{\text{.......}}{25} = 0.\text{.....}\,\text{.....}$$

You can change a decimal to a fraction by writing it as a fraction
with a denominator of 10, 100 or 1000, then simplifying.

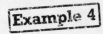 **Write these decimals as fractions.**
Give your answers in their simplest terms.

a) 0.4

1. The final digit is in the tenths column, so write a fraction using 10 as the denominator.

2. Simplify the fraction.

$$0.4 = \frac{4}{10} \overset{\div 2}{\underset{\div 2}{=}} \frac{2}{5}$$

b) 0.142

1. The final digit is in the thousandths column, so write a fraction using 1000 as the denominator.

2. Simplify the fraction.

$$0.142 = \frac{142}{1000} \overset{\div 2}{\underset{\div 2}{=}} \frac{71}{500}$$

Exercise 3

1 Write these decimals as fractions without using a calculator.

a) 0.3 **b)** 0.7 **c)** 0.01 **d)** 0.003 **e)** 0.13 **f)** 0.017

2 Write these decimals as fractions without using a calculator.
Give your answers in their simplest terms.

a) 0.5 **b)** 0.8 **c)** 0.2 **d)** 0.12 **e)** 0.44 **f)** 0.38

g) 0.64 **h)** 0.04 **i)** 0.05 **j)** 0.225 **k)** 0.045 **l)** 0.008

3 Write down a fraction that lies between 0.42 and 0.43.

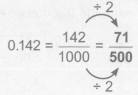

Investigate — Recurring Decimals

*Recurring decimals are ones that keep on
going forever, filling up all the decimal places
with a repeated digit or string of digits.*

$$\frac{1}{2} \quad \frac{1}{3} \quad \frac{1}{4} \quad \frac{1}{5} \quad \frac{1}{6} \quad \frac{1}{7} \quad \frac{1}{8} \quad \frac{1}{9}$$

a) Use a calculator to write each of the fractions in the box as a decimal.

b) Which denominators give recurring decimals? Are there any patterns?

c) Investigate, first using different numerators, then different denominators,
to test out any rules you come up with.

Percentages

A <u>percentage</u> is a fraction out of 100, so 45% is the same as $\dfrac{45}{100}$, which cancels down to $\dfrac{9}{20}$.

Example 5 **Write each of these amounts as a percentage without using a calculator:**

a) 3 out of 10

1. Write the amount as a fraction.
2. Write this with a denominator of 100.
3. The numerator is the percentage.

$$\overset{\times 10}{\frown} \quad \frac{3}{10} = \frac{30}{100} = \mathbf{30\%}$$
$$\underset{\times 10}{\smile}$$

b) 64 out of 200

1. Write the amount as a fraction.
2. Write this as an equivalent fraction over 100.
3. The numerator is the percentage.

$$\overset{\div 2}{\frown} \quad \frac{64}{200} = \frac{32}{100} = \mathbf{32\%}$$
$$\underset{\div 2}{\smile}$$

Exercise 4

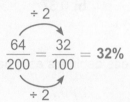

Answer questions 1 to 8 **without using a calculator**.

1 Write each of the following as a percentage:

a) 8 out of 10   b) 4 out of 10   c) 7 out of 50   d) 18 out of 50

e) 70 out of 200   f) 16 out of 200   g) 122 out of 200   h) 2 out of 20

i) $\dfrac{13}{20}$ j) $\dfrac{8}{25}$ k) $\dfrac{15}{25}$ l) $\dfrac{400}{1000}$

2 Jill scored $\dfrac{18}{25}$ in a test. What is her mark as a percentage?

3 A 200 g bar of chocolate contains 58 g of fat. What percentage of the chocolate is fat?

4 Rob buys 50 stamps. 41 are first class. What percentage are first class?

5 Peter flipped a coin 25 times. The coin landed showing 'heads' 12 times.
What percentage of flips landed with 'tails' showing?

To change from a <u>percentage</u> to a <u>decimal</u>, you can divide by 100.
To change from a decimal to a percentage, multiply by 100.

> **Example 6** Write $\dfrac{21}{35}$ first as a decimal and then as a percentage.
>
> 1. Divide the top number by the bottom number to get a decimal.
>
> $21 \div 35 = \mathbf{0.6}$
>
> 2. Then multiply by 100 to give the percentage.
>
> $0.6 \times 100 = \mathbf{60\%}$

6 Write each of the following decimals as a percentage.

   a) 0.12   **b)** 0.37   **c)** 0.94   **d)** 0.61   **e)** 0.03   **f)** 0.09

7 Write these decimals as **i)** percentages, and **ii)** fractions in their simplest form:

   a) 0.67   **b)** 0.77   **c)** 0.01   **d)** 0.84   **e)** 0.45   **f)** 0.05

8 Write these fractions as **i)** decimals, and **ii)** percentages:

   a) $\dfrac{49}{100}$ **b)** $\dfrac{33}{100}$ **c)** $\dfrac{3}{10}$ **d)** $\dfrac{9}{10}$ **e)** $\dfrac{1}{2}$ **f)** $\dfrac{1}{4}$ **g)** $\dfrac{3}{5}$

You **can** use a calculator for questions 9 to 12.

9 Write these fractions as: **i)** decimals   **ii)** percentages

   a) $\dfrac{18}{40}$ **b)** $\dfrac{42}{50}$ **c)** $\dfrac{39}{150}$ **d)** $\dfrac{48}{60}$ **e)** $\dfrac{36}{80}$ **f)** $\dfrac{30}{75}$

10 James sits an exam and gets a mark of $\dfrac{54}{75}$. What percentage did he get wrong?

11 325 students attend a school. 195 of the students are girls.
    Give the proportion of boys at the school as a decimal.

12 $\dfrac{18}{20}$ children in a class prefer dogs to cats. What percentage of the class prefer cats?

Example 7 **Write 45% as both a decimal and as a fraction in its simplest form.**

1. Divide the percentage by 100 to get a decimal.

$$45 \div 100 = \mathbf{0.45}$$

2. The final digit of 0.45 is in the hundredths column, so write 0.45 as 45 hundredths.

$$0.45 = \frac{45}{100}$$

3. Divide the top and bottom by 5 to simplify the fraction.

$$\overset{\div 5}{\overbrace{\frac{45}{100}}} = \frac{\mathbf{9}}{\mathbf{20}}$$
$$\underset{\div 5}{}$$

Exercise 5

Answer these questions **without using a calculator**.

1 This grid is made from 100 small squares.

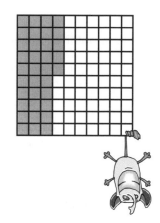

  a) How many of the squares are shaded?

  b) What fraction of the grid is shaded?

  c) Write the amount of the grid that is shaded as a decimal.

  d) What percentage of the grid is shaded?

  e) What percentage of the grid is not shaded?

  f) Write the amount of the grid that is not shaded as a fraction in its simplest form.

2 Write these percentages as **i)** decimals, and **ii)** fractions in their simplest form:

  a) 39%   **b)** 48%   **c)** 50%   **d)** 13%   **e)** 9%   **f)** 60%

  g) 25%   **h)** 30%   **i)** 55%   **j)** 75%   **k)** 5%   **l)** 22%

3 85% of customers in a cafe ordered soup for lunch.
Write this percentage as a fraction in its simplest form.

4 53% of the people who visited a museum one day were men.
What proportion of the visitors that day were women? Give your answer as a decimal.

5 The proportion of questions a student needs to get correct to pass an exam is 0.65.
How many questions out of 200 would she be able to get wrong and still pass?

Example 8

a) Write 6 out of 20 as a percentage without using a calculator.

1. Write the proportion as a fraction.

2. Write an equivalent fraction with a denominator of 100.

$$\overset{\times\,5}{\underset{\times\,5}{\frac{6}{20} = \frac{30}{100}}} = \mathbf{30\%}$$

3. The numerator is the percentage.

b) Write 87 out of 120 as a percentage. You may use a calculator.

1. Divide the numerator by the denominator to write the proportion as a decimal.

$$87 \div 120 = 0.725$$

2. Multiply the decimal by 100.

$$0.725 \times 100 = \mathbf{72.5\%}$$

Exercise 6

1 Work out the following without using a calculator:

a) 3 as a percentage of 25   **b)** 19 as a percentage of 50 **c)** 178 as a percentage of 200

2 Paul scored 81 out of 90 in a maths exam.
Work out his mark as a percentage, without using a calculator.

3 Sally saves up £225 for a shopping trip. She spends £207.
What percentage of her savings did she spend?

4 1120 people bought a raffle ticket and 28 of them won a prize.
What percentage of people who bought a ticket won a prize?

5 Emma has 68 pairs of socks. 51 pairs are purple and the other pairs are all orange.
What percentage of Emma's socks are orange?

6 27 out of 60 counters in a bag are red and the rest are green.
What percentage of the counters are green?

7 A gym has 460 members. 207 of the members use the swimming pool.
What percentage of members do not use the swimming pool?

Comparing Proportions

If you need to compare some proportions (fractions, decimals or percentages), convert them to the same type of proportion first. It's usually easiest to change everything to a percentage.

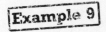 **In a school, 48% of Year 8 are girls.**
90 out of 200 pupils in Year 9 are girls.
Which year has the higher proportion of girls?

1. Change the fraction into a percentage. $\dfrac{90}{200}$ = 90 ÷ 200 = 0.45

   0.45 × 100 = 45%

2. Compare the two percentages.   48% is bigger than 45%, so **Year 8** has the higher proportion of girls.

Exercise 7

Answer questions 1 to 4 **without using a calculator**.

1   Which is bigger:

   a) 27% or $\dfrac{1}{4}$?   **b)** 49% or $\dfrac{1}{2}$?   **c)** 0.81 or $\dfrac{4}{5}$?   **d)** 60% or 0.66?

2   Write each set of numbers in order, starting with the smallest:

   a) 30%, $\dfrac{28}{100}$, 0.32   **b)** 0.56, $\dfrac{1}{2}$, 58%   **c)** $\dfrac{1}{5}$, 0.22, 19%

   d) $\dfrac{69}{100}$, 0.7, 71%   **e)** $\dfrac{4}{10}$, 0.42, 41%   **f)** $\dfrac{1}{4}$, 0.04, 26%

3   **a)** Write 63% as a decimal.

   b) Write $\dfrac{3}{5}$ as a decimal.

   c) Put 63%, $\dfrac{3}{5}$ and 0.66 in order, from smallest to largest.

4   For each of the following pairs, write down which is larger.

   a) 0.44, 40%   **b)** 0.3, 3%   **c)** 0.65, 60%   **d)** 0.08, 80%

   e) 0.3, $\dfrac{29}{100}$ **f)** 0.1, $\dfrac{1}{100}$ **g)** 0.8, $\dfrac{3}{4}$ **h)** 0.01, $\dfrac{2}{20}$

You **can** use a calculator to answer the questions 5 to 12 if you need to.

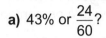

5 Which is bigger:

a) 43% or $\frac{24}{60}$?

b) $\frac{18}{30}$ or 0.51?

c) 0.85 or $\frac{36}{45}$?

d) 0.41 or $\frac{22}{55}$?

e) $\frac{5}{25}$ or 0.25?

f) 0.9 or $\frac{19}{20}$?

6 Write each set of numbers in order, starting with the smallest:

a) $\frac{11}{44}$, 0.11, 24%

b) 2%, 0.8, $\frac{8}{40}$

c) 0.7, $\frac{21}{28}$, 76%

7 For each of the following lists, write down which amount is **not** equal to the others.

a) 0.25, 40%, $\frac{4}{10}$

b) 0.6, 60%, $\frac{6}{100}$

c) 0.12, 12%, $\frac{1}{12}$

d) 0.3, 3%, $\frac{3}{10}$

e) 0.6, 6%, $\frac{3}{5}$

f) 0.4, 44%, $\frac{22}{50}$

g) 0.33, 33%, $\frac{33}{50}$

h) 0.12, 25%, $\frac{3}{25}$

8 Put the numbers in each of the following lists in order, from largest to smallest.

a) 0.91, 95%, $\frac{18}{20}$

b) 0.5, 51%, $\frac{1}{5}$

c) 0.6, 23%, $\frac{6}{25}$

d) 0.03, 31%, $\frac{3}{10}$

9 Two shops are having a sale.

Shop A is offering $\frac{1}{5}$ off all items, while Shop B is offering 25% off all items.

Which shop is reducing its prices by the greater percentage?

10 Jo is buying a television. She needs to pay $\frac{1}{5}$ of the total cost as a deposit.

She can afford to pay 22% of the cost of the television. Is this enough to pay the deposit?

11 In a test, Sophie scores 78% and Calum scores $\frac{66}{75}$. Who got the higher mark?

12 Tom wins at chess 180 times in every 250. Daisy wins three quarters of the time.
Who has the better percentage score?

5.4 Percentages of Amounts

Finding Percentages Without a Calculator

Finding a <u>percentage</u> of an amount just means finding a <u>proportion</u> of the total number.

Example 1 **Without using a calculator, find:**

a) **20% of £40**

　　1. 20% is the same as $\frac{1}{5}$. 　　　　　$20\% = \frac{20}{100} = \frac{1}{5}$

　　2. So find 20% of £40 by dividing by 5. 　$40 \div 5 = \textbf{£8}$

b) **60% of £40**

　　1. 60% is 3 lots of 20%, and from **a)** 　$60\% = 3 \times 20\%$
　　　we know that 20% of £40 is £8...

　　2. ...So multiply £8 by 3. 　　　　　　$60\% \text{ of } £40 = 3 \times £8 = \textbf{£24}$

Exercise 1

Answer these questions **without using a calculator**.

1　Find each of these percentages:

　　a) 50% of 8　　　**b)** 25% of 40　　　**c)** 50% of 24 cm　　　**d)** 25% of 20 kg　　　**e)** 50% of £7

2　**a)** Find 20% of £25.　　　　　**b)** Use your answer to **a)** to find 80% of £25.

3　50% of a bag of 36 counters are blue. How many counters are blue?

4　Grace gets paid £1200 each month. She saves 25% of everything she gets paid.
　　How much does she save each month?

5　8000 tickets went on sale for a pantomime. 75% of the tickets were sold to children.
　　How many tickets were sold to children?

6　Adam counted 160 cars. 25% of them were red. How many red cars did Adam count?

7　Of the 32 passengers on a train, 75% were adults. How many adults were on the train?

> **Example 2** Find 45% of 80 without a calculator.
>
> 1. First, find 10% of 80.
>   10% is the same as $\frac{1}{10}$, $80 \div 10 = 8$
>   so divide 80 by 10.
> 2. Next, find 40% and 5% of 80:
>   40% is 10% × 4. $8 \times 4 = 32$
>   5% is 10% ÷ 2. $8 \div 2 = 4$
> 3. Add these two values
>   together to find 45%   45% of 80 is 32 + 4 = **36**

8   **a)** Find 10% of 60.   **b)** Hence find 20% of 60.

9   **a)** Find 10% of 90.   **b)** Hence find 30% of 90.

10   **a)** Find 10% of 70 kg.   **b)** Hence find 40% of 70 kg.

11   **a)** Find 10% of £30.   **b)** Hence find 60% of £30.

12   Find each of these percentages:

    a) 20% of £120   **b)** 30% of 80   **c)** 40% of 30 cm   **d)** 70% of 50 miles

13   **a)** Find 10% of 40.   **b)** Hence find 5% of 40.

14   **a)** Find 10% of 160 km.   **b)** Hence find 5% of 160 km.

15   **a)** Find 10% of 60.   **b)** Find 5% of 60.   **c)** Find 15% of 60.

16   **a)** Find 10% of £300.   **b)** Find 5% of £300.   **c)** Find 35% of £300.

17   Lily buys a pack of charity Christmas cards for £6.
     15% of the cost is donated to charity. How much is the donation?

18 Find each of these percentages:

   a) 10% of 15   **b)** 30% of £120   **c)** 70% of 70 m   **d)** 15% of 90

   e) 35% of 60 cm   **f)** 5% of £500   **g)** 45% of £220   **h)** 80% of 200

19 Dan buys a bike costing £450. He has to leave a 20% deposit at the shop.
How much is the deposit?

20 240 people filled in a survey about pets. 10% owned a cat and 35% owned a dog.

   a) How many people owned a cat?

   b) How many people owned a dog?

21 Find each of these percentages:

   a) 20% of 10   **b)** 15% of 20   **c)** 50% of 86 kg   **d)** 2% of 400

   e) 50% of £680   **f)** 5% of 80 cm   **g)** 30% of 80   **h)** 75% of 24 ml

   i) 5% of £5.40   **j)** 15% of £90   **k)** 25% of 56   **l)** 3% of 1000

   m) 70% of 220 miles   **n)** 4% of 200 m   **o)** 25% of 900   **p)** 13% of 300 g

22 Find each of these percentages:

   a) 1% of £200   **b)** 1% of 6000 km   **c)** 3% of 600   **d)** 1% of 800

   e) 2% of 500   **f)** 6% of 600   **g)** 1% of 400   **h)** 1% of 1000 kg

   i) 4% of 450   **j)** 3% of 150 miles   **k)** 27% of 150   **l)** 16% of £70

23 Ashley made £60 by selling cupcakes. She donated 31% of this to charity.
How much did she donate to charity?

24 Adam gets paid £14 000 each year. He spends 3% of this on clothes.
How much does he spend on clothes each year?

25 Mark gets 98% on a science test.
How many questions did he get right out of 600?

Finding Percentages Using a Calculator

You can also work out percentages of amounts by multiplying the amount by the percentage as a <u>decimal</u>. This decimal is sometimes called a <u>multiplier</u>.

> **Example 3**   **Find 87% of 2.8 using your calculator.**
>
> 1. Change 87% to a decimal equivalent $87 \div 100 = 0.87$
>   by dividing by 100.
> 2. Multiply the amount by this decimal. $2.8 \times 0.87 = \mathbf{2.436}$

Exercise 2

Use a calculator to answer these questions.

1   Find each of the following.

    a) 15% of 150   **b)** 8% of 16   **c)** 27% of 65   **d)** 48% of 56

    e) 79% of 265   **f)** 52% of 480   **g)** 46% of 250   **h)** 82% of 600

    i) 57% of 216   **j)** 38% of 684   **k)** 9% of 542   **l)** 99% of 214

2   Answer each of the following.

    a) What is 12% of 68 kg?   **b)** What is 65% of 46 cm?

    c) What is 93% of 178 miles?   **d)** What is 7% of 360 km?

    e) What is 71% of £69?   **f)** What is 28% of £28?

3   Work out:

    a) 16% of 28.4   **b)** 17% of 16.8   **c)** 66% of 26.6   **d)** 18% of 88.8

    e) 69% of 120.6 cm   **f)** 73% of 36.5 kg   **g)** 24.5% of 860 g   **h)** 6.5% of £120

4   Paul is 88% of the way through a 250 mile journey.
    How many miles does he have left to travel?

5   The cost of an adult's ticket for a theme park is £36. A child's ticket is
    62.5% of the price of an adult's ticket. How much does it cost for
    one adult and two children to enter the theme park?

5.5 Percentage Change

Percentage Change Using Multipliers

If something <u>increases</u> by 10%, you've now got 110% of it.

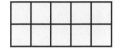 + =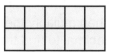

original amount $\frac{1}{10}$ (10% of the original amount) $\frac{11}{10}$ (110% of the original amount)

If something <u>decreases</u> by 10%, you've now got 90% of it left.

 − 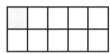 =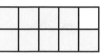

original amount $\frac{1}{10}$ (10% of the original amount) $\frac{9}{10}$ (90% of the original amount)

| **Example 1** | **Increase 250 by 20%.** |

1. Find the new total as a percentage of the original number.   100% + 20% = 120%

2. You can write this as a fraction... $120\% = \frac{120}{100}$

3. ...and a decimal.   120% ÷ 100 = 1.2

4. Multiply the amount by the decimal to find the answer.   250 × 1.2 = **300**

Exercise 1

1 For each of these:

i) write the new total as a decimal proportion of the original number

ii) calculate the new amount

a) Increase 140 by 10%   **b)** Increase 40 by 30%

c) Increase 600 by 20%   **d)** Increase 180 by 15%

2 Work out the new amounts when you:

a) Increase 150 kg by 70%   **b)** Increase 225 km by 98%

c) Increase 40 cm by 8%   **d)** Increase 15 g by 15%

e) Increase 580 m by 2%   **f)** Increase 2000 ml by 16%

Example 2	Decrease 150 by 20%

1. Find the new total as a percentage of the original number.　　100% − 20% = 80%

2. Convert the percentage to a decimal.　　80% × 100 = 0.8

3. Then multiply the amount by the decimal to find the new amount.　　150 × 0.8 = **120**

3 For each of these:

i) write the new total as a decimal proportion of the original number

ii) calculate the new amount

a) Decrease 160 by 20%　　　　　**b)** Decrease 90 by 40%

c) Decrease 800 by 30%　　　　　**d)** Decrease 160 by 25%

4 Work out the new amounts when you:

a) Decrease 800 by 24%　　　　　**b)** Decrease 224 by 20%

c) Decrease 720 by 25%　　　　　**d)** Decrease 200 by 13%

e) Decrease 84 by 45%　　　　　**f)** Decrease 90 by 37%

5 Work out the new amounts when you:

a) Increase £16 by 20%　　　　　**b)** Decrease 45 cm by 14%

c) Increase 124 kg by 9%　　　　　**d)** Decrease 18 km by 6%

6 Richard's phone bill is £35 each month. The price goes up by 6%. How much will he pay each month now?

> ### Investigate — Finding The Original Amount
>
> | Full Price | × | ? | = | Sale Price |
> | --- | --- | --- | --- | --- |
>
> **a)** Dan is using the calculation above to work out sale prices for items in his shop. What number should go in the middle box if he's reducing prices by 10%? What about 20%? What about x%?
>
> **b)** Can you write a similar calculation to change prices back from the sale price to the full price? Try it out using different numbers to check that it works.

Section 6 — Ratio and Proportion

6.1 Comparing Quantities Using Fractions and Ratios

Comparing Quantities Using Fractions

You can write one number as a <u>fraction</u> of another by putting the first number over the second and <u>cancelling down</u>. If the first number is bigger than the second, you'll end up with a fraction greater than 1.

If you multiply the fraction by the second number, you end up with the first number again.

Example 1

a) **Write 27 as a fraction of 36.**

Put 27 over 36 and cancel down.

$$\overset{\div 9}{\overbrace{\frac{27}{36}}} = \frac{3}{4}$$
$$\underset{\div 9}{\underbrace{\phantom{\frac{27}{36}}}}$$

b) **What fraction must you multiply 36 by to get 27?**

This is the fraction you've just found.

Check your answer by doing the multiplication: $36 \times \frac{3}{4} = 27$.

$\frac{3}{4}$

Exercise 1

For this exercise, give any **fractions** as improper fractions in their **simplest terms**.

1   a) Write 16 as a fraction of 20.   b) Write 25 as a fraction of 40.

c) Write 7 as a fraction of 21.   d) Write 32 as a fraction of 64.

2   a) Write 9 as a fraction of 6.   b) Write 18 as a fraction of 8.

c) Write 49 as a fraction of 28.   d) Write 38 as a fraction of 24.

3   a) i) Write 22 as a fraction of 32.   ii) Write 32 as a fraction of 22.

b) What fraction must you multiply 32 by to get 22?

4   a) i) Write 45 as a fraction of 54.

ii) Write 54 as a fraction of 45.

b) What fraction must you multiply 45 by to get 54?

5 **a)** Write 32 as a fraction of 40.

b) Use your answer to part **a)** to write 32 as a percentage of 40.

6 **a)** Write 35 as a fraction of 25.

b) Use your answer to part **a)** to write 35 as a percentage of 25.

7 **a)** Write 14 as a percentage of 20.

b) Write 24 as a percentage of 80.

c) Write 39 as a percentage of 52.

d) Write 75 as a percentage of 125.

8 **a)** Write 10 as a percentage of 8.

b) Write 18 as a percentage of 15.

c) Write 48 as a percentage of 24.

d) Write 92 as a percentage of 80.

9 The contents of a packet of jelly sweets are as follows:

Colour	Number of jelly sweets
Red	7
Yellow	5
Pink	4
Green	6
Orange	11

a) Write the number of orange jelly sweets as a fraction of the total number of jelly sweets in the packet.

b) Write the number of red jelly sweets as a fraction of the number of pink jelly sweets.

c) Complete this sentence:

The number of ⬚ sweets as a fraction of the number of ⬚ sweets is $\frac{3}{2}$.

10 There are 15 Year 7 students, 12 Year 8 students and 14 Year 9 students on a trip.

a) Write the number of Year 8 students as a percentage of the number of Year 7 students.

b) Write the number of Year 9 students as a fraction of the number of Year 8 students.

11 What fraction must you multiply 48 by to get 64?

12 Fill in the gap in the following multiplication: 39 × ⬚ = 65

Comparing Quantities Using Ratios

You can use ratios to compare amounts of things.

To write quantities in ratios, you have to translate the information into maths.

So 'twice as many apples as oranges' would be the ratio 2:1 (apples:oranges), and 'half as many dogs as cats' would be 1:2 (dogs:cats).

You can turn a ratio into a fraction by putting one bit of the ratio on top of the other.

> **Example 2** A recipe calls for three times as much flour as sugar.
>
> **a) Write the amount of flour to the amount of sugar as a ratio.**
>
> 'Three times' as much flour means that for every 1 part of sugar, there must be 3 parts of flour. So write this as a ratio.
>
> flour:sugar
> = 3:1
>
> **b) Write the amount of sugar compared to the amount of flour as a fraction.**
>
> Put the numbers from your ratio into a fraction. You want the amount of sugar, so put that part of the ratio on the top of the fraction.
>
> The recipe needs $\frac{1}{3}$ as much sugar as flour.

Exercise 2

1   Write the following statements as ratios of CDs to DVDs.

   a) Lucy has twice as many CDs as DVDs.

   b) Ricky has four times as many DVDs as CDs.

   c) Amir has half as many CDs as DVDs.

   d) Nancy has five times are many DVDs as CDs.

2   A choir has 6 times as many female members as male members.

   a) Write the ratio of female to male members.

   b) Complete the statement: There are ☐ times as many males as females.

3   Harry is given a box of toy lorries and cars. $\frac{4}{5}$ of the vehicles in the box are lorries.

   a) What fraction of the vehicles are cars?

   b) Write down the ratio of lorries to cars.

   c) Write the number of cars as a fraction of the number of lorries.

4 A bakery sells only white and wholemeal loaves of bread.
The ratio of white loaves to wholemeal loaves sold is 5:2.

a) Write the number of wholemeal loaves sold as a fraction
of the number of white loaves sold.

b) Write the number of white loaves sold as a fraction
of the number of wholemeal loaves sold.

c) Write the number of white loaves sold as a fraction
of the total number of loaves sold.

5 The ratio of Irish Setters to Labradors to Great Danes in a class at a dog show is 3:4:1.
All the dogs in the class are either Irish Setters, Labradors or Great Danes.

a) Write the number of Irish Setters as a fraction of the number of Labradors.

b) Write the number of Irish Setters as a percentage of the number of Great Danes.

c) Write the number of Labradors as a fraction of the total number of dogs in the class.

6 Neil has three times as many sheep as cows on his farm,
and half as many goats as sheep. Write this information as a ratio.
Give your answer in the form sheep:cows:goats.

Investigate — Recipes

a) Write the amounts of flour,
butter and sugar in this scone
recipe as a ratio.

To make 10 scones you need:

200 g flour, 50 g butter,
25 g sugar, 150 ml milk.

b) Rewrite the recipe giving the amounts of flour,
butter and sugar as fractions of the amount of flour.

c) Repeat part b), this time giving the amounts as fractions of the
amount of butter, then of sugar.

d) Think about how you could use your ratios and fractions in the
following situations.

i) You haven't got enough of one of the ingredients to make
the recipe as it is.

ii) You have to make scones for a huge tea party with
hundreds of guests.

6.2 Ratio and Proportion Problems

Simplifying Ratios

You can <u>simplify</u> ratios by dividing the numbers by a <u>common factor</u>.

Example 1   **Write the ratio 16 : 40 in its simplest form.**

1. Look for a number that divides into both 16 and 40.

   8 divides into 16 and 40

2. Divide both sides of the ratio by this number.

   $16 \div 8 = 2$ and $40 \div 8 = 5$

3. Make sure no other numbers divide into both sides of the ratio — that means it's in its simplest form.

   So the ratio can be written as **2 : 5**, which is the simplest form.

Example 2   **Write the ratio 3.5 cm : 21 mm in its simplest form.**

1. Rewrite the ratio so that the units are the same on both sides. Then remove the units altogether.

   1 cm = 10 mm, so 3.5 cm = 35 mm. 3.5 cm : 21 mm = 35 mm : 21 mm, so the ratio is 35 : 21.

2. 7 divides into both 35 and 21, so use this to simplify the ratio.

   $35 \div 7 = 5$ and $21 \div 7 = 3$

   So the ratio can be written as **5 : 3**, which is the simplest form.

Exercise 1

1   Write each of the following ratios in its simplest form.

   a) 4 : 8   b) 3 : 6   c) 6 : 18   d) 5 : 20

   e) 12 : 3   f) 16 : 8   g) 21 : 7   h) 24 : 12

   i) 4 : 6   j) 15 : 25   k) 12 : 30   l) 22 : 55

   m) 20 : 16   n) 27 : 18   o) 45 : 30   p) 42 : 28

2   Write down the ratio of squares to circles. Give your answer in its simplest form.

3   Write down the ratio of big squares to little squares. Give your answer in its simplest form.

4   A necklace is made up of 15 gold beads, 27 silver beads and 35 blue beads.

   a) What is the ratio of gold beads to silver beads in its simplest form?

   b) What is the ratio of gold beads to blue beads in its simplest form?

5   On a school bus there are 24 girls and 36 boys.
   What is the ratio of girls to boys?
   Give your answer in its simplest form.

6   A salad dressing is made by mixing 15 tablespoons of olive oil with 6 tablespoons
   of balsamic vinegar. Find the ratio of oil to vinegar in its simplest form.

7   On a street of 40 houses, 10 of them are empty.

   a) How many houses are not empty?

   b) Write the ratio of empty houses to not empty houses in its simplest form.

8   Write each of the following ratios in its simplest form.

   a) 20 cm : 1 m   **b)** 20 seconds : 1 minute   **c)** 30p : £1.20

   d) 45 minutes : 1 hour   **e)** 600 g : 1 kg   **f)** 4 cm : 25 mm

   g) 3 km : 900 m   **h)** 2 kg : 300 g   **i)** 6 mm : 18 cm

9   Write each of the following ratios in its simplest form.

   a) 6 : 3 : 3   **b)** 30 : 18 : 6   **c)** 80 mm : 12 cm : 16 cm

10 Cereal A comes in boxes of 800 g. Cereal B comes in boxes of 1.4 kg.
   Find the ratio of the weight of a box of cereal A to the weight of a box of cereal B.
   Give your answer in its simplest form.

11 For this rectangle, find the ratio of the longer side to the shorter side in its simplest form.

1.4 m

70 cm

12 On a map, a distance of 10 cm represents a real-life distance of 20 km. Find the scale of the map, giving your answer as a ratio in its simplest form.

13 A bag contains 16 red sweets and 12 green sweets.

a) Write the ratio of red sweets to green sweets in its simplest form.

b) Chloe eats some of the red sweets. The ratio of red to green sweets is now $1:2$. How many sweets did Chloe eat?

> ## Investigate — Simplifying Ratios
>
> **a)** Write the ratio $20:25$ in its simplest form.
>
> **b)** Now write it in the form $1:n$ by dividing both sides by the number on the left-hand side.
>
> **c)** Repeat steps **a)** and **b)** for the ratios $40:60$, $50:125$ and $200:450$.
>
> **d)** Why might it be useful to write ratios in the form $1:n$?

Using Ratios

You can use ratios to solve problems.

You can scale up a ratio by multiplying each side of the ratio by the same number.

Example 3
The ratio of apples to oranges on a fruit stall is $5:3$. If there are 30 apples on the stall, how many oranges are there?

1. Work out what you need to multiply by to go from 5 to 30 on the left-hand side.

2. Multiply the right-hand side by the same number to find the number of oranges.

apples : oranges

$$\times 6 \left(\begin{array}{c} 5:3 \\ 30:18 \end{array} \right) \times 6$$

So there are **18 oranges**.

Exercise 2

1   At a pet shop, the ratio of hamsters to guinea pigs is 5 : 2.
    If there are 20 hamsters, how many guinea pigs are there?

2   In a class, the ratio of left-handed people to right-handed people is 2 : 9.
    If there are 6 left-handed people in the class, how many right-handed people are there?

3   In a car park, the ratio of black cars to red cars is 3 : 4.
    If there are 12 black cars in the car park, how many red cars are there?

4   Georgia is sharing sweets with her brother in the ratio 3 : 5.
    If her brother gets 25 sweets, how many sweets does Georgia get?

5   In a garden, for every 4 rose bushes there are 7 azaleas.
    If there are 21 azaleas, how many rose bushes are there?

For questions **6-10**, remember to give the correct units in your answer.

6   Purple paint is made by mixing blue paint and red paint in the ratio 2 : 3.
    If 4 litres of blue paint are used, how many litres of red paint are needed?

7   In a recipe, flour and butter are used in the ratio 3 : 1.
    If 600 g of flour are used, how much butter is needed?

8   Bill and Ben share some money in the ratio 7 : 3. Ben gets £21. How much does Bill get?

9   The ratio of Tom's height to Lisa's height is 8 : 5. If Tom is 168 cm tall, how tall is Lisa?

10 Milly and Lotte are knitting scarves. For every 6 cm that Milly knits, Lotte knits 11 cm.
    If Milly knits a scarf that is 1.2 m long, how long will Lotte's scarf be in metres?

11 The ratio of Niko's age to Louise's age is 2 : 3. Louise is 15 years old.
    How many years will it be until the ratio of their ages is 3 : 4?

You can use ratios to <u>divide</u> an amount into two or more shares. Use the total number of parts to work out the size of one part, then use this to find the size of each share.

Example 4 **Divide £40 in the ratio 2:3.**

1. Add up the numbers in the ratio to find the total number of parts.

    2 + 3 = 5 parts altogether

2. Work out the amount for one part.

    5 parts = £40,
    so 1 part = £40 ÷ 5 = **£8**

3. Then multiply the amount for one part by the number of parts for each share (to check, if you add up the shares, you should get the original amount).

    £8 × 2 = £16
    £8 × 3 = £24

    So the shares are **£16** and **£24**
    (and £16 + £24 = £40).

Exercise 3

1 **a)** Divide 16 in the ratio 1:3. **b)** Divide 21 in the ratio 3:4.

2 **a)** Divide 22 in the ratio 3:8. **b)** Divide 130 in the ratio 6:7.

3 Divide £30 in the following ratios:

   a) 1:5 **b)** 2:3 **c)** 3:7 **d)** 7:8

4 Share 64 kg in the following ratios:

   a) 1:3 **b)** 1:7 **c)** 5:11 **d)** 15:17

5 Find the larger amount when each quantity below is divided in the given ratio.

   a) 120 ml in the ratio 7:13 **b)** 75 mm in the ratio 11:14

   c) £150 in the ratio 12:13 **d)** 420 g in the ratio 4:17

   e) 1000 m in the ratio 23:27 **f)** 96p in the ratio 7:25

6 Justin and Lee share £2000 in the ratio 7:18. How much does each person get?

7 In a school of 500 pupils, the ratio of pupils who wear glasses to pupils who don't wear glasses is 33:67. How many pupils don't wear glasses?

8 Ann bakes 200 cakes. She puts $\frac{2}{5}$ of the cakes in the freezer.

She ices the remaining cakes with either white icing or blue icing in the ratio 1:2. Work out how many cakes she ices with blue icing.

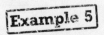 **Example 5** | Green paint is made by mixing blue paint and yellow paint in the ratio 4:9. It takes 26 litres of paint to paint a room. How much yellow paint is needed?

1. Add up the numbers in the ratio to find the total number of parts.

   4 + 9 = 13 parts altogether

2. Work out the amount for one part.

   13 parts = 26 litres, so 1 part = 26 litres ÷ 13 = 2 litres

3. Then multiply the amount for one part by the number of parts for yellow paint.

   2 litres × 9 = **18 litres** of yellow paint

Exercise 4

1 Leanne and Kyle have a combined age of 72. Their ages are in the ratio 2:7. How much older than Leanne is Kyle?

2 Katie is making bags of flour and sugar for a cake mix.
Each bag weighs 750 g, and the ratio of flour to sugar in each bag is 16:9.
How many grams of sugar will she need to make 6 bags of cake mix?

3 Sonya and Alfonse each have a job that pays them £5 per hour.
The ratio of the hours they work is 2:3, and they work for 125 hours in total between them.
How much does Alfonse earn?

4 Alyssa and Paul have a combined height of 240 cm. Their heights are in the ratio 5:7.
To ride a rollercoaster at a theme park, you must be over 1.1 m tall.
Is Alyssa tall enough to ride the rollercoaster?

5 A ship is carrying a load of gold bars and silver bars in the ratio 13:17.
The ship's load weighs 600 kg in total. If one bar of gold or silver weighs 5 kg, how many gold bars is the ship carrying?

Proportion Problems

If two things are in <u>direct proportion</u>, then the <u>ratio</u> between them is always the same. So if you increase one thing, the other increases at the same rate.

| Example 6 | To make 2 litres of squash, you need to use 0.5 litres of cordial. How much cordial would you need to make 3 litres of squash? |

1. Find the amount of cordial needed for 1 litre of squash by dividing by 2.

    2 litres of squash needs 0.5 litres of cordial, so 1 litre of squash needs $0.5 ÷ 2 = 0.25$ litres of cordial.

2. Then multiply this amount by 3 to find the amount needed for 3 litres.

    3 litres of squash needs $0.25 × 3 = $ **0.75 litres of cordial.**

Exercise 5

1 Olaf uses 3 loaves of bread to make sandwiches for 15 people.
How many loaves will he need to use to make sandwiches for 25 people?

2 To make 6 jugs of custard, you need to use 3 pints of milk.
How much milk is needed to make 4 jugs of custard?

3 It takes 8 oz of flour to make 12 scones.
How much flour is needed to make:

a) 6 scones?   **b)** 18 scones?   **c)** 36 scones?

4 It takes Marissa 2 hours to wash 8 cars. How long will it take her to wash 20 cars?

5 200 g of sugar makes 24 cupcakes.
How many cupcakes can you make with 500 g of sugar?

6 It takes Theo 45 minutes to plant 9 trees.
How many trees can he plant in 3 hours?

7 A recipe for 6 people uses 720 g of mince. Rob is cooking for 10 people.
How much mince will he need?

8 It takes Suri 18 minutes to address 27 envelopes.
How many envelopes could she address in half an hour?

9 Carys cooks 600 g of pasta to feed 8 people.
How much pasta would she need to cook to feed 5 people?

10 64 people travel to a rugby match on 2 identical coaches. There are no spare seats.
How many of these coaches are needed to take 160 people to the match?

11 It takes Shaun 9 days to read a 432-page book.
How long will it take him to read a 720-page book?

12 5 pizzas use 4 peppers and 2 onions. How many peppers and onions would be needed
for 12.5 pizzas if the ratio of peppers to onions is always the same?

13 Jimmy walks 15 km in 200 minutes. He then walks a further 45 km.
How many minutes does Jimmy walk for in total?

14 A car uses 8 litres of petrol per 100 km. Can it make a 450 km trip
with 35 litres of petrol in its tank (without stopping to refuel)?

15 Jake has 3 cats. Each cat eats 560 g of cat food every week. Jake has two 3 kg bags
of cat food. Does he have enough food to feed all of his cats for 24 days?

16 Daisy the cow produces 104 litres of milk in 4 days. Azalea the cow produces
162 litres of milk in 6 days. Which cow is producing milk faster?

17 Justin's wellies are sinking in quicksand. The right welly has sunk 17.5 cm in 7 minutes,
and the left welly has sunk 24 cm in 10 minutes. Which welly is sinking faster?

6.3 Percentage Change Problems

Percentage Increase and Decrease Problems

To increase or decrease something by a percentage, first find the percentage change as a decimal (the multiplier), then multiply the original amount by the multiplier to find the new amount.

> For a percentage increase, the multiplier is greater than 1
> (so for an increase of 20%, multiply by 1 + 0.2 = 1.2).
>
> For a percentage decrease, the multiplier is less than 1
> (so for a decrease of 20%, multiply by 1 − 0.2 = 0.8).

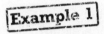 **A 10% service charge is added onto a meal costing £70. What is the total price of the meal?**

1. Work out the multiplier as a decimal.   100% + 10% = 110% = 1.1

2. Multiply the original amount by the multiplier to find the new amount.   £70 × 1.1 = £77
So the meal costs **£77**.

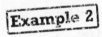 **A dress costing £40 is reduced by 15% in a sale. What is the new price of the dress?**

1. Work out the multiplier as a decimal.   100% − 15% = 85% = 0.85

2. Multiply the original amount by the multiplier to find the new amount.   £40 × 0.85 = £34
So the dress costs **£34** in the sale.

Exercise 1

1   A tax of 40% is added to the price of a luxury item costing £200.
What is the new price of the luxury item?

2   A bag costing £80 is reduced by 10% in a sale. What is the new price of the bag?

3   After a baby boom, the number of penguins in a zoo increases by 30%.
There were 30 penguins originally. How many are there after the baby boom?

4   A TV costing £400 is reduced by 20% in a sale. What is the new price of the TV?

5 Standard concert tickets cost £60. A front-row ticket costs 75% more.
How much does a front-row ticket cost?

6 In one week, a castle had 800 visitors.
The following week, the number of visitors decreased by 35%.
How many people visited the castle in the second week?

7 In a coffee shop, it costs 5% more to sit inside the shop than to get a takeaway.
If a takeaway coffee costs £2, how much would it cost to have the same coffee inside?

8 A cardigan usually costs £16, but is being sold at a 15% discount
because it has a button missing. What is the new price of the cardigan?

9 After a meal at a restaurant, the Snow family decide to leave a tip of 12%.
Their meal cost £150 before the tip. What was the cost of the meal including the tip?

10 A hotel bill came to £300. The hotel decided to knock 16% off the bill because of building
work going on in the hotel. What was the bill after the discount?

11 Morgan earns £650 a month. He gets a pay rise of 2%.
How much does he now earn each month?

12 One year, there were 700 girls and 500 boys in a school.
The following year, the number of girls had dropped by 4% and the number of boys had
increased by 6%. How many pupils were there in the school in the second year?

13 Bus fares increase by 8.5%. How much will a £2 ticket cost after the increase?

14 In a sale, all items are reduced by 12.5%. A bed cost £600 before the sale.
Find the sale price of the bed.

15 In January, the cost of a TV is £400. In February, the cost of the TV increases by 10%.
In March, the TV is in a '15% off' sale. How much does the TV cost in March?

To find a percentage change (either an increase or decrease):
- calculate the difference between the new amount and the original amount
- find this as a percentage of the original amount using the formula:

$$\text{percentage change} = \frac{\text{change}}{\text{original}} \times 100$$

Example 3   **In a sale, the cost of a pair of shoes is reduced from £50 to £45. Find the percentage decrease.**

1. Find the difference between the new cost and the original cost.

2. Put the numbers into the formula to find the percentage decrease.

£50 − £45 = £5

$$\text{percentage change} = \frac{5}{50} \times 100$$

$$= \textbf{10\%}$$

Exercise 2

1   Find the percentage increase when:

a) a price of £20 is increased to £25.

b) a price of £40 is increased to £52.

c) a price of £150 is increased to £180.

2   Find the percentage decrease when:

a) a price of £10 is decreased to £7.

b) a price of £20 is decreased to £15.

c) a price of £60 is decreased to £30.

3   At 8 am there are 52 cars parked in a car park.
At 9 am there are 65 cars parked in the same car park.

a) Find the difference between the number of cars parked in the car park at 8 am and 9 am.

b) Find the percentage increase in the number of cars parked in the car park between 8 am and 9 am.

4   The price of a sandwich drops from 80p to 68p.

a) Find the amount the price has been reduced by.

b) Find the percentage decrease in the price.

5 There are 25 pupils in a class. A new pupil joins the class.
Work out the percentage increase in the number of pupils in the class.

6 At the start of a race, the mass of fuel in a car is 150 kg. Halfway through the race, the mass has dropped to 82.5 kg. Find the percentage decrease in fuel.

7 Moyo's monthly rent increases from £450 to £472.50. Find the percentage increase.

8 Eddie's swimming pool has sprung a leak.
At the start of the day, the depth of water in the pool was 1.75 m, and by the end of the day the depth was 1.54 m.
Find the percentage decrease in the depth of the water.

9 The price of a pair of jeans is reduced from £60 to £49.80.
What is the percentage decrease?

10 The price of a house increases from £250 000 to £305 000.
What is the percentage increase?

11 Bridie buys a necklace for £12 and sells it for £15.24. What is her percentage profit?

12 It costs £55 to make 20 gingerbread houses. They are sold at a Christmas fair for £4.29 each. Work out the percentage profit.

13 Noah buys a boat for £134. It loses £5.36 in value each month.
Find the percentage loss in value after 6 months.

14 A motorbike is bought for £8300. Two years later, it is sold for £5976.
After another five years, it is sold for £2689.20.

   a) Find the percentage decrease in the motorbike's price over the first two years.

   b) Find the percentage decrease in the motorbike's price over the next five years.

   c) Find the percentage decrease in the motorbike's price over the whole seven years.

Finding the Original Value

If you know the <u>percentage change</u> and the new value,
you can use this information to find the original value:

* First find the <u>multiplier</u> (remember that for a 10% increase, the multiplier is 1.1, and for a 10% decrease the multiplier is 0.9).
* Divide the new value by the multiplier — this will give you the original value.

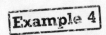

Example 4

a) A painting increases in value by 30% to £390.
Find what it was worth before the rise.

1. Find the multiplier.	100% + 30% = 130% = 1.3
2. Divide the new amount by the multiplier to find the original amount.	£390 ÷ 1.3 = £300 So the painting was worth **£300** before the rise.

b) In a sale, a t-shirt is reduced by 20% to £12.80.
Find what it cost before the sale.

1. Find the multiplier.	100% − 20% = 80% = 0.8
2. Divide the new amount by the multiplier to find the original amount.	£12.80 ÷ 0.8 = £16 So the t-shirt cost **£16** before the sale.

Exercise 3

1   A shop is having a 10% off sale. The sale prices of a number of items are given below. Find the original price of each item.

a) A scarf costing £9 in the sale.

b) A skirt costing £13.50 in the sale.

c) A belt costing £5.40 in the sale.

2   A restaurant automatically adds on a 20% service charge to every bill. Find the cost of the meal before the service charge for a bill of:

a) £36

b) £60

c) £78

3 An armchair costs £175 after a 30% discount. Find the original price of the armchair.

4 Brandon receives an electricity bill of £32.55, which is 5% higher than the bill for the previous month. How much was his bill for the previous month?

5 A statue worth £840 has increased in value by 40%. Find the original value of the statue.

6 Linda is selling her car for £6600, which is 45% less than the price she paid for it. How much did she pay for the car?

7 A house increases in value by 12% to £252 000. How much was it originally worth?

8 A red dress costs £55.20 after an 8% discount. A blue dress costs £56.96 after an 11% discount. Which dress cost more before the discounts?

Simple Interest

<u>Simple interest</u> is where a certain percentage of an initial investment or loan is added on to it at regular intervals (e.g. once a month or once a year). This means that the amount of interest is **the same** every time it's added on.

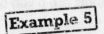 **Grace invests £500 in an account that pays 3% simple interest each year.**

a) Work out how much interest she will earn in one year.

This is just finding 3% of £500 — so multiply by 0.03.

£500 × 0.03 = £15
So she earns **£15** interest in 1 year.

b) How much will be in the account after 4 years?

1. In one year she earns £15 interest, so multiply this by 4 to find the interest earned in 4 years.

£15 × 4 = £60

2. Now add this amount onto the original amount.

£500 + £60 = **£560**

Exercise 4

1 Theo invests £800 in an account that pays 2% simple interest each year.

   a) Work out how much interest is earned in a year.

   b) Work out how much there will be in the account after 5 years.

   c) Work out how much there will be in the account after 10 years.

2 Kamui invests £2000 in an account that pays 1% simple interest each month. Work out how much will be in the account:

   a) after 3 months   **b)** after 8 months   **c)** after 1 year

3 When Jessica was born, her parents invested £2500 in an account that pays 2.5% simple interest each year. Work out how much will be in the account on Jessica's 21st birthday.

4 Emilia invests £5000 in an account that pays 2% simple interest each year and leaves it for 5 years. Lucy invests £4500 in an account that pays 5% simple interest each year and leaves it for 3 years.

   a) Who will have the most money at the end of the investment period?

   b) How much more money will she have?

Investigate — Compound Interest

Compound interest is where each amount of interest is calculated using the new total, rather than the original amount, so the amount of interest changes each time it's added. Banks often pay compound interest instead of simple interest.

£1000 is invested in an account that pays 2% compound interest each year.

a) Find the amount in the account after 1 year.

b) Find the amount in the account after 2 years.
Remember to use your answer to part **a)** in your calculation.

c) Repeat step **b)** to find the amount in the account after 3, 4 and 5 years.

d) Can you think of a formula you could use to make these calculations easier? Try repeating part **c)** using powers, then replace any numbers with words or letters. Try using your formula to find the amount in the account after 25 years.

Section 7 — Units and Scales

7.1 Changing Units

Time

The standard units of time are <u>hours</u>, <u>minutes</u> and <u>seconds</u>.
There are 60 seconds in a minute and 60 minutes in an hour.
You can use these to convert between hours, minutes and seconds.

 **A music video lasts for 165 seconds. What is this in minutes and seconds?**

1. Change 165 seconds into minutes by dividing by 60.
   $165 \div 60 = 2.75$ minutes

2. Then convert the decimal bit to seconds by multiplying by 60.
   $0.75 \times 60 = 45$ seconds

3. Put the two bits together.
   165 seconds **= 2 mins 45 seconds**

Exercise 1

1 Rewrite these times in minutes:

    a) 2 hours   **b)** 6 hours   **c)** 3.5 hours

    d) 0.25 hours   **e)** 4 hours and 30 minutes   **f)** 5 hours and 25 minutes

2 Rewrite these times in seconds:

    a) 5 minutes   **b)** 8 minutes   **c)** 15 minutes

    d) 2.5 minutes   **e)** 3 minutes and 15 seconds   **f)** 4 minutes and 10 seconds

3 Rewrite these times in hours:

    a) 270 minutes   **b)** 105 minutes   **c)** 3 hours and 12 minutes

4 Rewrite these times in hours and minutes:

    a) 180 minutes   **b)** 150 minutes   **c)** 225 minutes   **d)** 247 minutes

5 Rewrite these times in minutes and seconds:

    a) 360 seconds   **b)** 90 seconds   **c)** 136 seconds   **d)** 199 seconds

6 A song lasts for 3.25 minutes. What is this time in seconds?

7 **a)** Write 1.5 hours in minutes.

b) Use your answer to part **a)** to write 1.5 hours in seconds.

8 There are 24 hours in a day. Find:

a) the number of minutes in a day

b) the number of seconds in a day.

9 Leo wants to watch a film that is 145 minutes long.
He has two and a quarter hours to spare. Is this enough time to watch the film?

> ## Investigate — Time
>
> The standard conversions for time are 60, 60 and 24 (i.e. 60 seconds in a minute, 60 minutes in an hour and 24 hours in a day).
>
> **a)** Use the internet to investigate the history of measuring time.
> Why do you think we use the current system?
>
> **b)** How else could you divide up time?
> Think about good and bad ways to do it.

Metric Units

To convert between different units, you need to know the conversion factor.
This tells you how many times bigger or smaller one unit is than another.

When converting to a smaller unit (e.g. m to cm), multiply by the conversion factor.
When converting to a bigger unit (e.g. cm to m), divide by the conversion factor.

You can convert between different metric units using these conversions:

Length:	Mass:	Volume:
1 cm = 10 mm	1 kg = 1000 g	1 litre (l) = 1000 ml
1 m = 100 cm	1 tonne = 1000 kg	1 ml = 1 cm^3
1 km = 1000 m		

You can use these conversions to convert areas too — but you have to use the conversion factor twice. So to convert mm^2 to cm^2, divide by 10, then divide by 10 again.

Example 2 Convert:

a) 1.36 litres into cm³

1. There are 1000 cm³ in 1 litre, so the conversion factor is 1000.

$\qquad$ 1 litre = 1000 cm³

2. cm³ are smaller than litres, so multiply by the conversion factor.

$\qquad$ 1.36 litres = (1.36 × 1000) cm³
$\qquad\qquad$ = **1360 cm³**

b) 12 245 cm into km

1. First, convert cm to m by dividing by the conversion factor (100).

$\qquad$ 1 m = 100 cm
$\qquad$ 12 245 cm = (12 245 ÷ 100) m
$\qquad\qquad$ = 122.45 m

2. Then convert 122.45 m into km by dividing by the conversion factor (1000).

$\qquad$ 1 km = 1000 m
$\qquad$ 122.45 m = (122.45 ÷ 1000) km
$\qquad\qquad$ = **0.12245 km**

c) 0.182 m² into cm²

1. The conversion factor is 100 (remember, for areas use the conversion factor twice).

$\qquad$ 1 m = 100 cm

2. cm² are smaller than m², so multiply by the conversion factor twice.

$\qquad$ 0.182 m² = (0.182 × 100 × 100) cm²
$\qquad\qquad$ = **1820 cm²**

Exercise 2

1 For each of these conversions, write down **i)** the conversion factor, and **ii)** whether you should multiply or divide by the conversion factor.

    a) m into cm   **b)** ml into litres   **c)** g into kg

    d) tonnes into kg   **e)** km into m   **f)** mm into cm

For questions **2-4**, convert each measurement into the units given.

2   **a)** 6 cm into mm   **b)** 4 litres into ml   **c)** 6 kg into g

    d) 3 km into m   **e)** 7 tonnes into kg   **f)** 48 cm³ into ml

    g) 2.6 cm into mm   **h)** 5.1 litres into cm³   **i)** 9.6 km into m

    j) 3.15 tonnes into kg   **k)** 2.25 m into cm   **l)** 5.26 kg into g

3 **a)** 30 mm into cm   **b)** 5000 g into kg   **c)** 8000 ml into litres

     d) 4000 kg into tonnes   **e)** 2000 m into km   **f)** 100 ml into cm^3

     g) 3400 g into kg   **h)** 63 mm in cm   **i)** 2800 kg into tonnes

     j) 9430 ml into litres   **k)** 375 cm into m   **l)** 2670 m into km

4 **a)** 12.8 cm into mm   **b)** 2150 ml into litres   **c)** 4400 m into km

     d) 1.74 tonnes into kg   **e)** 495 cm into m   **f)** 8700 g into kg

     g) 4.15 litres into cm^3 **h)** 6.89 m into cm   **i)** 7.65 km into m

5 A caterpillar is 42 mm long. What is its length in cm?

6 Bethany makes 800 ml of pink lemonade. How much lemonade does she make in litres?

7 Ryan has 2.75 m of ribbon. He cuts it into 25 cm pieces.

     a) Convert 2.75 m into cm.

     b) Use your answer to part **a)** to work out how many 25 cm lengths he has.

8 **a)** Convert 6 km into m.

     b) Use your answer to part **a)** to convert 6 km into cm.

9 Convert the following area measurements into the units given.

     a) 4 cm^2 into mm^2 **b)** 5 km^2 into m^2 **c)** 1600 cm^2 into m^2

10 Convert the following measurements into the units given.

     a) 4 m into mm   **b)** 2 tonnes into g   **c)** 250 000 cm into km

11 A pot of paint will cover an area of 8000 cm^2.
How many pots will be needed to paint a wall with area 3.2 m^2?

Imperial Units

Imperial units are things like inches, feet and miles for lengths, ounces and pounds for mass and pints and gallons for volume.

You can convert between different imperial units using these conversions:

Length:

1 foot = 12 inches

1 yard = 3 feet

Mass:

1 pound = 16 ounces

1 stone = 14 pounds

Volume:

1 gallon = 8 pints

Example 3 Convert:

a) 3.5 gallons into pints

1. There are 8 pints in 1 gallon, so the conversion factor is 8.

1 gallon = 8 pints

2. Pints are smaller than gallons, so multiply by the conversion factor.

3.5 gallons = (3.5 × 8) pints
            = **28 pints**

b) 32 pounds into stones and pounds

1. The conversion factor is 14, and stones are bigger than pounds, so divide by 14. Give your answer with a remainder.

1 stone = 14 pounds

32 pounds = (32 ÷ 14) stone
          = (2 remainder 4) stone

2. The bit before the remainder is the number of stones, and the remainder is the number of pounds.

So 32 pounds = **2 stone 4 pounds**

Exercise 3

1 For each of these conversions, write down **i)** the conversion factor, and **ii)** whether you should multiply or divide by the conversion factor.

a) feet into yards

b) pounds into ounces

c) pints into gallons

d) feet into inches

e) pounds into stones

f) inches into feet

For questions **2-5**, convert each measurement into the units given.

2 **a)** 4 feet into inches **b)** 3 stone into pounds **c)** 5 gallons into pints

  d) 2 pounds into ounces **e)** 12 yards into feet **f)** 0.5 stone into pounds

3 **a)** 36 inches into feet **b)** 80 pints into gallons **c)** 28 pounds into stones

  d) 21 feet into yards **e)** 40 ounces into pounds **f)** 30 pints into gallons

4 **a)** 27 feet into yards **b)** 3.5 pounds into ounces

  c) 120 pints into gallons **d)** 160 ounces into pounds

5 **a)** 18 inches into feet and inches **b)** 104 pounds into stones and pounds

6 Joshua is 56 inches tall. What is his height in feet and inches?

7 Caitlin has made 5 gallons of fruit punch for a village gala. If the punch is served in half-pint glasses, how many glasses of punch can she serve?

Metric and Imperial Conversions

You can convert between <u>metric</u> and <u>imperial</u> units using these conversions:

Length:
1 inch ≈ 2.5 cm
1 foot ≈ 30 cm
1 yard ≈ 90 cm
1 mile ≈ 1.6 km

Mass:
1 ounce ≈ 28 g
1 pound ≈ 450 g
1 stone ≈ 6400 g
1 kg ≈ 2.2 pounds

Volume:
1 pint ≈ 0.57 litres
1 gallon ≈ 4.5 litres

'≈' means 'approximately equal to'.

Example 4 **Convert 5 ounces into g.**

1. The conversion factor is 28. 1 ounce ≈ 28 g

2. Grams are smaller than ounces, 5 ounces ≈ (5 × 28) g
   so multiply by the conversion factor. = **140 g**

1. First, convert 2.25 m into cm
    by multiplying by 100.   2.25 m = 225 cm

2. The conversion factor between   1 inch ≈ 2.5 cm
    cm and inches is 2.5.

3. Inches are bigger than cm, so divide   225 cm ≈ (225 ÷ 2.5) inches
    by the conversion factor.   = **90 inches**

Exercise 4

1   Which is larger:

    a) 1 inch or 1 cm?   **b)** 1 kg or 1 pound?   **c)** 1 pint or 1 litre?

2   Convert these measurements from imperial units to metric.

    a) 10 inches into cm   **b)** 6 pounds into g   **c)** 2 stone into g

    d) 15 yards into cm   **e)** 3 ounces into g   **f)** 4 gallons into litres

    g) 15 feet into cm   **h)** 8 miles into km   **i)** 7 pints into litres

3   Convert these measurements from metric units to imperial.

    a) 360 cm into yards   **b)** 64 000 g into stones   **c)** 72 litres into gallons

    d) 114 litres into pints   **e)** 210 cm into feet   **f)** 1350 g into pounds

    g) 75 cm into inches   **h)** 8 kg into pounds   **i)** 182 g into ounces

4   **a)** Convert 5 feet into cm.

    b) Use your answer to part **a)** to convert 5 feet into m.

5   A wind-up robot can travel 20 m on a single wind. How many times
will it need winding to cover a distance of half a mile?

6   Convert 1.75 m into feet and inches.

7.2 Compound Measures — Speed

Calculating Speed

Speed, distance and time are connected by the formula: $\text{Speed} = \dfrac{\text{Distance}}{\text{Time}}$

Speed units (e.g. km/h) are a combination of the distance units (e.g. km)
and time units (e.g. hours).

Example 1   **Graham cycles 30 km in 2 hours.**
What is his average speed?

1. Write down the formula for speed.

$\text{Speed} = \dfrac{\text{Distance}}{\text{Time}}$

2. Put your numbers for distance and time into the formula.

$= \dfrac{30}{2} = 30 \div 2$

3. Give your answer in the correct units —
the distance is in km and the time is in hours,
so the speed will be in km per hour (km/h).

$= \textbf{15 km/h}$

Exercise 1

1   Find the average speed in km/h of each of these journeys:

a) distance = 15 km, time = 3 hours

b) distance = 20 km, time = 5 hours

c) distance = 40 km, time = 8 hours

d) distance = 90 km, time = 3 hours

e) distance = 120 km, time = 6 hours

f) distance = 5000 km, time = 10 hours

2   A car travels 180 miles in 3 hours.
Find its average speed in miles per hour (mph).

3   A dog runs 125 m in 25 seconds.
Find its average speed in metres per second (m/s).

4   A plane flies 2000 miles in 4 hours.
Find its average speed in miles per hour (mph).

5 Find the speed of the following. Give your answer using the units given in each question.

    a) a man running 16 km in 2 hours

    b) a lorry travelling 140 miles in 4 hours

    c) a bird flying 500 m in 80 seconds

    d) a cyclist travelling 48 km in 5 hours

    e) a skier travelling 700 m in 140 seconds

    f) a snail crawling 1 m in 40 seconds

6 A rocket travels 4250 miles in 15 minutes.

    a) Convert 15 minutes into hours.

    b) Find the average speed of the rocket in miles per hour (mph).

7 Find the speeds for each of the following journeys. Give your answers in the units stated.

    a) Distance = 315 miles, time = 4 and a half hours, speed = mph

    b) Distance = 27 km, time = 45 minutes, speed = km/h

    c) Distance = 11 000 m, time 2 hours and 30 minutes, speed = km/h

    d) Distance = 1600 km, time = 2 hours, speed = mph

8 Find the speed of the following in km/h.
You will need to convert the units to km and hours first.

    a) a car travelling 90 km in 1 hour and 15 minutes

    b) a cyclist travelling 6 km in 30 minutes

    c) a monorail travelling 2 km in 15 minutes

    d) a cable car travelling 1500 m in 0.75 hours

    e) a boy running 800 m in 10 minutes

9 Mo can run a mile in 6 minutes.
Use conversions to work out his average speed in km/h.

Calculating Distance and Time

You can rearrange the speed formula to find distance or time:

$$\text{Distance} = \text{Speed} \times \text{Time} \qquad \text{Time} = \frac{\text{Distance}}{\text{Speed}}$$

The units of the answer will be in terms of the units of the bits you know —
so if you had a speed in mph and a time in hours, the distance would be in miles.

Example 2 **A car travels for 45 minutes at an average speed of 40 km/h. How far does it travel?**

1. The speed is in km/h,
   so convert the time into hours.

   45 minutes = 0.75 hours

2. Use the formula for distance and put
   in the numbers for speed and time.
   The units of distance will be km.

   Distance = Speed × Time
   = 40 × 0.75
   = **30 km**

Example 3 **Sunita walks 4 km to her friend's house at an average speed of 6 km/h. She sets off at 10:30 am. What time will she arrive at her friend's house?**

1. Use the formula for time and put in the
   numbers for speed and distance.

   $\text{Time} = \dfrac{\text{Distance}}{\text{Speed}} = \dfrac{4}{6} = 0.666...$ hours

2. Convert your answer into minutes.

   (0.666... × 60) mins = 40 mins

3. Add on the number of minutes to the
   time she set off to find her arrival time.

   Arrival time = 10:30 am + 40 mins
   = **11:10 am**

Exercise 2

1 For each of the following, use the speed and time given to find the distance travelled.

   a) speed = 40 km/h, time = 5 hours

   b) speed = 60 mph, time = 3 hours

   c) speed = 5 m/s, time = 20 seconds

   d) speed = 5 km/h, time = 6 hours

2 Find the distance travelled by a cyclist who cycles at 11 km/h for 3 hours.

3 Find the distance travelled by a spider that crawls at 0.5 m/s for 40 seconds.

4 For each of the following, use the speed given to find the time taken to travel the distance.

   a) speed = 7 km/h, distance = 35 km   **b)** speed = 25 mph, distance = 100 miles

   c) speed = 8 m/s, distance = 36 m   **d)** speed = 18 km/h, distance = 9 km

5 Two villages are 16 miles apart. Louise sets off from one village and cycles at an average speed of 10 mph. How long does it take her to reach the other village?

6 Kara rollerblades at an average speed of 14 km/h. How far does she rollerblade in 15 minutes?

7 Jack sets off on a 25 km hike at 9 am. He walks at an average speed of 4 km/h. What time will he finish the hike?

8 Jess cycles for 15 minutes at an average speed of 24 km/h. Charlie cycles for 30 minutes at an average speed of 10 mph. Who cycled the furthest?

9 Joe starts work at 9 am. He sets off for work at 8.45 am. He works 18 miles away from home, and drives at an average speed of 45 mph. How many minutes late for work will he be?

10 A car travels 16 km at an average speed of 20 mph. How long does this journey take in minutes?

Investigate — Distance-Time Graphs

The distance-time graph shows the Hutton family's journey one Sunday afternoon.

a) What do you think is happening in each section of the graph?

b) Use the graph to describe the journey.

c) Write a story describing a journey, then draw a distance-time graph to explain it.

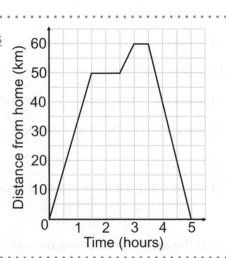

7.3 Scale Drawings

Maps and Map Scales

Maps use a scale to accurately show large distances on a smaller drawing. So a scale of 1 cm : 100 m means that 1 cm on the map represents an actual distance of 100 m.

A scale without units (e.g. 1 : 100) means you can use any units — but you must put the same units on both sides. For example, 1 cm : 100 cm or 1 mm : 100 mm.

Example 1   The scale on a map is 1 : 500.
What is the actual distance (in metres) between
two points which are 25 cm apart on the map.

1. Write the scale down using cm
   (to match the units given in the question).   1 cm : 500 cm

2. Multiply both sides of the scale   1 cm represents 500 cm
   by the same number (here it's 25).   so 25 cm represents 12 500 cm

3. Give your answer using the correct units.   12 500 cm = (12 500 ÷ 100) m
                                                          = **125 m**

Exercise 1

1   A map scale is given as 1 cm : 20 km.

   a) Convert these lengths on the map to actual distances:

     i) 5 cm   **ii)** 8 cm

     iii) 20 cm   **iv)** 0.5 cm

     v) 7.5 cm   **vi)** 5.25 cm

   b) Convert these actual distances to lengths on the map:

     i) 40 km   **ii)** 120 km

     iii) 200 km   **iv)** 50 km

     v) 110 km   **vi)** 75 km

2   The scale on a map of America is 1 cm : 100 km.
Find the lengths used on the map to represent these actual distances.

   a) New York to Boston, 300 km   **b)** Denver to Salt Lake City, 600 km

   c) Nashville to Oklahoma City, 970 km   **d)** San Francisco to Los Angeles, 560 km

3 Updale and Downdale are 2.5 km apart.
They are drawn on a map with a scale of 1 cm : 0.5 km.

a) How far apart will the villages be on the map?

b) The same map shows the distance from Highburrow to Lowburrow as 4.5 cm.
What is the actual distance between these two villages?

4 A map scale is given as 1 : 500. Convert these lengths on the map
to actual distances. Give your answers in m.

a) 3 cm
b) 5 cm
c) 8 cm

d) 6.5 cm
e) 2.25 cm
f) 9.75 cm

5 The scale of a map is given as 1 : 250.

a) Convert these lengths on the map to actual distances. Give your answers in metres.

i) 4 cm
ii) 10 cm

iii) 12 cm
iv) 2.5 cm

v) 6.2 cm
vi) 8.4 cm

b) Convert these actual distances to lengths on the map. Give your answers in cm.

i) 20 m
ii) 50 m

iii) 12 m
iv) 2.5 m

v) 7.5 m
vi) 2.25 m

6 A 20 km road is to be drawn on a map with a scale of 1 : 500 000.
How long will the road be on the map? Give your answer in cm.

7 A map uses the scale 1 : 50 000. Find the actual distances in km represented by:

a) 2.5 cm
b) 5.6 cm
c) 9.7 cm

8 Karen is drawing a plan of the grounds of a stately home on a piece of A4 paper.
The drive is 2.5 km long. Suggest a suitable scale for her plan, and work out
how long the drive would be on the plan using this scale.

Scale Drawings

Scale diagrams and plans also use <u>scales</u> to show actual distances on a drawing.

Example 2 The diagram shows a rough sketch of a park. Use the scale **1 cm : 5 m** to draw an accurate plan of the park.

1. Use the scale to work out the lengths for the plan.
   1 cm = 5 m, so divide the lengths in m by 5 to find the lengths in cm on the plan.
   5 m: 5 ÷ 5 = 1 cm
   2.5 m: 2.5 ÷ 5 = 0.5 cm
   20 m: 20 ÷ 5 = 4 cm
   10 m: 10 ÷ 5 = 2 cm

2. Use these lengths to draw an accurate plan.

Exercise 2

1 An architect has been asked to draw the plans for a building using a scale of 1 cm : 2 m. Find the lengths he should draw on the plan to represent these actual distances.

a) 6 m   **b)** 20 m   **c)** 7 m   **d)** 5.5 m

2 A plan of an office is drawn using a scale of 2 cm : 1 m. Find the actual dimensions if they are given on the plan as:

a) 6 cm   **b)** 10 cm   **c)** 7 cm   **d)** 1.5 cm

3 The scale drawings below have been drawn using the scale 1 cm : 1 m. By measuring these scale drawings, give the actual lengths of sides a, b and c in each shape.

a)
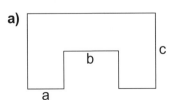

b)
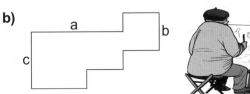

4 A model of a building uses a scale of 1 : 1000. The height of the tower on the model is 5 cm. Work out its actual height, giving your answer in m.

5 A model plane uses a scale of 1 : 250.
Use the actual measurements given here
to find the measurements of the model in cm.

a) Height of tail: 5 m

b) Length of body: 10 m

c) Width of cockpit: 3 m

d) Length of wing: 7.5 m

6 A sketch of part of a zoo has been drawn.

a) Use the scale 1 cm : 5 m to draw an accurate plan of the zoo.

b) Use your plan to find the real-life distance between the two points labelled A and B on the sketch.

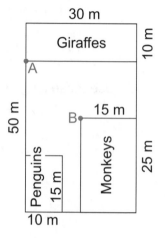

7 Isabel has made a sketch of her shed. Draw an accurate plan of the shed, using a scale of 1 : 50.

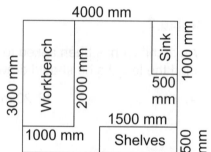

. . . .

Investigate — Scale Drawings

a) Draw a shape on squared paper and calculate its area.

b) Scale up the shape by a factor of 2 (remember to double all the dimensions). Work out its area.

c) Scale up the original shape by a factor of 3 and work out its area.

d) Repeat steps **a)**-**c)** for different shapes.

e) What happens to the area of a shape when you enlarge it? Can you find a rule for the scale factor of the area given the scale factor for the dimensions?

Section 8 — Algebraic Expressions

8.1 Expressions

An algebraic <u>expression</u> uses letters to represent unknown numbers (called <u>variables</u>). Expressions do not contain an equals sign (=).

An expression consists of a number of <u>terms</u> separated by + or − signs. Terms can be letters, numbers or a mixture of both.

Each term has a + or a − sign attached to the front of it. Terms at the start of an expression that don't have a sign in front of them are <u>positive</u>.

one term

two terms

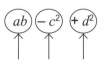

three terms

In expressions, there is a standard algebraic notation (a kind of 'shorthand') which is used to write terms more easily:

$$ab = a \times b$$
$$3y = 3 \times y \text{ (or } y + y + y)$$
$$a^2 = a \times a$$
$$3a^2 = 3a \times a \text{ (or } 3 \times a \times a \text{ or } 3 \times a^2)$$

$$a^3 = a \times a \times a$$
$$a^2b = a \times a \times b \text{ (or } a^2 \times b)$$
$$\frac{a}{b} = a \div b$$

A <u>coefficient</u> is a number placed before a letter in an algebraic expression, e.g. the '5' in $5y$. Non-integer coefficients are normally written as fractions, not decimals.

Exercise 1

1 How many terms are in each of these expressions?

a) $6y + z - c$ b) $a + b$ c) $3r - 7 + u$ d) $11b + x - 3$

e) ab f) $ab + 7$ g) $6 + c + xy$ h) $abc + 9$

i) $2v + x^2$ j) $ab^2 - b$ k) $3 + c^3$ l) $12 - abc + d^3$

2 List all the terms in each expression. Remember to include the signs.

a) $m + 9 + n$ b) $a - bc + d^2$ c) $11r - 2 + t$ d) $-p - q + 7$

e) $ab + cd$ f) $y + 7 - yz$ g) xyz h) $q - rs + 4 + t$

i) $f^2 + g^2h$ j) $-v^2 - v + 2$ k) $8 - c^3 - c^2$ l) $1 - xyz + z^3 - y$

3 Choose the correct rewriting of each expression. One has been done for you.

a) $x + x + y$ $x^2 + y$ ⟨$2x + y$⟩ x^2y

b) $b \times c \times b \times b$ b^3c $3bc$ bc^3

c) $u \times 9 \div p$ $9u - p$ $\dfrac{u^9}{p}$ $\dfrac{9u}{p}$

d) $3 + m \div n$ $3 + \dfrac{m}{n}$ $3 + m - n$ $3m - n$

4 Rewrite these expressions using the correct algebraic notation.

a) $4 \times a$ **b)** $x \times y$ **c)** $a \times a$ **d)** $c \times 2 \times d$

e) $f \div 3$ **f)** $m \times m \times m$ **g)** $8 \times c \times c$ **h)** $f \times p \times q$

i) $p \times k \times p$ **j)** $g \div k$ **k)** $u + u + u + u$ **l)** $p + l \times l$

m) $k \div 6p$ **n)** $t + t + t$ **o)** $r \times r \times s \times s$ **p)** $u \times r \div q$

Investigate — Expressions

Expressions can be used to represent many situations, e.g. the area of a shape, or a sequence of numbers. For example, n^2 is the area of a square with side length n and $2n - 1$ will generate a series of odd numbers when $n = 1, 2, 3...$

a) Write down an expression that will generate a series of even numbers when $n = 1, 2, 3...$

b) Write down an expression for the area of a rectangle with side lengths a and b.

c) Write down expressions for the perimeter of a square and the perimeter of a rectangle. How many terms does each expression have? Why do they have different numbers of terms?

d) Find an expression for the total number of handshakes needed if n people all shake hands with each other.

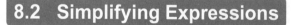

8.2 Simplifying Expressions

Expressions can sometimes be <u>simplified</u> by collecting <u>like terms</u>. 'Like terms' contain exactly the same letters raised to the same <u>powers</u>, but may have different <u>coefficients</u>. Numbers on their own in an expression are treated as like terms.

Example 1 Simplify the expression $6a + 2b - 4a - 8b$.

1. '$6a$' and '$-4a$' are like terms. '$2b$' and '$-8b$' are like terms.

2. Rewrite the expression with the like terms collected together.

$6a - 4a + 2b - 8b$

3. Combine the like terms.

$6a - 4a = 2a$
$2b - 8b = -6b$

4. Write out the simplified expression.

$2a - 6b$

Exercise 1

1 Simplify these expressions.

a) $2x + x + 3y + y$

b) $4a - a + 6b + 2b$

c) $9m - 3m + n + 4n$

d) $p + 5q + 2p - 4q$

e) $6f - 5g - 2g + 3f$

f) $3a + 3c - a + 3c$

g) $4x - 3x - 5y - y$

h) $2p + q + 4p - 6q$

i) $6f + 7g - 2f - 3g$

j) $10s - 4t - 2s + 6t$

k) $7x + 2y - y - x$

l) $8m + 4n - n + 7m$

m) $5d + 3e - 8e - d$

n) $11p - 6q - 3p - 8q$

o) $-7i + 3j - 5i - 6j$

2 Simplify these expressions.

a) $f + 4 + 11f + 9$

b) $5x + 8 + 12x + 4$

c) $9y - 6y - 11 + 6$

d) $s + 2s + 6 - 12$

e) $9f + 12 - 2 - 2f$

f) $6a - a + 14 - 3$

g) $12 + 7x - 2x - 5$

h) $2q + 7q + 11 - 12$

i) $3 - 2g + 7g - 10$

j) $10 - 6y + 7y - 3$

k) $11s + 12 + 10 - 7s$

l) $-4 + 6h - 4h - 11$

3 Add together the following pairs of expressions and simplify your answers.

a) $4y + 2x$ and $7y - 5x$

b) $8c + 6d$ and $6c + d$

c) $11r - 2s$ and $5r + 8s$

d) $12g + 4j$ and $-15g - 7j$

e) $11w - 5u$ and $5w - 11u$

f) $-9y + 11z$ and $12y - 15z$

g) $-7v - 3w$ and $8v - 10w$

h) $12g + 5h$ and $g - 11h$

4 Simplify the following expressions by collecting like terms.

a) $2y + 7y + 10 + 7 + 5x + 2x$

b) $8a - 2c + 6 - 12 + 9a + 7c$

c) $12 - 5r + 7s - 3 + 8s - 6r$

d) $9t + 11t - 11 + 10s + 4 - 6s$

e) $8a - 5b + 12a + 9 - 4 + 3b$

f) $7m + 8 + 7m - 4p + 3 - 9p$

g) $7y + 11 - 6 - 8y - 5z + 8z$

h) $2 - 6c + 9b + 2c - 11b + 8$

i) $11 + 7p - 9q + 4p - 2q + 8$

j) $5g + 11g - 12 + 9h - 7 - 11h$

5 Simplify the following expressions by collecting like terms.

a) $x^2 + x^2 + 6 + 8$

b) $2a^2 - a^2 + 9 - 3$

c) $4c^2 + c^2 - 5 + 7$

d) $6 + 12 + 6f^3 - 3f^3$

e) $4n^2 - 6n^2 - 3 - 4$

f) $5k^3 + 11 + 7k^3 - 2$

g) $11z^2 + 10 - 3 + 2z^2$

h) $10 - 11 + 4b^3 + 10b^3$

i) $9c^2 + 9 - 8c^2 + 12$

j) $7g^2 + 3 + 12 - 5g^2$

k) $11w^2 - w^2 + 7 + 6$

l) $10u^3 - 8 + 5u^3 - 8$

6 Simplify the following expressions by collecting like terms.

a) $2y^2 + 4y^2 + y + 5y + 4 + 2$

b) $8g^2 - 2g^2 + 4 - 6g + 7g + 8$

c) $6v - 1 + v^2 - 2v + 9v^2 + 6$

d) $11d^2 - 7 + 4d + 6d^2 + 2d + 3$

e) $7p^3 - 4p^3 + 5 + 9p^2 + 8p^2 - 6$

f) $6a^2 + a^3 + 2 + 9 + a^2 + 9a^3$

g) $2y^2 + 8y - 3 - 11 - y^2 - 12y$

h) $12h^3 - 3h + 9 + 6h - 12 + 4h^3$

7 Simplify these expressions.

a) $3wv + 7wv - 9w + 3w$

b) $2g^4 + 8g^4 - 3gh - 8gh$

c) $5xy + y - 3xy + 12x$

d) $10ab + 8b^3 + a - 7ab$

e) $2p + 8pq - 3pq + 9q$

f) $5fg + fg + 8fg + 3f^2$

8 Simplify the following expressions.

a) $9xy + yx + 2x - 3x$

b) $8ab - 7a + 8ba + 3a$

c) $5pq - qp + p^2 + 4p^2$

d) $11rt + 4tr - t^2 + r^2$

e) $7yz - 2yz + 7zy + z^2$

f) $2mn + nm + 7m + 6m$

g) $4g + 7h - gh + 7hg$

h) $2jk - 3j^2 + 4k^2 + 9kj$

i) $3u + 7uv - 9uv^2 + 8v^2u$

8.3 Expressions with Brackets

Expanding Brackets

You can '<u>expand</u>' (or 'multiply out') brackets by multiplying everything inside the brackets by the letter or number in front of the brackets.
This removes the brackets from the expression.

| Example 1 | Expand $7(x - 6)$. |

1. Multiply both x and -6 by 7. $(7 \times x) + (7 \times -6)$
                                         $7x + -42$

2. Simplify the expression. $7x - 42$

Exercise 1

1 Expand the brackets in the following expressions.

a) $3(a + 4)$ b) $2(b + 1)$ c) $4(p + 6)$ d) $5(5 + y)$

e) $6(h - 3)$ f) $8(q - 2)$ g) $2(t + 11)$ h) $9(b - 7)$

i) $6(k + 7)$ j) $9(3 + p)$ k) $4(9 + g)$ l) $2(5 - y)$

2 Expand the brackets in the following expressions.

a) $-8(d + 3)$ b) $-5(x + 4)$ c) $-11(4 - r)$ d) $-12(9 - r)$

e) $-4(r + 8)$ f) $-11(5 + q)$ g) $-3(t - 12)$ h) $-7(2 + x)$

i) $-11(a - 6)$ j) $-9(8 + p)$ k) $-8(8 + s)$ l) $-7(11 - y)$

3 Expand the brackets in the following expressions.

a) $2(s + b - 8)$ b) $5(a + 4 + c)$ c) $5(p + q + 7)$ d) $6(2 + x - y)$

e) $9(t - 3 + p)$ f) $6(h - k + 5)$ g) $11(t + 11 - r)$ h) $9(b - 12 - f)$

4 Expand the brackets in the following expressions.

a) $-7(a + 8 - d)$ b) $-4(b + 2 + c)$ c) $-5(p + 7 + f)$ d) $-8(r + 5 - y)$

e) $-2(c - b + 5)$ f) $-6(q - v + 7)$ g) $-11(s + 12 - q)$ h) $-6(b - 10 - f)$

| Example 2 | Expand the brackets in $3a(a + 4)$. |

1. Multiply both a and 4 by $3a$. $\qquad$ $(3a \times a) + (3a \times 4)$

2. Simplify the expression $\qquad$ $3a^2 + 12a$

Exercise 2

1 Expand the brackets in the following expressions.

a) $c(c + 2)$ **b)** $m(5 + m)$ **c)** $q(11 + q)$ **d)** $r(r - 5)$

e) $v(v + 7)$ **f)** $y(y - 5)$ **g)** $k(k - 10)$ **h)** $b(8 + b)$

2 Expand the brackets in the following expressions.

a) $-d(d + 7)$ **b)** $-b(b + 9)$ **c)** $-v(5 + v)$ **d)** $-x(x - 9)$

e) $-y(y - 12)$ **f)** $-z(z + 5)$ **g)** $-r(11 - r)$ **h)** $-p(p + 8)$

i) $-q(q - 10)$ **j)** $-j(j + 6)$ **k)** $-k(8 - k)$ **l)** $-l(-5 - l)$

3 Expand the brackets in the following expressions.

a) $3a(a + 3)$ **b)** $2v(v + 5)$ **c)** $4r(5 - r)$ **d)** $11x(x + 11)$

e) $5h(h - 3)$ **f)** $8q(q - 7)$ **g)** $6t(t - 12)$ **h)** $9y(y - 8)$

i) $11b(7 + b)$ **j)** $4w(12 - w)$ **k)** $12z(8 + z)$ **l)** $7q(9 - q)$

4 Expand the brackets in the following expressions.

a) $7f(f + 2 + g)$ **b)** $4h(h + 1 + j)$ **c)** $9k(l + k - 6)$ **d)** $5r(8 + r - s)$

e) $6d(11 + g - d)$ **f)** $8n(n - m - 9)$ **g)** $2j(12 + j - k)$ **h)** $9a(b - a - 12)$

i) $5p(6 + p + q)$ **j)** $3s(12 - t - s)$ **k)** $12b(11 + b + c)$ **l)** $3a(a - b + 10)$

5 Expand the brackets in the following expressions.

a) $-2f(f + 2 + g)$ **b)** $-5c(b + c - 2)$ **c)** $-4r(r - s + 2)$ **d)** $-7b(c - 4 - b)$

e) $-5j(j + 6 + k)$ **f)** $-3n(5 - n - m)$ **g)** $-6y(y - 10 + z)$ **h)** $-11v(w + v + 9)$

i) $-8h(j - h + 9)$ **j)** $-2c(d + c - 10)$ **k)** $-2r(11 - r - s)$ **l)** $-12x(5 + y - x)$

Factorising

Factorising is the opposite of expanding brackets. It's putting brackets into an expression.

You look for the highest common factor (HCF) of all the terms in an expression, and 'take it outside' the brackets.

Example 3 Factorise these expressions:

a) **$12p + 8$**

1. 4 is the highest common factor of $12p$ and 8.
   So write a pair of brackets with a 4 outside.

   $12p + 8 = 4(\ +\ )$

2. Divide each term in the expression by 4
   and write the results in the brackets.

   $12p \div 4 = 3p$

   $8 \div 4 = 2$

   $4(3p + 2)$

b) **$7a + 15a^2$**

1. There are no common factors of 7 and 15, but
   'a' is a factor of both terms. So write a pair of
   brackets with 'a' outside.

   $7a + 15a^2 = a(\ +\ )$

2. Divide each term in the expression by 'a' and
   write the results in the brackets.

   $7a \div a = 7$

   $15a^2 \div a = 15a$

   $a(7 + 15a)$

Exercise 3

1 **a)** Find the highest common factor of $9a$ and 27.

   b) Divide both $9a$ and 27 by your answer to **a)**.

   c) Using your answers to **a)** and **b)**, factorise the expression $9a + 27$.

2 **a)** Find the highest common factor of $12b$ and 16.

   b) Divide both $12b$ and 16 by your answer to **a)**.

   c) Using your answers to **a)** and **b)**, factorise the expression $12b - 16$.

3 **a)** Find the highest common factor of 15 and 24x.

b) Factorise the expression 15 − 24x.

4 Factorise these expressions.

a) 9 + 18a **b)** 12 + 4b **c)** 5 − 25c **d)** 8x + 20

e) 6d − 33 **f)** 12x + 60 **g)** 14y + 42 **h)** 35 + 15v

i) 8c − 52 **j)** 16p − 12 **k)** 49 − 14x **l)** 18x + 66

5 Find the highest common factor in each of these expressions.

a) 6a + 5a^2 **b)** 11u^2 + 4u **c)** 5h + 12h^3 **d)** 6j + 3j^2

e) 4b^3 + 20b **f)** 3h + 30h^2 **g)** 6s^3 + 33s **h)** 12r^3 + 45r

6 **a)** Find the highest common factor of 16x and 20x^2.

b) Use your answer to **a)** to factorise the expression 16x + 20x^2.

7 Fully factorise these expressions.

a) 14a + 3a^2 **b)** 15v^2 + 4v **c)** 7c + 12c^2 **d)** 16f − 5f^2

e) 2d^3 + 8d **f)** 7q + 14q^2 **g)** 6y^2 + 9y **h)** 15r − 10r^3

i) 6c − 32c^3 **j)** 16p − 6p^2 **k)** 18y + 12y^2 **l)** 20x^2 − 32x

8 **a)** Find the highest common factor of 12x^2y and 20xy.

b) Factorise the expression 12x^2y + 20xy.

9 Fully factorise these expressions.

a) 2xy − xy^2 **b)** 8ab − 3a **c)** 4p^2q − 12pq **d)** 15su^2 + 25u^2

e) 21df − 7d^2f^2 **f)** 3v^2 + 30vy **g)** 5rw − 10r **h)** 8xy^2 + 16xy + 4y

10 Fully factorise these expressions.

a) 6pq^2 + 15p^2q **b)** 9x^2y − 3xy^2 **c)** 21cd^2 + 35c^2d **d)** 12gh^2 − 6g^2h

Two Brackets

To <u>expand</u> two sets of brackets, you need to multiply each term in the right bracket by each term in the left bracket.

$$(a + b)(c + d) = ac + ad + bc + bd$$

Example 4 Expand $(x + 2)(x + 3)$.

1. Multiply each term in the right bracket by each term in the left bracket.

$$(x + 2)(x + 3) = x^2 + 3x + 2x + 6$$

2. Simplify by collecting like terms. $x^2 + 5x + 6$

Exercise 4

1 Expand the brackets in the following expressions.

a) $(b + 2)(b + 1)$ **b)** $(a + 3)(a + 3)$ **c)** $(x + 4)(x + 1)$

d) $(y + 5)(y + 2)$ **e)** $(c + 5)(c + 9)$ **f)** $(a + 2)(a + 6)$

g) $(r + 8)(r + 3)$ **h)** $(z + 7)(z + 11)$ **i)** $(d + 8)(d + 4)$

j) $(p + 12)(p + 4)$ **k)** $(q + 9)(q + 9)$ **l)** $(t + 11)(t + 6)$

m) $(j + 7)(j + 9)$ **n)** $(g + 4)(g + 12)$ **o)** $(y + 8)(y + 10)$

2 Expand the brackets in the following expressions.

a) $(a - 5)(a + 6)$ **b)** $(u + 3)(u - 7)$ **c)** $(j - 7)(j + 6)$

d) $(g + 4)(g - 11)$ **e)** $(f - 6)(f + 2)$ **f)** $(n + 11)(n - 3)$

g) $(k + 7)(k - 9)$ **h)** $(b - 5)(b + 12)$ **i)** $(v + 9)(v - 1)$

j) $(s + 3)(s - 11)$ **k)** $(h + 12)(h - 7)$ **l)** $(q - 10)(q + 9)$

m) $(q - 4)(q + 11)$ **n)** $(g - 10)(g + 6)$ **o)** $(q + 8)(q - 12)$

3 Expand the brackets in the following expressions.

a) $(r - 5)(r - 9)$

b) $(x - 3)(x - 8)$

c) $(h - 7)(h - 4)$

d) $(f - 3)(f - 5)$

e) $(w - 7)(w - 1)$

f) $(c - 10)(c - 3)$

g) $(n - 7)(n - 2)$

h) $(a - 9)(a - 4)$

i) $(r - 5)(r - 11)$

j) $(y - 4)(y - 12)$

k) $(b - 7)(b - 8)$

l) $(x - 6)(x - 10)$

4 Expand the brackets in these expressions.

a) $(p + 1)(6 + p)$

b) $(7 + x)(x - 6)$

c) $(j - 2)(6 + j)$

d) $(g + 5)(5 + g)$

e) $(4 + x)(x - 9)$

f) $(z - 5)(2 + z)$

g) $(t + 3)(12 - t)$

h) $(10 - s)(s - 4)$

i) $(d - 8)(3 + d)$

j) $(q - 6)(2 + q)$

k) $(a - 7)(8 + a)$

l) $(v + 2)(1 + v)$

m) $(3 - f)(f + 10)$

n) $(h + 5)(4 - h)$

o) $(11 - b)(2 + b)$

Investigate — Factorising into Two Brackets

Expressions such as $x^2 + 12x + 27$ (where the highest power of x is 2) can be factorised into two brackets in the form $(x + a)(x + b)$, where a and b are numbers, using steps **a)-c)**:

a) List all the pairs of factors of 27.

b) Find a factor pair that will multiply together to give 27 and add together to make 12.

c) These two factors are a and b.
Put these two factors into two brackets in the form $(x + a)(x + b)$.

d) Expand the brackets to check that you get the original expression.
Does it matter which way round you put a and b? If not, why not?

e) Look at your answers to questions **1** to **3** in the previous exercise.
How do the signs in the brackets match the signs in the expressions?

f) Can you factorise the expression $x^2 - 3x - 40$?
Use the steps **a)-c)** to help you. Pay attention to the signs in the expression.

Section 9 — Equations

9.1 Solving Equations

One-Step Equations

An equation is made up of two expressions, one on each side of an equals sign.

Equations contain one (or more) unknown variable, usually shown by a letter. Solving an equation involves finding the value of the letter that makes both sides of the equation equal.

Example 1 | **Solve the following equations.**

a) $x + 7 = 12$

1. You need to get x on its own on one side of the equation. $\quad x + 7 = 12$

   The easiest way to do this is to subtract 7 from the left-hand side. You have to do the same to both sides of an equation, so subtract 7 from the right-hand side too. $\quad x + 7 - 7 = 12 - 7$

2. Now find the solution to the equation. $\quad x = 12 - 7$

   $x = 5$

b) $\dfrac{t}{6} = 9$

1. You need to get t on its own.
   To do this, you need to do the opposite of dividing by 6 which is multiplying by 6. You have to do the same to both sides of an equation, so multiply the right-hand side by 6 too. $\quad \dfrac{t}{6} = 9$

   $\dfrac{t}{6} \times 6 = 9 \times 6$

2. Now find the solution to the equation. $\quad t = 9 \times 6$

   $t = 54$

c) $10 - r = 4$

1. Start by adding r to both sides of the equation to get rid of the minus sign in front of the r. $\quad 10 - r + r = 4 + r$

   $10 = 4 + r$

2. Now you can solve the equation as before by subtracting 4 from both sides. $\quad 10 - 4 = 4 + r - 4$

   $10 - 4 = r$

3. You'd usually write your answer with the variable on the left (i.e. $r = 6$). $\quad 6 = r \quad \text{or} \quad r = 6$

Exercise 1

1 Work out the value of x in these equations.

 a) $x + 9 = 17$ b) $x - 7 = 11$ c) $14 = x - 8$ d) $6 + x = 18$

 e) $x + 4 = 29$ f) $15 = x - 12$ g) $x - 17 = 29$ h) $55 = x + 5$

 i) $22 = x - 14$ j) $x + 16 = 31$ k) $29 = x - 12$ l) $21 + x = 29$

2 Solve these equations.

 a) $6a = 18$ b) $8x = 48$ c) $\dfrac{l}{3} = 10$ d) $56 = 7x$

 e) $3 = \dfrac{m}{15}$ f) $32 = 16n$ g) $9 = \dfrac{y}{7}$ h) $r \div 11 = 8$

 i) $14q = 84$ j) $13c = 91$ k) $9 = \dfrac{z}{8}$ l) $\dfrac{s}{20} = 4$

3 Solve these equations.

 a) $9 - a = 6$ b) $18 - r = 3$ c) $22 - b = 6$ d) $5 = 17 - q$

 e) $25 - c = 15$ f) $12 = 39 - x$ g) $27 = 42 - d$ h) $52 - z = 31$

 i) $63 - f = 36$ j) $22 = 45 - s$ k) $21 = 61 - p$ l) $80 - m = 54$

4 Solve these equations.

 a) $34 - x = 6$ b) $44 = 13 + x$ c) $81 + x = 90$ d) $84 = 7x$

 e) $\dfrac{x}{26} = 4$ f) $87 - x = 12$ g) $150 = 41 + x$ h) $40x = 920$

 i) $45 + x = 171$ j) $76 = 151 - x$ k) $16 = \dfrac{x}{8}$ l) $\dfrac{x}{13} = 3$

5 Solve these equations.

 a) $7 - r = -6$ b) $14 - t = 21$ c) $18 + x = 12$ d) $-3 = 11 - p$

 e) $20 - s = 22$ f) $-2 = 15 - y$ g) $12 = 30 + u$ h) $40 - l = -22$

6 Solve these equations. Express your answers as simplified fractions.

 a) $20x = 5$ b) $16x = 8$ c) $25x = 10$

 d) $8x = 6$ e) $4 = 14x$ f) $4x = 18$

Two-Step Equations

Some equations need to be solved in two stages.
You need to do these stages in the right order.

Example 2   **Solve the equation $3x + 6 = 18$.**

1. $3x + 6$ means "take your value of x and then: i) multiply it by 3,
         ii) add 6".

To get x on its own, "undo" these steps, but in the opposite order.

2. First, subtract 6 from both sides.

$$3x + 6 - 6 = 18 - 6$$
$$3x = 12$$

3. Then divide both sides by 3.

$$3x \div 3 = 12 \div 3$$
$$x = 4$$

4. Check your answer by substituting 4 in for x.

$$(3 \times 4) + 6 = 12 + 6 = 18$$

When you've got an equation containing brackets, expand
the brackets to get rid of them and solve the equation as usual.

Example 3   **Solve the equation $4(y - 2) = 12$.**

1. First, multiply out the brackets and rewrite the equation.

$$4(y - 2) = (4 \times y) + (4 \times -2) = 4y - 8$$
$$4y - 8 = 12$$

2. Now solve the equation as normal:

Add 8 to both sides.

$$4y - 8 + 8 = 12 + 8$$
$$4y = 20$$

Then divide both sides by 4.

$$4y \div 4 = 20 \div 4$$
$$y = 5$$

3. Check your answer by substituting 5 in for y.

$$4(5 - 2) = 4(3) = 12$$

Exercise 2

1 Work out the value of a in these equations.

   a) $2a + 3 = 7$ **b)** $3a + 4 = 13$ **c)** $11 = 2a + 1$ **d)** $6 + 4a = 14$

   e) $9a + 4 = 22$ **f)** $9 = 5a - 6$ **g)** $6a - 3 = 15$ **h)** $39 = 4a + 11$

   i) $37 = 7a - 12$ **j)** $6a + 14 = 44$ **k)** $50 = 7a - 6$ **l)** $21 + 9a = 66$

   m) $41 = 3a + 11$ **n)** $12a - 25 = 35$ **o)** $26 = 4a - 22$ **p)** $9 + 6a = 75$

2 Solve the following equations.

   a) $8 - 2x = 4$ **b)** $11 - 3x = 2$ **c)** $18 - 2x = 4$ **d)** $6 = 30 - 6x$

   e) $17 - 2x = 1$ **f)** $16 = 56 - 8x$ **g)** $8 = 56 - 4x$ **h)** $14 = 32 - 6x$

   i) $57 - 6x = 21$ **j)** $75 - 8x = 3$ **k)** $14 = 47 - 3x$ **l)** $60 - 4x = 8$

3 Solve the following equations.

   a) $4p + 2 = 50$ **b)** $30 - 5p = 5$ **c)** $53 = 6p + 11$ **d)** $21 = 48 - 9q$

   e) $8q - 35 = 61$ **f)** $13 = 58 - 5q$ **g)** $12q + 9 = 81$ **h)** $6 = 72 - 11q$

   i) $17 = 39 - 2p$ **j)** $8q + 39 = 63$ **k)** $4 = 100 - 8q$ **l)** $111 - 9p = 12$

   m) $12p + 14 = 86$ **n)** $19 = 55 - 4p$ **o)** $20 = 90 - 5q$ **p)** $13 = 145 - 11q$

4 Solve the following equations.

   a) $3(n + 2) = 15$ **b)** $2(2 + n) = 14$ **c)** $44 = 4(n - 1)$

   d) $5(n + 1) = 45$ **e)** $6(n + 4) = 72$ **f)** $2(n - 4) = 12$

   g) $9(n - 3) = 72$ **h)** $75 = 5(n + 2)$ **i)** $48 = 12(n - 11)$

   j) $108 = 9(n + 8)$ **k)** $84 = 6(n - 2)$ **l)** $12(n + 1) = 144$

5 Solve the following equations.

   a) $6(8 - a) = 36$ **b)** $3(11 - t) = 27$ **c)** $12 = 4(6 - u)$ **d)** $7(8 - c) = 49$

   e) $4(8 - b) = 8$ **f)** $63 = 7(20 - w)$ **g)** $11(12 - y) = 110$ **h)** $42 = 14(8 - x)$

   i) $28 = 7(15 - q)$ **j)** $8(25 - p) = 80$ **k)** $81 = 9(18 - z)$ **l)** $11(20 - x) = 88$

6 Solve the following equations. Express your answers as simplified fractions.

a) $4y + 5 = 7$　　**b)** $3y + 7 = 8$　　**c)** $14 = 5y + 11$　　**d)** $10 - 12y = 2$

e) $12y - 8 = 1$　　**f)** $13 = 16y - 1$　　**g)** $22 - 6y = 19$　　**h)** $33 = 18y + 27$

i) $2 = 18y - 6$　　**j)** $24y + 18 = 24$　　**k)** $23 = 8y + 19$　　**l)** $28 + 9y = 34$

7 Solve the following equations.

a) $2x - 14 = -6$　　**b)** $5x - 11 = -1$　　**c)** $4x + 25 = 9$　　**d)** $14 + 7x = -14$

e) $4x - 36 = -4$　　**f)** $32 = 12 - 4x$　　**g)** $7x + 30 = -19$　　**h)** $4 = 6x + 40$

i) $-18 = 30 - 4x$　　**j)** $71 - 8x = -17$　　**k)** $57 = 5 - 4x$　　**l)** $11x - 97 = -9$

8 Solve the following equations.

a) $6(x - 7) = -30$　　**b)** $4(5 - x) = -28$　　**c)** $-33 = -3(6 + x)$

d) $6(8 - x) = 72$　　**e)** $8(x - 6) = -24$　　**f)** $35 = 5(x + 9)$

g) $12(x + 5) = 24$　　**h)** $91 = 7(5 - x)$　　**i)** $-81 = 9(3 - x)$

Investigate — Simultaneous Equations

Look at the following equation:

$$x + y = 10$$

a) Write all the possible combinations of positive whole numbers for the letters x and y.

b) List some combinations of numbers where either x or y is negative.

c) List a few possibilities for values of x and y where they are both decimals.

d) Can you know for sure what x and y are?
What if you also knew that $x - y = 4$?
List the possible combinations of numbers for x and y that fit both equations.

e) $x + y = 10$ and $x - y = 4$ are **simultaneous** equations if x has the same value in both equations and y has the same value in both equations.
Write a new equation to go with $x + y = 10$ to make another pair of simultaneous equations.
Use different values of x and y from **a)** to write your new equation.

Section 10 — Formulas

10.1 Writing Formulas

A formula is like a set of instructions for working something out.

For example, $d = 2e + 5$ is a formula for d.
It tells you how to find d if you know the value of e.

The part after the = is an algebraic expression.

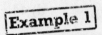 **Write a formula for P, the perimeter of a regular pentagon with sides of length x.**

1. The perimeter is the distance around the outside of the shape.

   $P = x + x + x + x + x$

2. Simplify the expression for the perimeter by adding up the side lengths.

   $x + x + x + x + x = 5x$

3. The formula should start with '$P = $'.
   P is called the subject of the formula.

   $P = 5x$

Exercise 1

1 m is 7 more than n. Write a formula for m in terms of n.

2 Write down a formula for P, the perimeter of each room shown below.

a)
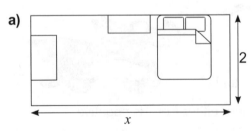

b)
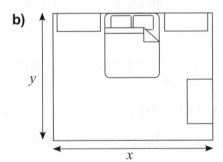

3 Write a formula for A, the area of a square with sides of length x.

4 It costs Eric 8p per minute to make a phone call.
Write a formula to show the cost, C, in pence, of making a call lasting m minutes.

5 It costs £6 per hour to hire a bike.
Write a formula for the cost, £C, of hiring a bike for h hours.

6 It takes Ben 5 minutes to cycle 1 mile.
Write a formula for the time taken, T minutes, for Ben to cycle m miles.

7 Alice gets paid w pounds for each hour she works.
Write a formula for the total amount Alice gets paid, £P, if she works for 11 hours.

8 Sara works 4 more hours per week than Ash.
Write a formula for the number of hours that Sara works, N, if Ash works for h hours.

9 Nadia jogs k kilometres more than Jack.
Write a formula for N, the number of kilometres Nadia jogs, if Jack jogs 5.5 kilometres.

Example 2	The total cost of calling out a plumber is made up of:

      i) **a cost of £12 for each hour,**
plus   ii) **a fixed cost of £18**

Write a formula for £C, the total cost of calling out a plumber for h hours.

1. Multiply h by 12 to find an expression for the total hourly cost.

   Cost (in pounds) for h hours:
   $h \times 12 = 12h$

2. Then add on the fixed cost of £18.

   $12h + 18$

3. The formula should start with '$C =$'.

   So $C = 12h + 18$

---

10 Write a formula for the cost, £C, of hiring a boat for b hours
if it costs £15 for each hour plus a fixed charge of £36.

11 Renting a holiday cottage costs a £250 fixed fee plus £40 per day.
Write a formula for the cost, £C, of renting the cottage for d days.

12 Paul gets paid £12.50 an hour.
At the end of each month, £5 is taken off his total wages as a charity donation.
Write a formula to show how much Paul will be paid each month, £P, if he works for h hours.

10.2 Substituting into a Formula

Substituting numbers into a <u>formula</u> or <u>expression</u> means replacing letters with numbers.

Example 1 $S = 5 + t$. **Find the value of S when $t = 6$.**

1. Write down the formula. $S = 5 + t$
2. Replace t with 6 and do the calculation. $= 5 + 6 = 11$

So $S = 11$

Exercise 1

1 $D = 5 + e$. Find the value of D when $e = 4$.

2 Find the value of s in each of the following when $t = 2$.

a) $s = 4 + t$ b) $s = 2 + t$ c) $s = t - 1$ d) $s = t - 5$

3 If $q = 8$ and $r = 6$, find the value of s in each of the following.

a) $s = q + 3$ b) $s = r - 2$ c) $s = q + r$ d) $s = q - r$ e) $s = r - q$

4 $B = 5c$. Find the value of B when:

a) $c = 3$ b) $c = 7$ c) $c = 20$ d) $c = 100$

5 Find the value of y in each of the following when $x = 4$.

a) $y = \dfrac{8}{x}$ b) $y = \dfrac{16}{x}$ c) $y = \dfrac{20}{x}$ d) $y = \dfrac{40}{x}$

6 If $x = 9$ and $y = 3$, find the value of z in each of the following.

a) $z = xy$ b) $z = x^2$ c) $z = \dfrac{x}{y}$ d) $z = \dfrac{y}{x}$

7 The number of chocolates, C, needed for a party is worked out using the formula $C = 6n$, where n is the number of people attending.

How many chocolates are needed if there are:

a) 8 people? b) 12 people? c) 40 people? d) 50 people?

The cost of hiring a car is worked out using the formula $C = 25d + 40$, where C is the cost in pounds and d is the number of days the car is hired for.

Use the formula to work out the cost of hiring a car for 4 days.

1. Write down the formula.

   $C = 25d + 40$

2. Replace d with the number of days (4), and do the calculation.

   $C = (25 \times 4) + 40$
   $= 100 + 40 = 140$

   So it costs **£140** to hire the car for 4 days.

8 Find the value of G in each of the following if $h = 8$.

a) $G = 2h + 1$ b) $G = 40 - 4h$ c) $G = 7 - 3h$ d) $G = 9 + 3h$

9 a) Use the formula $d = ef$ to find d if $e = 4$ and $f = 5$.

    b) Use the formula $d = ef + g$ to find d if $e = 3$, $f = 4$ and $g = 5$.

10 If $x = 3$ and $y = 6$, find the value of z in each of the following.

a) $z = 3x - y$ b) $z = 4x + y$ c) $z = x + \dfrac{y}{2}$ d) $z = 3x + 3y$

11 A teacher hires a coach for a school trip. The cost is worked out using $C = \dfrac{m}{3} + 40$, where C is the cost in pounds and m is the number of miles the coach travels.

Work out how much it would cost to hire the coach for a distance of:

a) 27 miles   b) 36 miles   c) 120 miles   d) 300 miles

12 The price, in pence, of a bag of pick 'n' mix sweets, S, is worked out using the formula $S = 2w + 15$, where w is the weight of the sweets in grams.

Work out how much bags of sweets with the following weights will cost in pence:

a) 100 g   b) 150 g   c) 220 g   d) 540 g

13 The cost of hiring a boat is worked out using $C = 5h + 4.5$, where C is the cost in pounds and h is the number of hours the boat is hired for. Find the cost of hiring a boat for two and a half hours.

Using Formulas in Maths and Science

Formulas are used a lot in maths and science. Here are some examples:

Maths

area of rectangle = length × width   area of triangle = $\frac{1}{2}$ × base × height

Science

speed = $\dfrac{\text{distance}}{\text{time}}$ pressure = $\dfrac{\text{force}}{\text{area}}$ moment = force × distance

Exercise 2

1   The formula for finding the perimeter of a square, P, can be written as $P = 4l$, where l is the length of one side. Work out the perimeter of a square with a side length of 12 cm.

2   The formula for the area of a rectangle, A, is A = length × width.
    Work out the area of a rectangle with a length of 8 m and a width of 11 m.

3   The distance Katie cycles can be worked out using this formula:

$$\text{distance} = \text{speed} \times \text{time}$$

Work out the distance Katie cycles in miles if she cycles at 9 mph for 2 hours.

4   Use the formula to work out the area of this triangle.

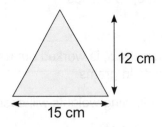

12 cm

15 cm

area of triangle = $\frac{1}{2}$ × base × height

5   Force, F, can be calculated using the formula $F = ma$. Work out the value of F when:

a) $m = 8$, $a = 3$ b) $m = 4$, $a = 13$ c) $m = 12$, $a = 9$

d) $m = 0.5$, $a = 10$ e) $m = 5$, $a = 2.5$ f) $m = 1.5$, $a = 3.5$

6 Use the formula to work out the areas of these parallelograms.

area = base × height

a)

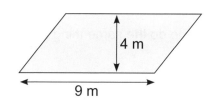

4 m

9 m

b)

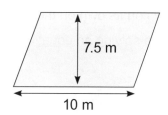

7.5 m

10 m

7 Use the formula $v = u + at$ to find v if:

a) $u = 5$, $a = 3$, $t = 2$ **b)** $u = 7$, $a = 4$, $t = 8$ **c)** $u = 6.5$, $a = 5$, $t = 7$

d) $u = 6$, $a = 12$, $t = 3$ **e)** $u = 7$, $a = 0.5$, $t = 16$ **f)** $u = 4.5$, $a = 6$, $t = 4$

8 Use the formula $C = \dfrac{5}{9}(F - 32)$ to convert the following temperatures
in degrees Fahrenheit (F) to degrees Celsius (C).

a) 113 °F **b)** 95 °F **c)** 140 °F

9 Use the formula $s = ut + \dfrac{1}{2}at^2$ to find s when:

a) $a = 6$, $u = 4$, $t = 3$ **b)** $a = 8$, $u = 7$, $t = 2$ **c)** $a = 4$, $u = 4$, $t = 4$

d) $a = 8$, $u = 3$, $t = 5$ **e)** $a = 8$, $u = 3.5$, $t = 2$ **f)** $a = 4$, $u = 2.5$, $t = 3$

Investigate — Units and Formulas

a) Write down some units, for example, cm³, m², km/hour, etc.
Can you work out what measurements have been multiplied
or divided to get these units?

b) Now look at this formula:

$$\text{speed} = \frac{\text{distance in metres}}{\text{time in seconds}}$$

Can you work out the units that speed would be in?

c) List some more formulas. Can you work out what units could go into
each formula, and what the units of the subject would be?

10.3 Rearranging Formulas

Making a letter the subject of a formula means rearranging the formula so that the letter you want is on its own on the left.

It's a bit like solving an equation — you always have to do the same thing to both sides.

> **Example 1**   **Make e the subject of the formula $f = eg$.**
>
> 1. Write down the original formula.
>
> 2. Divide both sides by g.
>   Then e is on its own, since $eg \div g = e$.
>
> 3. In your final answer, always write the letter that's on its own on the left-hand side of the formula. All the other letters should be on the right-hand side.
>
> $f = eg$
>
> $f \div g = eg \div g$
>
> $\dfrac{f}{g} = e$
>
> $e = \dfrac{f}{g}$

Exercise 1

1   Make s the subject of the following formulas. All your answers should begin "$s =$".

  a) $r = s + 4$ **b)** $p = s - 8$ **c)** $h = 12 + s$

  d) $d = s + 6.4$ **e)** $t = s - 2.7$ **f)** $j = 28 + s$

2   Make time the subject of this formula: distance = speed × time

3   Make force the subject of this formula: pressure = $\dfrac{\text{force}}{\text{area}}$

4   Make x the subject of the following formulas.

  a) $f = x + r$ **b)** $9t = x + 16r$ **c)** $15g = 18h + x$

5   Make y the subject of the following formulas.

  a) $a = 7y$ **b)** $b = 15y$ **c)** $c = 6.7y$

  d) $d = 1.5y$ **e)** $e = 8y$ **f)** $f = 4.9y$

6   Make acceleration the subject of this formula: force = mass × acceleration

7 Make time the subject of this formula: $\text{speed} = \dfrac{\text{distance}}{\text{time}}$

8 Make x the subject of the following formulas.

a) $p = \dfrac{x}{7}$ **b)** $q = \dfrac{x}{11}$ **c)** $r = \dfrac{x}{1.3}$

d) $s = \dfrac{x}{10}$ **e)** $t = \dfrac{x}{7.5}$ **f)** $u = \dfrac{x}{13.8}$

9 Make b the subject of the following formulas.

a) $s = bt$ **b)** $xyz = 3b$ **c)** $ef + g = 2b$

d) $3j = kb$ **e)** $rst = 5b$ **f)** $3c + 2 = 5b$

10 The formula to find the area of a parallelogram, A, is $A = b \times h$, where b stands for base and h stands for vertical height.

a) Rearrange the formula to make b the subject.

b) Find the base length of a parallelogram which has an area of 42 cm² and a height of 6 cm.

11 Make x the subject of the following formulas.

a) $b = 2x + 7$ **b)** $c = 5x - 1$ **c)** $y = 3x + 14$

d) $p = 5x + 3$ **e)** $f = 7x + 2$ **f)** $h = 1.5x - 6$

12 **a)** Rearrange the formula $v = u + at$ to make a the subject.

b) Find a if $u = 2$, $v = 12$ and $t = 2$.

c) Find a if $u = 4$, $v = 20$ and $t = 4$.

d) Find a if $u = 5$, $v = 17$ and $t = 3$.

13 The formula to find the area of a triangle is:

$$\text{area of triangle} = \frac{1}{2} \times \text{base} \times \text{height}$$

The area of a triangle is 30 cm² and its height is 4 cm. What is the length of its base?

Section 11 — Sequences

11.1 Generating Terms

Term to Term Rules

A <u>sequence</u> is a pattern of numbers or shapes that follow a certain rule.
To write down a sequence you need to know two things:

1. The **first** <u>term</u> of the sequence.

2. The rule for **extending** the sequence.

Example 1 | The first term of a sequence is 4 and the rule is "multiply by 2 and subtract 1 each time". Write down the first five terms.

1. To find the second term, multiply the first term by 2, $4 \times 2 = 8$
   and then subtract 1. $8 - 1 = 7$

2. To find the third term, multiply the second term by 2, $7 \times 2 = 14$
   and then subtract 1. $14 - 1 = 13$

3. Carry on until you have the first five terms $(13 \times 2) - 1 = 25$
   of the sequence. $(25 \times 2) - 1 = 49$

   4, 7, 13, 25, 49

Exercise 1

1   Use each rule to generate the first five terms of the sequence.

a) The first term is 9 and the rule is "add 4 each time".

b) The first term is 37 and the rule is "subtract 3 each time".

c) The first term is 6 and the rule is "multiply by 10 each time".

d) The first term is 160 and the rule is "divide by 2 each time".

e) The first term is 10 and the rule is "add 16 each time".

f) The first term is 7 and the rule is "multiply by 2 each time".

2   The rule for extending a sequence is "subtract 14 each time".
       Find the first five terms of the sequence if the first term is:

a) 154   **b)** 200   **c)** 68   **d)** 133   **e)** 16

Example 2 **Find the rule for extending each of these sequences. Then use the rule to find the next term in the sequence.**

a) 6, 10, 14, 18, 22

1. Write the difference between the neighbouring terms in the gaps.

6   10   14   18   22
  +4   +4   +4   +4

2. Identify the rule.

"add 4 each time"

3. Apply the rule to the last term to find the next term.

22 + 4 = **26**

b) 3, 6, 12, 24, 48

1. First, try writing the difference between the neighbouring terms.

3   6   12   24   48
  +3   +6   +12   +24

2. If this doesn't give an obvious 'addition' rule, see if each term is being multiplied by some number.

3   6   12   24   48
  ×2   ×2   ×2   ×2

3. This works, so the rule is:

"multiply by 2 each time"

4. Apply the rule for the last term to find the next term.

48 × 2 = **96**

---

3 For each of these sequences, find: **i)** the rule for extending the sequence.
                                                 ii) the next two terms in the sequence.

a) 4, 10, 16...   **b)** 11, 23, 35...   **c)** 3, 9, 27...   **d)** 53, 44, 35...

e) 80, 40, 20...   **f)** 24, 18, 12...   **g)** 4, 8, 16...   **h)** 1, 4, 16...

i) 12, 29, 46...   **j)** 127, 101, 75...   **k)** 10, 100, 1000...   **l)** 60, 81, 102...

---

4 For each sequence: **i)** Draw the next three patterns in the sequence.
                                ii) Explain the rule for finding the number of circles in the next pattern.
                                iii) Work out how many circles will be in the 8th pattern.

a)

b)

c)

d)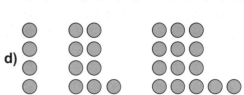

5 How many matchsticks are needed to make the next shape in each of these sequences?

a)

b)

c)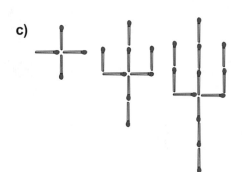

d)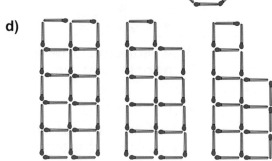

6 Use these rules to generate the first five terms of each sequence.

a) The first term is 8 and the rule is "multiply by 2 and subtract 5 each time".

b) The first term is 52 and the rule is "add 4 and divide by 2 each time".

c) The first term is 5 and the rule is "subtract 3 and multiply by 4 each time".

d) The first term is 166 and the rule is "divide by 2 and subtract 5 each time".

e) The first term is 171 and the rule is "divide by 3 and add 6 each time".

7 Choose the rule that describes each of these sequences.

a) 2, 12, 42, 132...   "multiply by 4 then add 4"   "add 2 then multiply by 3"

b) 8, 12, 18, 27...   "divide by 2 then multiply by 3"   "multiply by 2 then subtract 4"

c) −1, 8, 44, 188...   "add 3 then multiply by 4"   "multiply by 2 then add 10"

d) 1, 15, 155, 1555...   "multiply by 14 then add 1"   "multiply by 10 then add 5"

e) 2, 3, 6, 15...   "divide by 2 then multiply by 3"   "subtract 1 then multiply by 3"

8 For each of these sequences: **i)** Describe the rule for extending the sequence.
                                       ii) Use the rule to generate the next 3 terms.

a) 1, 3, 7, 13, 21...   **b)** 4, 5, 7, 10, 14...   **c)** 4, 7, 12, 19, 28...

d) 11, 14, 20, 29, 41...   **e)** 5, 15, 30, 50, 75...   **f)** 6, 10, 16, 24, 34...

Position to Term (*n*th Term) Rules

You can work out a <u>term</u> by using its position in the sequence. A term's position in a sequence is described by the letter *n*. For example, the 1st term has $n = 1$, the 2nd term has $n = 2$, the 3rd term has $n = 3$, and so on.

| Example 3 | The *n*th term in a sequence is $3n + 8$.

a) Find the first four terms.

   1. To find the 1st, 2nd, 3rd and 4th terms of the sequence, substitute the values $n = 1$, $n = 2$, $n = 3$ and $n = 4$ into the expression.

      $(3 \times 1) + 8 = 11$
      $(3 \times 2) + 8 = 14$
      $(3 \times 3) + 8 = 17$
      $(3 \times 4) + 8 = 20$

   2. Write the terms in order to form the sequence.   **11, 14, 17, 20**

b) Find the 10th term.

   Substitute $n = 10$ into the expression $3n + 8$. $(3 \times 10) + 8 = \mathbf{38}$

Exercise 2

1   The *n*th term of a sequence is $2n + 9$. Find the value of the *n*th term when:

    a) $n = 1$ **b)** $n = 2$ **c)** $n = 4$ **d)** $n = 10$

2   The *n*th term of a sequence is $5n - 2$. Find the value of the *n*th term when:

    a) $n = 1$ **b)** $n = 4$ **c)** $n = 9$ **d)** $n = 11$

3   The *n*th term of a sequence is $26 - 4n$. Find the value of:

    a) the first term   **b)** the third term   **c)** the fourth term   **d)** the seventh term

4   Find the first five terms of the sequence where the *n*th term is given by:

    a) $n + 6$ **b)** $3n + 3$ **c)** $4n - 2$ **d)** $7n + 2$

    e) $3 + 9n$ **f)** $8 + 5n$ **g)** $6n - 3$ **h)** $23 - n$

    i) $8n - 1$ **j)** $51 - 4n$ **k)** $25 - 2n$ **l)** $12 + 7n$

5 Each of these expressions gives the nth term for a different sequence.
For each sequence, find: **i)** the 8th term   **ii)** the 12th term   **iii)** the 16th term

a) $11n - 6$ **b)** $308 - 4n$ **c)** $-2n + 17$ **d)** $12n + 4$

e) $5(n - 2)$ **f)** $190 - 7n$ **g)** $821 - 6n$ **h)** $2(2n - 9)$

6 Draw the next three shapes in each of these sequences and
state the number of matchsticks in each shape.

a) Matchsticks in nth term: $3n + 2$

b) Matchsticks in nth term: $2n + 2$

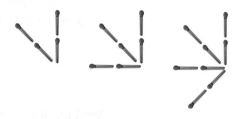

c) Matchsticks in nth term: $2n + 3$

d) Matchsticks in nth term: $3n$

Example 4	The nth term of a sequence is $5n - 3$. Which term has the value 32?

1. Set the nth term equal to 32. $5n - 3 = 32$

2. Solve the equation to find n. $5n - 3 + 3 = 32 + 3$

$5n = 35$

$5n \div 5 = 35 \div 5$

$n = 7$

32 is the **7th term**

Exercise 3

1 The nth term of a sequence is $6n + 2$. Which term has the value:

a) 20?   **b)** 38?   **c)** 62?   **d)** 74?

2 The nth term of a sequence is $80 - 4n$. Which term has the value:

a) 60?   **b)** 48?   **c)** 72?   **d)** 32?

3 **a)** The nth term rule of a sequence is $2n + 8$. Which term has the value 26?

b) The nth term rule of a sequence is $19 - 3n$. Which term has the value 1?

c) The nth term rule of a sequence is $84 - 7n$. Which term has the value 35?

4 Which pattern in these sequences would you be able to make with:

a) 23 matchsticks?

Matchsticks in nth term: $4n - 1$

b) 42 matchsticks?

Matchsticks in nth term: $5n + 2$

11.2 Finding the Rule for the nth Term

You can work out the expression for the nth term by looking at the differences between the terms of a sequence.

Example 1 **Find the nth term of the sequence 5, 9, 13, 17...**

1. Find the difference between each term and the next term.

$$5 \quad 9 \quad 13 \quad 17$$
$$+4 \quad +4 \quad +4$$

2. The terms increase by 4 each time, so the expression for the nth term will include '$4n$'.

3. List the values of $4n$.

$$4 \quad 8 \quad 12 \quad 16$$

4. Work out what you have to add or subtract to get from $4n$ to the same term in the sequence.

$$\downarrow +1 \quad \downarrow +1 \quad \downarrow +1 \quad \downarrow +1$$
$$5 \quad 9 \quad 13 \quad 17$$

5. Combine '$4n$' and '$+1$' to get the expression for the nth term.

$$4n + 1$$

6. Check your expression by using it to find at least one of the terms you know.

(2nd term is $(4 \times 2) + 1 = 9$)

Example 2 Find the nth term of the sequence 11, 9, 7, 5...

1. Find the difference between each term and the next term.

11   9   7   5
   −2   −2   −2

2. The terms decrease by 2 each time, so the expression for the nth term must include '$-2n$'.

3. List the values of $-2n$.

−2   −4   −6   −8

4. Work out what you have to add or subtract to get from $-2n$ to the same term in the sequence.

+13 +13 +13 +13

11   9   7   5

5. Combine '$-2n$' and '+13' to get the expression for the nth term.

$-2n + 13$ or **$13 - 2n$**

6. Check your expression by using it to find at least one of the terms you know.

(2nd term is $13 - (2 \times 2) = 9$)

Exercise 1

1   The first four terms of a sequence are 7, 9, 11 and 13.

   a) Find the difference between each term and the next.

   b) Write out the first 4 numbers in the corresponding times table.

   c) Find the difference between each times table value and the corresponding term in the sequence.

   d) Write down and check your expression for the nth term of the sequence.

2   The first four terms of a sequence are 5, 11, 17 and 23.

   a) Find the difference between each term and the next.

   b) Write out the first 4 numbers in the corresponding times table.

   c) Find the difference between each times table value and the corresponding term in the sequence.

   d) Write down and check your expression for the nth term of the sequence.

3   Work out the expression for the nth term for the following sequences.

   a) 11, 15, 19, 23...   **b)** 8, 11, 14, 17...   **c)** 10, 19, 28, 37...

   d) 3, 7, 11, 15...   **e)** 14, 21, 28, 35...   **f)** 32, 42, 52, 62...

   g) 4, 10, 16, 22...   **h)** 6, 15, 24, 33...   **i)** 17, 22, 27, 32...

4 The first four terms of a sequence are 21, 18, 15 and 12.

   a) Find the difference between each term and the next.

   b) Write out the first 4 multiples of the difference.

   c) Find the difference between each multiple and the corresponding term in the sequence.

   d) Write down and check your expression for the nth term of the sequence.

5 Work out the expression for the nth term for these sequences.

   a) 20, 15, 10, 5...   **b)** 14, 12, 10, 8...   **c)** 8, 7, 6, 5...

   d) 23, 20, 17, 14...   **e)** 25, 21, 17, 13...   **f)** 41, 31, 21, 11...

   g) 42, 33, 24, 15...   **h)** 29, 23, 17, 11...   **i)** 33, 27, 21, 15...

6 For each of these sequences: **i)** Work out the expression for the nth term.
                                        ii) Use the expression to work out the 8th term.

   a) 1, 3, 5, 7...   **b)** 11, 14, 17, 20...   **c)** 18, 20, 22, 24...

   d) 41, 46, 51, 56...   **e)** 5, 12, 19, 26...   **f)** 3, 12, 21, 30...

7 For each of these sequences: **i)** Work out the expression for the nth term.
                                        ii) Use the expression to work out the 6th term.

   a) 11, 10, 9, 8...   **b)** 39, 35, 31, 27...   **c)** 28, 26, 24, 22...

   d) 40, 31, 22, 13...   **e)** 32, 26, 20, 14...   **f)** 45, 38, 31, 24...

8 Find an expression for the number of matchsticks in the nth pattern of each of these sequences.

a)
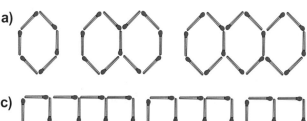

b)

c)
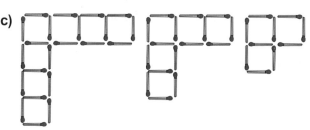

d)
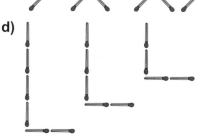

9 For the following sequences:
   i) Work out an expression for the number of matchsticks in the nth pattern.
   ii) Draw the 7th pattern in the sequence.

a)

b)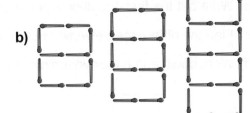

10 For the following sequences:
   i) Work out an expression for the number of matchsticks in the nth pattern.
   ii) Draw the next two patterns in the sequence.

a)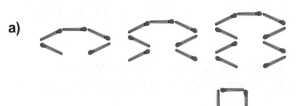

b)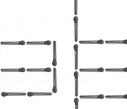

c)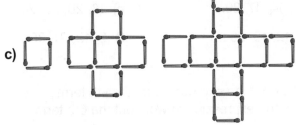

Investigate — Non-linear Sequences

A sequence which increases or decreases by the same amount between each term is known as a linear sequence. In non-linear sequences, the differences between the terms change.

a) Look at the sequence: 2, 8, 18, 32, 50, 72. Work out the difference between each term and the next term. Is this a linear or a non-linear sequence? Why?

b) Can you see a pattern between the differences you worked out in **a)**? Write a rule for extending the sequence in **a)**.

c) Now write out the first six terms of the sequence with the nth term n^2. Compare this sequence with the sequence in **a)**. What do you notice?

d) Use your observations to write an expression for the nth term of the sequence in **a)**.

e) Work out the expression for the nth term of the sequence: 5, 11, 21, 35, 53, 75. Write out the first 6 terms of some similar sequences.

Section 12 — Graphs and Equations

12.1 Coordinates

Coordinates tell you the position of a point
on the grid made by the *x*-axis (horizontal)
and the *y*-axis (vertical).

Coordinates are written in pairs inside
brackets, with the *x*-coordinate (across) first
and the *y*-coordinate (up and down) second.
Each coordinate can be positive or negative.

The *x*- and *y*-axes cross at the origin.
It has coordinates (0, 0).

Each quarter of the graph is called a quadrant.

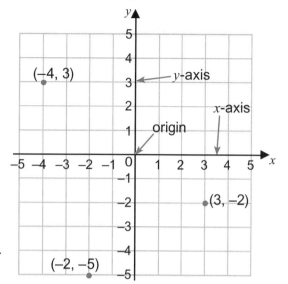

Example 1   Draw the shape *WXYZ* with vertices *W*(−4, 5),
X(3, 2), *Y*(4, −3) and *Z*(−5, −2).

1. Some of the coordinates are negative, so draw
   axes which go below zero.

2. Read across the horizontal axis for the
   x-coordinates and up and down the vertical
   axis for the *y*-coordinates.

3. Plot the points and connect them to draw the
   shape.

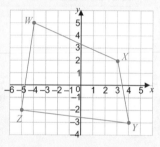

Exercise 1

1   Find the coordinates of points *A-H* shown on the grid.

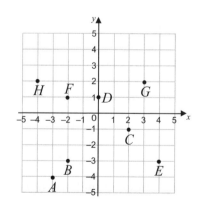

2 **a)** Draw a coordinate grid with *x*-values from −5 to 5
and *y*-values from −5 to 5. Plot the following points
on your grid. Join the points in alphabetical order.

I(0, 4)	*J*(3, 2)	*K*(3, −2)
L(0, −4)	*M*(−3, −2)	*N*(−3, 2)

b) What is the name of the shape you have drawn?

12.2 Plotting Graphs

Linear Graphs

Equations containing x and y describe a connection between x- and y- coordinates.

If you find some coordinate pairs that fit the equation and join them up, you get the graph of that equation. Some equations produce straight line graphs when you do this.

You can draw these graphs by filling in a table of values and plotting points.

Example 1 | **Complete the table to show the values of y when $y = x + 3$ and x has values from −4 to 4. Use your table to draw the graph of $y = x + 3$ for values of x from −4 to 4.**

1. $y = x + 3$, so add 3 to each x-value to fill in the second row of the table.

2. Use the numbers from the first and second rows to fill in the third row.

x	−4	−3	−2	−1	0	1	2	3	4
y	−1	0	1	2	3	4	5	6	7
Coordinates	(−4, −1)	(−3, 0)	(−2, 1)	(−1, 2)	(0, 3)	(1, 4)	(2, 5)	(3, 6)	(4, 7)

3. Plot the coordinates from your table on a grid and join them up to draw the graph.

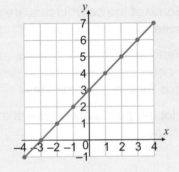

Exercise 1

1 a) Copy and complete the table to show the value of $y = x + 4$ for values of x from 0 to 5.

x	0	1	2	3	4	5
y	4	5				
Coordinates	(0, 4)					

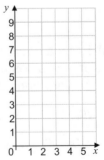

b) Copy the grid and plot the coordinates from your table.

c) Join up the points to draw the line $y = x + 4$ for values of x from 0 to 5.

2 a) Copy and complete the table to show the
value of $y = x - 5$ for values of x from 0 to 5.

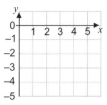

x	0	1	2	3	4	5
y	-5					
Coordinates						

b) Copy the grid and plot the coordinates from your table.

c) Join up the points to draw the line $y = x - 5$ for values of x from 0 to 5.

3 a) Copy and complete the table to show the value of
$y = 3x$ for values of x from −2 to 2.

x	−2	−1	0	1	2
y				3	
Coordinates					

b) Draw a set of axes with x-values from −4 to 4 and y-values from −12 to 12
and plot the coordinates from your table.

c) Join up the points to draw the line $y = 3x$ for values of x from −2 to 2.
Extend the line to show the graph of $y = 3x$ for values of x from −4 to 4.

4 For each of the following equations:

i) copy and complete the table to show the value of y for values of x from −1 to 2.

x	−1	0	1	2
y				
Coordinates				

ii) plot the points from your table and use these points to draw the graph of the
equation for values of x from −3 to 3.

a) $y = x + 2$ **b)** $y = x + 6$ **c)** $y = x - 4$

d) $y = x - 2$ **e)** $y = 2x$ **f)** $y = 2 - x$

g) $y = x + 10$ **h)** $y = x - 6$ **i)** $y = x + 9$

j) $y = 4 - x$ **k)** $y = -3x$ **l)** $y = -2x$

5 Draw a graph of the following equations for the given range of x-values.

a) $y = x + 1$ for x from -4 to 4

b) $y = x - 3$ for x from 0 to 6

c) $y = x + 5$ for x from -5 to 0

d) $y = 5 - x$ for x from -4 to 4

e) $y = -x$ for x from -5 to 5

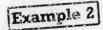 **Complete the table to show the value of $y = 2x + 1$ for values of x from 0 to 3.**

Use the table to draw the graph of $y = 2x + 1$ for values of x from 0 to 5.

1. Multiply each x-value by 2 to fill in the second row of the table, and then add 1 to fill in the third row.

x	0	1	2	3
$2x$	0	2	4	6
$2x + 1$	1	3	5	7
Coordinates	(0, 1)	(1, 3)	(2, 5)	(3, 7)

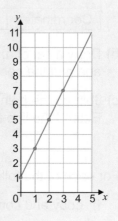

2. Fill in the fourth row of the table and plot the coordinates from your table on a grid. Join up the points and extend the line to draw the graph up to $x = 5$.

Exercise 2

1 a) Copy and complete the table to show the value of $y = 3x - 2$ for values of x from 0 to 3.

x	0	1	2	3
$3x$				
$3x - 2$	-2			
Coordinates	(0, -2)			

b) Copy the grid and plot the coordinates from your table.

c) Join up the points and extend the line to draw the graph of $y = 3x - 2$ for values of x from 0 to 5.

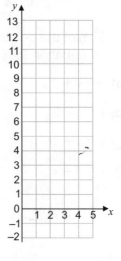

2 a) Copy and complete the table to show the value of $y = 5 - 2x$ for values of x from -1 to 2.

x	-1	0	1	2
$2x$			2	
$5 - 2x$			3	
Coordinates				

b) Draw a set of axes with x-values from -5 to 5 and y-values from -5 to 15 and plot the coordinates from your table.

c) Join up the points and extend the line to draw the graph of $y = 5 - 2x$ for values of x from -5 to 5.

3 For each of the following equations:

i) copy and complete the table to show the value of y for values of x from -1 to 2.

ii) draw a graph of the equation for values of x from -3 to 3.

x	-1	0	1	2
y				
Coordinates				

a) $y = 2x - 1$ **b)** $y = 3x + 1$ **c)** $y = 4x + 2$

d) $y = 4 - 2x$ **e)** $y = 6 - 3x$ **f)** $y = 3x - 3$

4 Draw a graph of the following equations for the given range of x-values.

a) $y = 5x - 3$ for x from 0 to 4

b) $y = 8 - 4x$ for x from 0 to 3

c) $y = -2x + 6$ for x from 0 to 5

Investigate — Linear Graphs

a) On the same grid, draw the graphs of $y = 2x$, $y = 2x + 1$, $y = 2x + 2$, $y = 2x - 1$ and $y = 2x - 2$.

What do you notice about the steepness of the lines that you have drawn? Which part of the equation do you think this might relate to?

b) On a new grid, draw the graphs of $y = x + 3$, $y = 2x + 3$, $y = -x + 3$ and $y = -2x + 3$.

What are the coordinates of the point where your lines cross? What do you notice about the y-coordinate?

c) What happens to the graphs when you change one number in the equation and keep the other fixed? Can you come up with a rule which describes the connection between the equations and their graphs?

Quadratic Graphs

<u>Quadratic equations</u> always include an x^2 term (but no higher powers of x, such as x^3, x^4...).

The graph of a quadratic equation is always a smooth curve, with no spikes, lumps or straight lines.

The curve can either be u-shaped or n-shaped and will always be <u>symmetrical</u>.

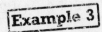

a) Complete the table to find the value of
$y = x^2 - 3$ **for values of x from −3 to 3.**

b) Draw the graph of $y = x^2 - 3$ for values of x from −3 to 3.

1. Fill in the table one row at a time. (Remember that the square of a negative number is positive.)

x	−3	−2	−1	0	1	2	3
x^2	9	4	1	0	1	4	9
$x^2 - 3$	6	1	−2	−3	−2	1	6

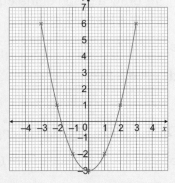

2. Now plot each x-value from the first row against the corresponding y-value from the third row, and join the points with a smooth curve.

Exercise 3

1 a) Copy and complete the table to find the value of $y = x^2$ for values of x from −3 to 3.

x	−3	−2	−1	0	1	2	3
x^2	9		1			4	

b) Copy the grid and plot the points from your table.

c) Join up the points to draw the graph of $y = x^2$ for values of x from −3 to 3.

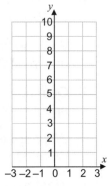

2 a) Copy and complete the table to find the value of $y = x^2 + 3$ for values of x from -3 to 3.

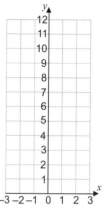

x	-3	-2	-1	0	1	2	3
x^2	9		1			4	
$x^2 + 3$	12		4			7	

b) Copy the grid and plot the points from your table.

c) Join up the points to draw the graph of $y = x^2 + 3$ for values of x from -3 to 3.

3 a) Copy and complete the table to show the value of $y = x^2 - 2$ for values of x from -3 to 3.

x	-3	-2	-1	0	1	2	3
x^2		4					9
$x^2 - 2$		2					7

b) Draw a set of axes with x-values from -3 to 3 and y-values from -2 to 7. Draw the graph of $y = x^2 - 2$ on your axes.

4 For each of the following equations:

   i) copy and complete this table to show the value of y for values of x from -3 to 3.

x	-3	-2	-1	0	1	2	3
y							

   ii) draw a graph of the equation on suitable axes.

a) $y = x^2 + 1$ **b)** $y = x^2 + 2$ **c)** $y = x^2 - 1$

d) $y = x^2 - 5$ **e)** $y = x^2 + 4$ **f)** $y = x^2 - 4$

5 For each of the following equations:

   i) complete a table to show the value of y for values of x from -3 to 3.

   ii) draw a graph of the equation on suitable axes.

a) $y = -x^2$ **b)** $y = 10 - x^2$ **c)** $y = 4 - x^2$

12.3 Interpreting Graphs

Identifying Graphs

You can work out the features of <u>straight line graphs</u> just by looking at their <u>equations</u>.

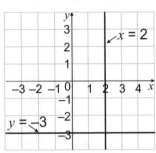

<u>Horizontal</u> lines have equations: y = **a number**.

For example, $y = -3$ is horizontal, with all the y-coordinates at -3.

<u>Vertical</u> lines have equations: x = **a number**.

For example, $x = 2$ is vertical, with all the x-coordinates at 2.

Sloping lines have equations containing both y and x.

For example, $y = 2x - 1$ and $y = 3x - 1$ are sloping.

The bigger the number before the x, the <u>steeper</u> the graph. ($y = x$ means $y = 1x$.)

The other number tells you where it crosses the <u>y-axis</u>.

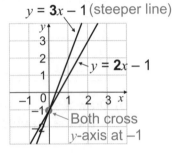

Exercise 1

1 **a)** Give the letter (A-E) of the graph that matches each equation.

  i) $x = 2$ **ii)** $y = 2$

  iii) $x = -6$ **iv)** $y = -6$

b) Give the equation of the remaining unmatched graph.

c) What is the equation of:

  i) the x-axis?

  ii) the y-axis?

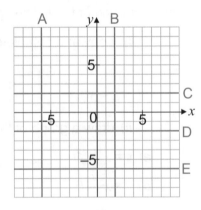

2 **a)** Give the letter (A-E) of the graph that matches each equation. The graph of $y = x$ is labelled to help you.

  i) $y = x + 3$

  ii) $y = 3x + 1$

  iii) $y = x - 8$

  iv) $y = 3x - 8$

b) Give the equation of the remaining unmatched graph.

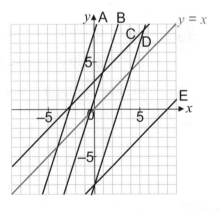

Calculating Gradients

The <u>gradient</u> is the steepness of a line or <u>line segment</u>.

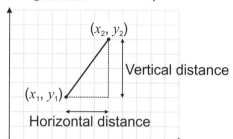

You can calculate the gradient by looking at the <u>coordinates</u> of two points on a line.

The gradient is the <u>vertical</u> distance between them divided by the <u>horizontal</u> distance.

$$\text{Gradient} = \frac{\text{Vertical distance}}{\text{Horizontal distance}} = \frac{y_2 - y_1}{x_2 - x_1}$$

Example 1 **Find the gradient of this line segment:**

1. Count the squares to find the vertical distance between the ends of the line segment.

2. Do the same for the horizontal distance.

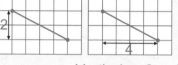

3. Divide the vertical distance by the horizontal distance:

$$\text{Gradient} = \frac{\text{Vertical}}{\text{Horizontal}} = \frac{2}{4} = \frac{1}{2}$$

4. Check if it slopes 'upwards' or 'downwards'.

It slopes downwards so...

5. The gradient is negative if it slopes downwards.

$$\text{Gradient} = -\frac{1}{2}$$

Exercise 2

1 Find the gradient of each of these line segments:

a)   b) 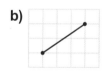 c)   d) 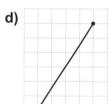 e)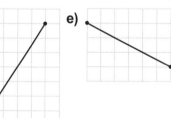

Example 2 **Find the gradient of the line that passes through points A(1, 1) and B(5, 9).**

1. Call A (x_1, y_1) and B (x_2, y_2).

$$x_1 = 1, y_1 = 1, x_2 = 5, y_2 = 9$$

2. Put the values for x_1, y_1, x_2 and y_2 in the formula.

$$\text{Gradient} = \frac{y_2 - y_1}{x_2 - x_1} = \frac{9 - 1}{5 - 1}$$

3. Calculate the gradient.

$$\text{Gradient} = \frac{8}{4} = 2$$

Exercise 3

1 Use the coordinates labelled on the lines to find the gradient of each one.

a) 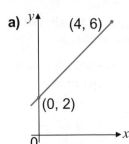 (4, 6) (0, 2)

b) 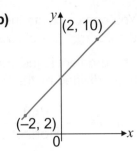 (2, 10) (−2, 2)

c) 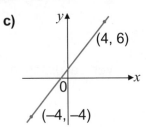 (4, 6) (−4, −4)

d) 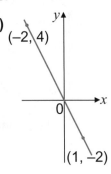 (−2, 4) (1, −2)

2 For each line, find the coordinates of the labelled points and use them to find the gradient of the line.

a)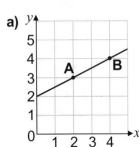

b)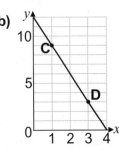

c)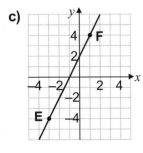

d)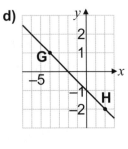

3 **a)** Plot the points (−3, 2) and (1, 7) on a set of axes and draw a straight line through them.

    b) Find the gradient of this line.

4 Find the gradient of each line that passes through points A and B.

    a) A:(0, 1) B:(2, 9)   **b)** A:(6, 1) B:(12, 4)   **c)** A:(3, 1) B:(4, −1)   **d)** A:(−2, 7) B:(1, 4)

    e) A:(1, 0) B:(5, −8)   **f)** A:(−5, 0) B:(−2, 2)   **g)** A:(−7, 9) B:(1, 7)   **h)** A:(−1, 5) B:(1, −1)

5 Using any two points on each line for reference, find the gradients of these lines.

a)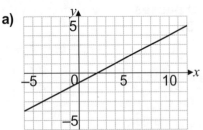

b)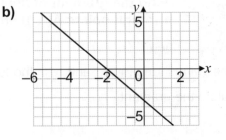

y = mx + c

Equations of straight lines can be written in the form: $y = mx + c$.
m and **c** are numbers, where:

- **m** is the <u>gradient</u> of the line, and
- **c** tells you the <u>y-intercept</u> — the point where the line crosses the y-axis.

If c is zero (so the equation is $y = mx$) then the graph goes through the <u>origin</u>, (0, 0).
If m is zero (equation $y = c$) then the graph is a <u>horizontal</u> line through c on the y-axis.

| **Example 3** | **Give the equation of this straight line graph in the form $y = mx + c$.** |

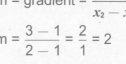

1. First find the gradient, m.
   The line passes through
   coordinates (1, 1) and (2, 3),
   so use the formula.

   $m = \text{gradient} = \dfrac{y_2 - y_1}{x_2 - x_1}$

   $m = \dfrac{3 - 1}{2 - 1} = \dfrac{2}{1} = 2$

2. Now find the y-intercept, c.
   The line crosses through −1 on
   the y-axis, coordinates (0, −1).

   $c = -1$

3. Put m and c into the equation.

   $y = 2x + (-1)$ or $y = 2x - 1$

Exercise 4

1 For each straight line graph given by these equations, write down:

   i) the gradient,   **ii)** the coordinates of the y-intercept.

   a) $y = 2x + 3$ **b)** $y = 6x + 1$ **c)** $y = 3x - 4$ **d)** $y = 5x$ **e)** $y = x + 7$

   f) $y = x - 2$ **g)** $y = -2x + 4$ **h)** $y = 4 - 2x$ **i)** $y = 6$ **j)** $y = \dfrac{x}{2}$

2 Write down a pair of equations from the box whose graphs have the same:

   a) gradient.

   b) y-intercept.

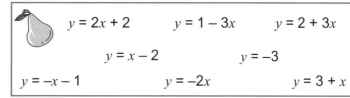

$y = 2x + 2$ $y = 1 - 3x$ $y = 2 + 3x$

$y = x - 2$ $y = -3$

$y = -x - 1$ $y = -2x$ $y = 3 + x$

3 Give an equation, in the form $y = mx + c$, of a graph that has:

   a) gradient 4 and passes through (0, 1).   **b)** gradient 2 and passes through (0, −3).

   c) gradient −2 and passes through (0, 5).   **d)** gradient 1 and passes through the origin.

4 For each of the graphs shown:

    i) Work out the gradient.

    ii) Write down the coordinates of the y-intercept.

    iii) Give the equation of the line in the form $y = mx + c$.

a)
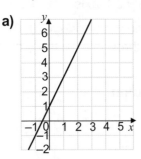

b)
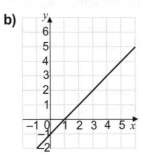

c)
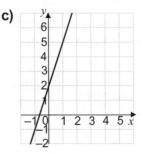

d)
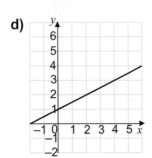

e)
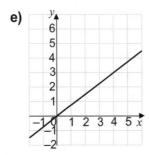

f)
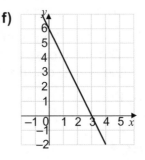

Investigate — Interpreting Quadratics

These quadratic graphs have the equations:

A: $y = 2x^2 + 3$, **B**: $y = x^2 + 3$, **C**: $y = x^2 - 1$

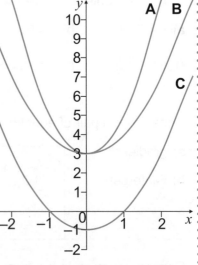

  a) What do graphs **A** and **B** have in common?
     How are they different?

  b) What do graphs **B** and **C** have in common?
     How are they different?

  c) What would $y = 2x^2 - 1$ look like?
     Plot it to see if you were right.

  d) Try to write a general rule for graphs with
     equations $y = \mathbf{a}x^2 + \mathbf{b}$, to say how the numbers for **a** and **b** affect the graph.

  e) Test your rule by plotting graphs with different numbers for **a** and **b**.

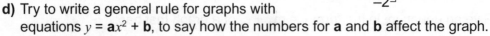

12.4 Modelling Using Graphs

Interpreting Real-Life Graphs

Graphs can be used to show real-life situations. For example, straight line graphs can be used to convert between different units or currencies.

Describing a real-life situation using a graph (or an equation) is called modelling.

Example 1 The graph shown can be used to convert between pounds (£) and euros (€).

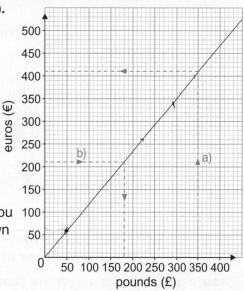

a) **Use the graph to change £350 to euros.**

Follow the grid up from £350 until you reach the line. Then follow the grid across to find the amount in euros.

£350 = **€410**

b) **Use the graph to change €210 to pounds.**

Follow the grid across from €210 until you reach the line. Then follow the grid down to find the amount in pounds.

€210 = **£180**

Exercise 1

Use this graph to answer questions **1** to **3**.

1 Convert the following amounts from one currency to the other. Give your answers to the nearest 10.

   a) £310   b) £50   c) £220

   d) €150   e) €400   f) €340

2 A coat costs €270. How much is this in pounds?

3 A laptop costs £370 in the UK and €440 in Germany. Is the laptop cheaper in Germany or the UK?

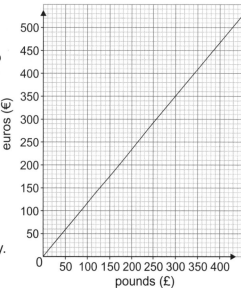

Use this graph to answer questions **4** to **7**.

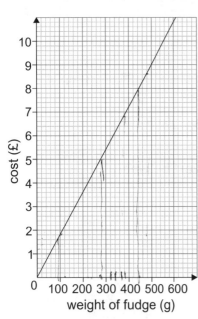

weight of fudge (g)

4 Estimate the cost of the following weights of fudge.

a) 100 g   **b)** 380 g   **c)** 480 g

5 Estimate the weight of fudge that could be bought with the following amounts of money.

a) £5   **b)** £9   **c)** £2.20

6 Estimate the cost of 1000 g of fudge.

7 Estimate how much fudge you could buy for £16.

Drawing Real-Life Graphs

Example 2 A plumber charges customers a fee of £40, plus £30 per hour of work she does.

Draw a graph to show how the cost of hiring the plumber varies with the amount of time the job takes.

1. Work out the cost of a few jobs of different lengths of time and put these values in a table.

2. Plot the values on a sheet of graph paper and join the points to draw the graph.

A job lasting 1 hour will cost
£40 + £30 = £70

A job lasting 2 hours will cost
£40 + (2 × £30) = £100

A job lasting 3 hours will cost
£40 + (3 × £30) = £130

Time (hours)	1	2	3
Cost (£)	70	100	130

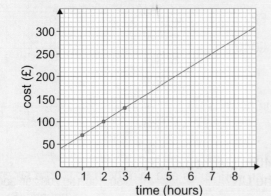

time (hours)

Exercise 2

1 The instructions for cooking different weights of chicken are:
'Cook for 40 minutes per kg, plus an extra 20 minutes'.

a) Copy and complete the table to show the
cooking times for chickens of different weights.

Weight (kg)	1	2	3	4	5
Time (minutes)					

b) Copy the coordinate grid, then plot the values
from your table.

c) Join the points to draw a graph showing
the cooking times for different weights of chicken.

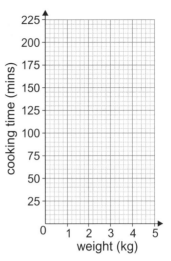

2 A delivery company charges £6.60 to deliver the first parcel in an order,
then £1.40 for every additional parcel in the order after that.

a) Copy and complete the table
to show the delivery cost for
different numbers of parcels.

No. of parcels in delivery	1	2	3	4	5
Cost (£)					

b) Draw a coordinate grid on a sheet of graph paper. Plot 'number of parcels' on the
horizontal axis and 'cost in pounds' on the vertical axis.

c) Draw a graph showing how the cost of a delivery
varies with the number of parcels in the delivery.

3 The cost of a hotel room is £90 per night for the first 3 nights,
then £40 per night for every night after that.

a) Draw a graph showing how the cost of staying at the hotel varies with the length of stay.
Plot the values for at least 7 nights on your graph.

b) A stay at the hotel cost £390. What was the length of the stay?

4 This table shows how the fuel efficiency of a car in miles per gallon (mpg) varies with the
speed of the car in miles per hour (mph).

Speed (mph)	55	60	65	70	75	80
Fuel Efficiency (mpg)	32.3	30.7	28.9	27.0	24.9	22.7

a) Draw a pair of axes with speed on the horizontal axis and fuel efficiency on the vertical
axis. Plot the points from the table on your axes and join them up with a smooth curve.

b) Use your graph to predict the fuel efficiency of the car when it is travelling at 73 mph.

Section 13 — Angles and Shapes

13.1 Angle Rules

Angles at a Point

Angles on a straight line add up to 180°.

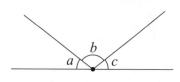

$$a + b + c = 180°$$

Angles around a point add up to 360°.

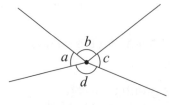

$$a + b + c + d = 360°$$

Angles within a right angle add up to 90°.

$$a + b = 90°$$

Example 1   Find the size of angle x.

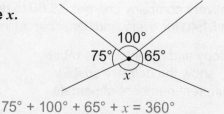

1. Use the fact that angles around a point add up to 360° to write an equation involving x.
2. Simplify the equation.
3. Solve the equation to find x.

$$75° + 100° + 65° + x = 360°$$
$$240° + x = 360°$$
$$x = 360° - 240°$$
$$x = \textbf{120°}$$

Exercise 1

The diagrams in this exercise are **not** drawn accurately, so don't try to measure the angles.

1   Find the size of angle x in each diagram.

a)

b)

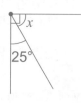

c)

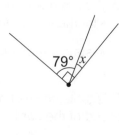

2   Find the size of angle u in each diagram.

a)

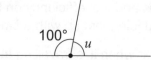

b)

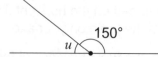

c)

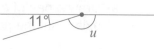

3 Find the size of angle a in each diagram.

a)

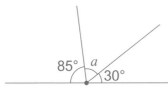

85° a 30°

b)

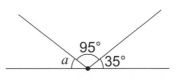

95° a 35°

c)

119° 27° a

4 Find the size of angle z in each diagram.

a)

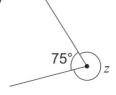

75° z

b)

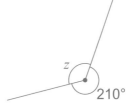

z 210°

c)

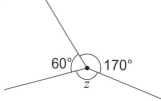

60° 170° z

5 Find the size of angle w in each diagram.

a)

95° 50° 60° w

b)

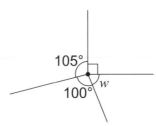

105° 100° w

c)

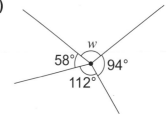

w 58° 94° 112°

6 Find the value of each letter in the following diagrams.

a)

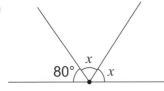

x 80° x

b)

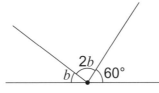

$2b$ b 60°

c)

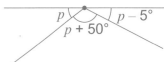

p $p-5°$ $p+50°$

d)

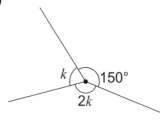

k 150° $2k$

e)

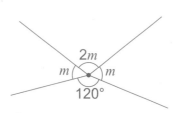

$2m$ m m 120°

f)

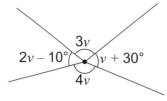

$2v-10°$ $3v$ $v+30°$ $4v$

Angles Around Intersecting Lines

<u>Intersecting lines</u> are lines that cross at a point.
At this point, opposite angles are equal —
they're known as <u>vertically opposite angles</u>.

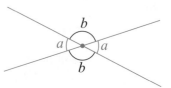

Because they're angles on a straight line, $a + b = 180°$.

Lines that intersect at <u>right angles</u> (90°) are called <u>perpendicular lines</u>.

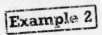 **Find the sizes of angles x, y and z
shown in the diagram.**

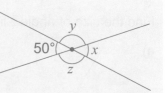

1. x and the 50° angle are vertically $x = $ **50°**
   opposite, so they are equal.

2. y and the 50° angle are on a straight $y + 50° = 180°$
   line, so they add up to 180°. $y = 180° - 50° = $ **130°**

3. y and z are vertically opposite,
   so they are equal. $z = y = $ **130°**

Exercise 2

The diagrams in this exercise are **not** drawn accurately, so don't try to measure the angles.

1 Find the sizes of the missing angles marked by letters.

a)
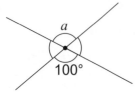

b)
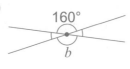

c)
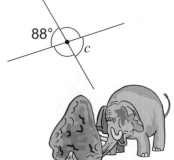

2 Find the sizes of the missing angles marked by letters.

a)
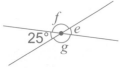

b)
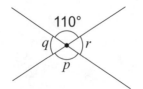

c)
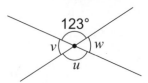

3 Find the value of each letter in the following diagrams.

a)

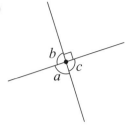

b)

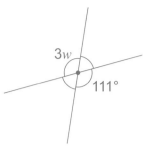

c)

d)

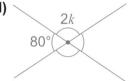

e)

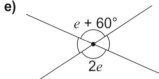

f)

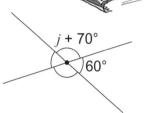

Angles Around Parallel Lines

Parallel lines are lines that are always the same distance apart and never meet.

Here are some special angles around parallel lines that you need to know.

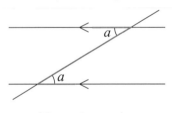

Alternate angles
are equal

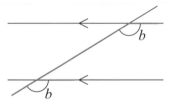

Corresponding angles
are equal

Example 3 Find the sizes of angles u, v and w shown in the diagram.

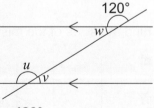

1. u and the 120° angle are corresponding angles, so they are equal.

$u = $ **120°**

2. u and v are on a straight line, so they add up to 180°.

$v + 120° = 180°$
$v = 180° - 120° = $ **60°**

3. v and w are alternate angles, so they are equal.

$w = v = $ **60°**

Exercise 3

The diagrams in this exercise are **not** drawn accurately, so don't try to measure the angles.

1 Say whether the angles shown on the diagrams are alternate, corresponding or neither.

a)

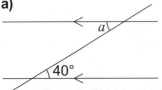

b)

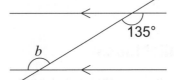

c)

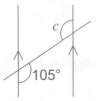

2 Find the size of each missing angle marked by a letter and give a reason for your answer.

a)

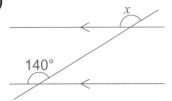

b)

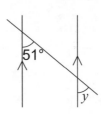

c)

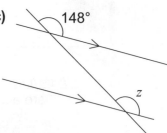

3 Find the size of each missing angle marked by a letter and give a reason for your answer.

a)

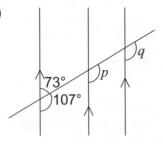

b)

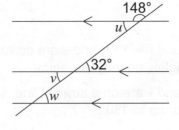

c)

4 Find the sizes of the missing angles marked by letters and give a reason for each answer.

a)

b)

5 Marco is building some horizontal shelves on the sloped wall of an attic.
One shelf makes an angle of 102° between the wall
and the shelf, as shown on the diagram.
Find the angle the other shelf makes with the wall,
labelled a on the diagram.

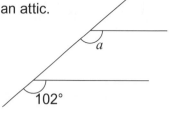

6 Part of a fire escape is shown in the diagram.
A ladder goes between two horizontal platforms,
making an angle of 49° with the upper platform, as shown.
Find the angle between the ladder and the lower platform,
marked f on the diagram.

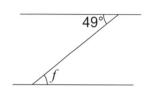

7 Find the sizes of the missing angles marked by letters.

a)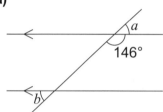

b)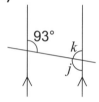

c)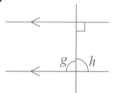

8 Use the angle rules you know to find the sizes
of the missing angles marked by letters.

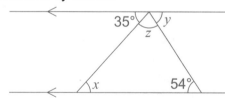

··

Investigate — Angles Around Parallel Lines

This diagram can be used to show that the angles in a triangle add up to 180°.

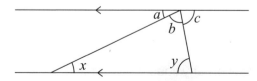

Use your knowledge of angle rules to show that the angles
in a triangle add up to 180°, using the diagram as a reference.
··

Symmetry

A line of symmetry is a mirror line, along which you can fold a shape so that both halves match up exactly. Either side of the line of symmetry is a reflection of the other.

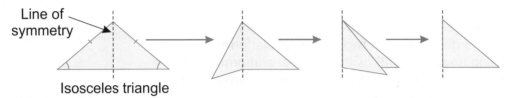

Line of symmetry

Isosceles triangle

The order of rotational symmetry of a shape is the number of positions you can rotate the shape into so that it looks exactly the same.

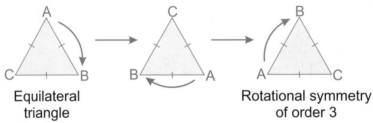

Equilateral triangle

Rotational symmetry of order 3

A shape that only looks the same once every complete turn has rotational symmetry of order 1.

Example 1

a) **Draw any lines of symmetry on to this H-shape.**

There are two ways you can fold this shape so that both halves match up exactly, so draw in the lines of symmetry.

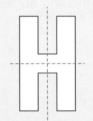

b) **What is the order of rotational symmetry for this shape?**

There are two positions in which this shape looks exactly the same.　　Order of rotational symmetry = **2**

Exercise 1

1   a) Copy the shape and draw on any lines of symmetry.

b) What is its order of rotational symmetry?

2 For each shape: **i)** copy the shape and draw on any lines of symmetry

                  ii) write down its order of rotational symmetry

a)

b)

c)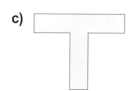

d)

e)

f)

3 For each shape: **i)** sketch the shape and write down the number of lines of symmetry

                  ii) write down its order of rotational symmetry

a) Regular hexagon   **b)** Isosceles triangle

c) Square   **d)** Regular octagon

e) Scalene triangle   **f)** Rhombus

4 a) How many lines of symmetry does this shape have?

  b) What is its order of rotational symmetry?

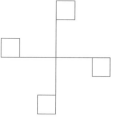

5 Copy each pattern and shade two more squares to make:

a) a pattern with 2 lines of symmetry
and rotational symmetry of order 2.

b) a pattern with 4 lines of symmetry
and rotational symmetry of order 4.

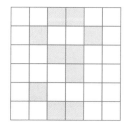

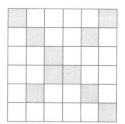

Properties of 2D Shapes

You need to know the different types of <u>triangles</u> and <u>quadrilaterals</u> and their properties.

Triangles

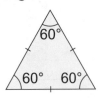   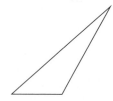

<u>Equilateral triangle</u>
3 equal sides
3 equal angles of 60°
3 lines of symmetry
Rotational symmetry
of order 3

<u>Isosceles triangle</u>
2 equal sides
2 equal angles
1 line of symmetry
Rotational symmetry
of order 1

<u>Right-angled triangle</u>
1 right angle (90°)
Rotational symmetry
of order 1

<u>Scalene triangle</u>
All three sides and
angles are different
No lines of symmetry
Rotational symmetry
of order 1

Quadrilaterals (four-sided shapes)

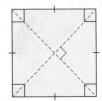 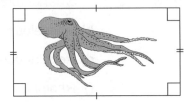 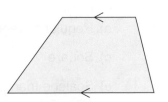

<u>Square</u>
4 equal sides
4 right angles (90°)
4 lines of symmetry
Rotational symmetry
of order 4
Diagonals cross at right angles

<u>Rectangle</u>
2 pairs of equal sides
(opposite sides are equal)
4 right angles (90°)
2 lines of symmetry
Rotational symmetry
of order 2

<u>Trapezium</u>
1 pair of parallel sides
Rotational symmetry
of order 1

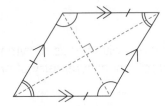 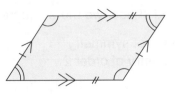 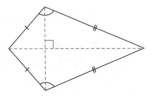

<u>Rhombus</u>
4 equal sides
(opposite sides are parallel)
2 pairs of equal angles
2 lines of symmetry
Rotational symmetry
of order 2
Diagonals cross at right angles

<u>Parallelogram</u>
2 pairs of equal sides
(opposite sides are
equal and parallel)
2 pairs of equal angles
No lines of symmetry
Rotational symmetry
of order 2

<u>Kite</u>
2 pairs of equal sides
1 pair of equal angles
1 line of symmetry
Rotational symmetry
of order 1
Diagonals cross at
right angles

Exercise 2

1 Write down the name of each shape.

a)

b)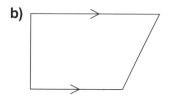

c)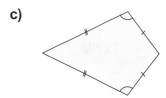

2 I am thinking of a shape with four sides. It has two pairs of equal angles and rotational symmetry of order 2. Its diagonals cross at right angles. What is the name of the shape I am thinking of?

3 Copy and complete this table.

Sketch	Name of shape	Number of lines of symmetry	Order of rotational symmetry
	Scalene triangle		
		3	3

4 Choose the correct option to finish the following sentences.

a) A parallelogram has (**one pair** / **two pairs**) of equal angles.

b) A (**rhombus** / **kite**) has one line of symmetry.

c) A trapezium has (**one pair** / **two pairs**) of parallel sides.

d) The diagonals of a (**rhombus** / **rectangle**) cross at right angles.

5 For each set of points: **i)** copy the grid and plot the points to draw the triangle

           ii) write down the type of triangle you've drawn

a) A(1, 1), B(8, 1), C(8, 7)

b) P(1, 2), Q(7, 2), R(4, 9)

c) X(3, 1), Y(7, 5), Z(5, 8)

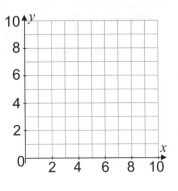

6 Copy each grid and add one more point to form:

a) a parallelogram

b) a kite

c) a trapezium with a line of symmetry

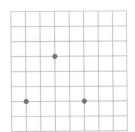

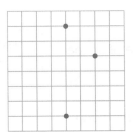

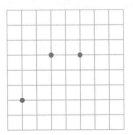

7 Sanjay and Eve are looking at the same triangle. Sanjay says, "this triangle is isosceles". Eve says, "this is a right-angled triangle". Can they both be correct? Explain your answer.

8 Write down all the different types of quadrilateral which have:

a) 2 pairs of parallel sides

b) diagonals that cross at right angles

c) 2 pairs of equal angles

d) 4 equal sides

Investigate — 2D Shapes

a) Design a flow chart to help you identify the different types of triangle. Use the question given as a starting point.

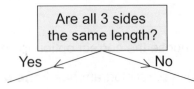

b) Now design a flow chart to help you identify the different types of quadrilateral.

c) Can you adapt your flow charts to make one that works for both triangles and quadrilaterals?

Angles in a Triangle

The angles in a <u>triangle</u> add up to 180°.

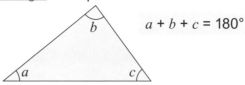

$$a + b + c = 180°$$

Example 2   a) **Find the size of angle x.**

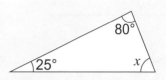

1. The angles in a triangle add up to 180°.
   Use this to write an equation involving x.

2. Solve your equation to find x.

$$x + 25° + 80° = 180°$$
$$x + 105° = 180°$$
$$x = 180° - 105° = \textbf{75°}$$

b) **Find the size of angle y.**

1. The triangle is isosceles, so the unmarked angle is the same size as the 40° angle.

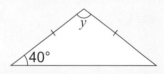

2. Now use the fact that angles in a triangle add up to 180° to write an equation involving y.

3. Solve your equation to find y.

$$y + 40° + 40° = 180°$$
$$y + 80° = 180°$$
$$y = 180° - 80° = \textbf{100°}$$

Exercise 3

The diagrams in this exercise are **not** drawn accurately, so don't try to measure the angles.

1   Find the sizes of the missing angles marked by letters.

a)

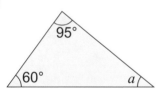

b)

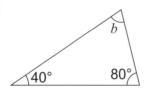

c)

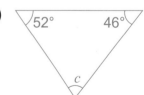

d)

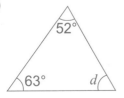

e)

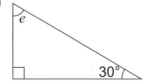

f)

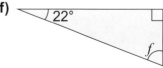

2 Find the sizes of the missing angles marked by letters.

a)
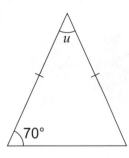

b)
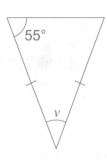

c)
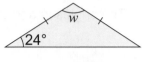

d)
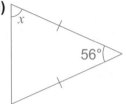

e)
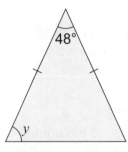

f)

3 Find the value of each letter in the following diagrams.

a)
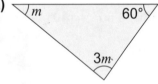

b)
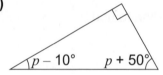

c)
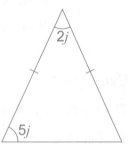

4 Find all the missing angles marked by letters in the diagrams.

a)
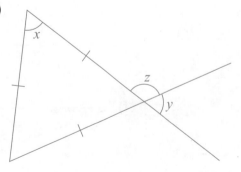

b)
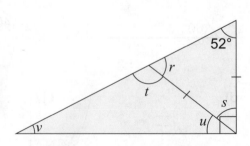

Angles in a Quadrilateral

The angles in a quadrilateral add up to 360°.

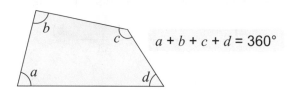

$a + b + c + d = 360°$

a) **Find the size of angle x.**

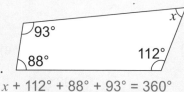

1. The angles in a quadrilateral add up to 360°. Use this to write an equation involving x.

$x + 112° + 88° + 93° = 360°$

2. Solve your equation to find x.

$x + 293° = 360°$
$x = 360° - 293° = \mathbf{67°}$

b) **Find the size of angle y.**

1. Opposite angles in a parallelogram are equal, so there are two 75° angles and two of angle y.

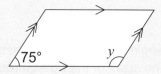

2. Now use the fact that angles in a quadrilateral add up to 360° to write an equation involving y.

$y + 75° + y + 75° = 360°$
$2y + 150° = 360°$
$2y = 360° - 150° = 210°$

3. Solve your equation to find y.

$y = 210° \div 2 = \mathbf{105°}$

Exercise 4

The diagrams in this exercise are **not** drawn accurately, so don't try to measure the angles.

1   Find the sizes of the missing angles marked by letters.

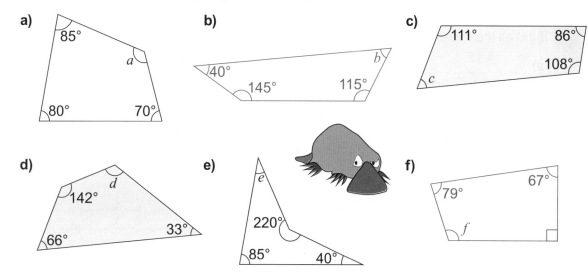

2 Find the sizes of the missing angles marked by letters.

a)

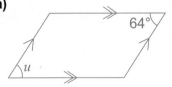

b)

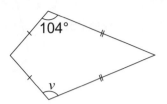

c)

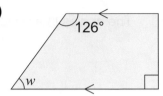

d)

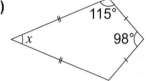

e)

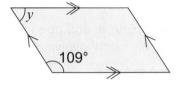

f)

3 One angle of a rhombus measures 27°.
Find the sizes of the other three angles.

4 Find the value of each letter in the following diagrams.

a)

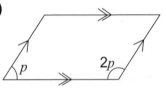

b)

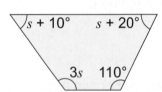

c)

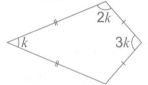

5 Find all the missing angles marked by letters in the diagrams.

a)

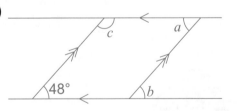

b)

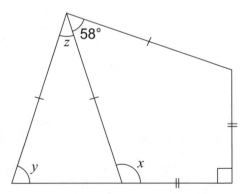

13.3 Angles in Polygons

A polygon is an enclosed shape whose sides are all straight.
A regular polygon has all sides of equal length and angles that are all equal.

The angles inside a polygon are called interior angles.
The sum of the interior angles depends on how many sides the polygon has.

To find the sum of the interior angles, divide the polygon up into triangles (by drawing lines from one corner to all the others). Then multiply the number of triangles by 180° (as there are 180° in a triangle) — this is the sum of the interior angles.

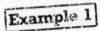 **Find the sum of the interior angles in a hexagon.**

1. Draw any hexagon (it doesn't have to be regular).

2. Split the hexagon into triangles by drawing lines from one corner to all the others.

3. Angles in a triangle add up to 180° and there are 4 triangles, so multiply 180° by 4.

Sum of interior angles:
4 × 180° = **720°**

Exercise 1

The diagrams in this exercise are **not** drawn accurately, so don't try to measure the angles.

1 By dividing each shape into triangles, find the sum of the interior angles of the following:

a)

b)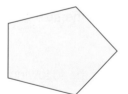

c)

2 Sketch the polygon shown.

a) Divide the polygon into triangles, starting from the 150° angle.

b) Find the sum of the interior angles of the polygon.

c) Use your answer to part **b)** to find the size of the angle marked x.

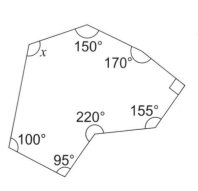

3 **a)** Find the sum of the interior angles of the polygon shown.

b) Use your answer to part **a)** to find the size of the angle marked y.

4 A hexagon has two angles measuring 130°, two right angles and one angle measuring 175°. Find the size of the missing angle.

5 Find the sizes of the missing angles marked by letters in the following shapes:

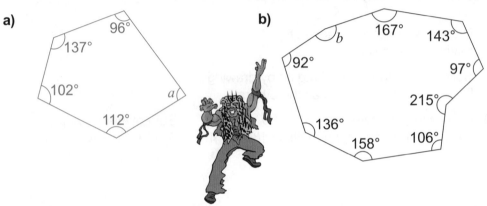

a)

96°
137°
102°
112°
a

b)

b
167°
143°
92°
97°
215°
136°
158°
106°

6 In a regular polygon, all the interior angles are the same size.

a) Find the sum of the interior angles in a dodecagon (a 12-sided shape).

b) Use your answer to part **a)** to find the size of one interior angle of a regular dodecagon.

7 Find the size of one interior angle in the following shapes:

a) a regular hexagon   **b)** a regular octagon   **c)** a regular 15-sided polygon

---

Investigate — Angles in Polygons

a) Starting with a quadrilateral and increasing the number of sides up to a decagon (a 10-sided shape), write down the number of sides the polygon has, the number of triangles it can be split into and the sum of the interior angles.

b) Can you find a link between the number of sides the polygon has and the number of triangles it can be split into? Try and use this link to write a formula to work out the sum of the interior angles for any polygon.

13.4 Properties of 3D Shapes

Here are the 3D shapes you need to know:

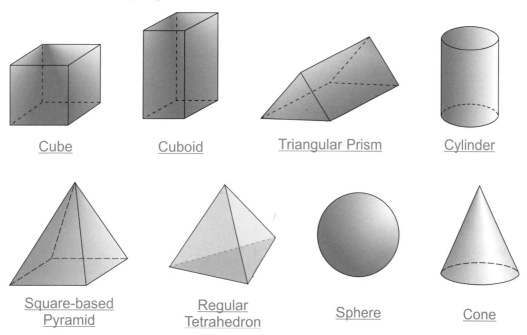

| Cube | Cuboid | Triangular Prism | Cylinder |

| Square-based Pyramid | Regular Tetrahedron | Sphere | Cone |

You need to be able to spot different parts of 3D shapes — vertices, faces and edges. Don't forget the hidden ones when you're counting them up.

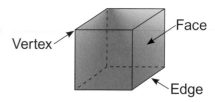

A prism is a 3D shape which is the same shape and size all the way through — it has a constant cross-section.

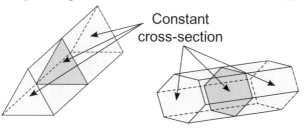

Constant cross-section

Not a prism:

Different cross-section

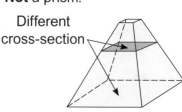

Exercise 1

1   For each shape, write down the number of: **i)** faces
                                            ii) vertices
                                            iii) edges

a) Cube   **b)** Square-based pyramid   **c)** Triangular prism

2 Which of these shapes are prisms?

 A 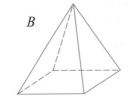 B 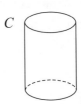 C

 D 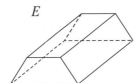 E   F

3 Look at this shape.

  a) Write down its name.

  b) Write down the number of:

   i) faces   **ii)** vertices   **iii)** edges

4 I am thinking of a 3D shape. It has 4 faces, 4 vertices and 6 edges. What is the name of the shape I am thinking of?

5 Sketch a pentagonal prism and use your sketch to write down how many faces, vertices and edges it has.

6 Pippa is making models of some 3D shapes out of cardboard. Write down the names of the shapes she can make by folding up the following designs:

a)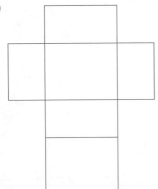

b)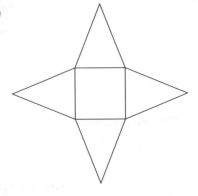

Section 14 — Constructions

14.1 Constructions

Perpendicular Lines

The <u>perpendicular</u> from a point to a line:
- passes through the point, and
- meets the line at a <u>right angle</u> (90°).

There are two different perpendicular lines you will need to be able to <u>construct</u>:

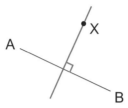

The perpendicular **from** the point X **to** the line AB. (This is the **shortest distance** between X and AB.)

The perpendicular **at** the point X **on** the line AB.

Example 1 Construct the perpendicular from a point X to a horizontal line using only a ruler and a compass.

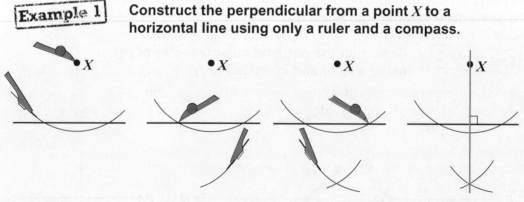

1. Draw an arc with the compass point on X that cuts the line twice.

2. Draw an arc with the compass point on one of the points where your arc meets the line. Do the same for the other point, keeping the radius the same.

3. Draw the perpendicular from X to where the arcs cross.

Exercise 1

1 a) Draw two points P and Q. Draw a long straight line passing through them.

b) Draw another point R above the line PQ.
Construct the perpendicular from R to the line PQ.

2 a) On squared paper, draw axes with x-values and y-values from –5 to 5.

b) Plot the points $A(-5, -1)$, $B(3, 3)$ and $C(4, -4)$. Join points A and B with a straight line.

c) Construct a line to show the shortest distance from point C to the line AB.

d) Give the coordinates of the point where the line you drew in **c)** meets AB.

3 Draw an equilateral triangle using a ruler and a protractor.
Construct a perpendicular from each of the triangle's corners to the opposite side.
What do you notice about where these lines cross?

4 Draw a straight line and label the ends A and B.
Mark a point C on the line. Construct the perpendicular to the line AB through point C.

Perpendicular Bisectors

The <u>perpendicular bisector</u> of a line between points A and B:

- is at <u>right angles</u> to the line AB
- cuts the line AB in half.

All points on the perpendicular bisector are
the same distance from both A and B.

Example 2 Construct the perpendicular bisector of PQ using a ruler and compass only.

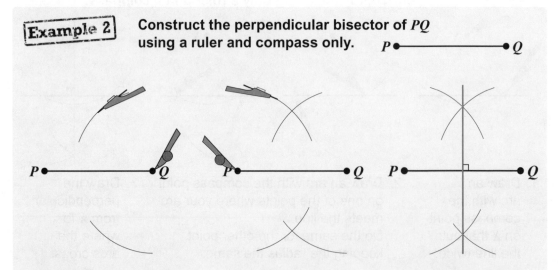

1. Place the compass point at Q, with the radius more than half of the length PQ. Draw two arcs as shown.

2. Keep the radius the same and put the compass point at P. Draw two more arcs, each crossing one of the first two arcs.

3. Use a ruler to draw a straight line through the points where the arcs meet. This is the perpendicular bisector.

Exercise 2

1 **a)** Draw a horizontal line AB 8 cm long.

b) Construct its perpendicular bisector using a ruler and compass only.

2 **a)** Draw a vertical line XY 12 cm long.

b) Construct its perpendicular bisector using a ruler and compass only.

3 **a)** Draw a slanting line XY 70 mm long.

b) Construct the perpendicular to XY that cuts XY 35 mm from point X.

4 **a)** On squared paper, draw axes with x-values and y-values from 0 to 10.

b) Plot the points $A(0, 4)$ and $B(8, 8)$ and join them to make the straight line AB.

c) Construct the perpendicular bisector of AB using a ruler and compass only.

d) Give the coordinates of the point where the line you drew in **c)** cuts the x-axis.

5 **a)** Draw a horizontal line EF 10 cm long.

b) Construct its perpendicular bisector and label the point where the two lines cross D.

c) Mark two points on the perpendicular bisector, one 5 cm above D and the other 5 cm below D. Label these points G and H.

d) Draw the quadrilateral $EGFH$. What shape have you constructed?

6 **a)** Use a ruler and a protractor to draw an equilateral triangle. Label the corners P, Q and R.

b) Construct perpendicular bisectors of sides PQ, QR and PR. Continue each line through the corner opposite. Label the point S, where the three bisectors cross.

c) Set your compass to the length of the line PS. Draw a circle with centre S.

d) What do you notice about the circle?

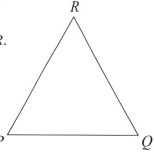

Angle Bisectors

An <u>angle bisector</u> cuts an angle exactly in half, leaving two equal angles.

Every point on the angle bisector is exactly the same distance away from the two original lines.

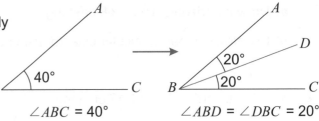

∠ABC = 40°   ∠ABD = ∠DBC = 20°

Example 3   Construct the bisector of an 80° angle.

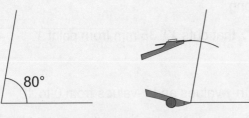
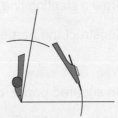

1. Place the point of the compass on the corner of the angle and draw arcs crossing both lines — using the same radius.

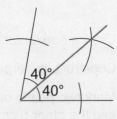

2. Now place the point of the compass where your arcs cross the lines, and draw two more arcs that cross — using the same radius.

3. Use a ruler to draw a straight line through the corner of the angle and the point where the arcs cross — this is the angle bisector.

Exercise 3

1   Draw the following angles using a protractor.
For each angle, construct the angle bisector using a ruler and compass.

a) 30°   b) 64°   c) 90°   d) 130°

e) 54°   f) 108°   g) 38°   h) 180°

Check each of your angle bisectors with a protractor.

2 a) Draw a straight line and label the end points A and B.

b) Construct the perpendicular bisector of the line AB.
Label the end points of the perpendicular bisector C and D and
label point E, where lines AB and CD cross.

c) Construct the angle bisector of $\angle BED$.
Measure and label the sizes of the angles between
this bisector and the lines BE and DE.

3 a) Use a protractor to draw an angle RST of 100°.

b) Construct the bisector of $\angle RST$. Label a point on the angle bisector U.

c) Construct the bisector of $\angle RSU$. Label a point on this angle bisector V.

d) What is the size of $\angle RSV$?

4 Laura has a slice of pizza with the angle shown in this diagram:

120°

Construct an angle of 120° to represent the pizza.
Laura wants to cut the pizza into four equal slices.
Construct three angle bisectors to show how Laura should cut the pizza up.

5 a) Use a ruler to draw a straight line AB.

b) Using only angle bisectors, draw an angle of 22.5° accurately.

Investigate — Angle Bisectors

a) Draw any triangle using a ruler to make sure all the sides are straight.

b) Construct the angle bisector for each of the three angles in the triangle.

c) Repeat parts **a)** and **b)** a few times for different triangles.

d) Do you notice anything about where the lines cross?
Will they always cross inside the triangle?

Triangles

When you are given all three side lengths of a <u>triangle</u> there is only one possible triangle you can construct.

Two <u>constructions</u> of the same triangle might look different (they could be a rotation or reflection of one another), but they will have the same shape and size. We say the two triangles are <u>congruent</u>.

Always label the corners of your triangle so you can describe the line that connects them.

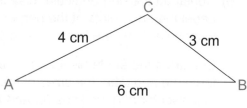

AB = 6 cm, BC = 3 cm and AC = 4 cm

Example 4 | Draw triangle ABC, where AB is 4 cm, BC is 2 cm and AC is 3.5 cm.

1. Start by sketching and labelling the triangle so you know roughly what is needed.

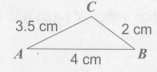

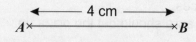

2. Draw and label the 4 cm side using a ruler.

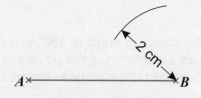

3. Set your compass to 2 cm. Draw an arc 2 cm from B.

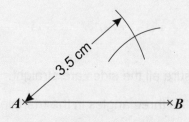

4. Set your compass to 3.5 cm. Draw an arc 3.5 cm from A.

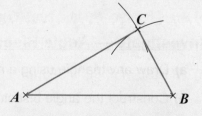

5. Label point C where the two arcs cross and use a ruler to draw the other two sides of the triangle.

Exercise 4

1 These triangles are not drawn accurately.
Draw them accurately with the measurements given using a ruler and compass.

a)

3 cm   4 cm

5 cm

b)

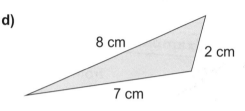

12 cm   5 cm

9 cm

c)

9 cm

4.5 cm   7.5 cm

d)

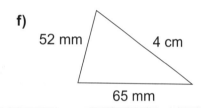

8 cm   2 cm

7 cm

e)

60 mm

40 mm

55 mm

f)

52 mm   4 cm

65 mm

2 Draw an equilateral triangle with side lengths of 5 cm using a ruler and compass.

3 Draw each of the following triangles ABC using a ruler and compass.

a) AB is 5 cm, BC is 11 cm, AC is 11 cm.

b) AB is 8.5 cm, BC is 4 cm, AC is 6.5 cm.

c) AB is 2.6 cm, BC is 4.4 cm, AC is 5.3 cm.

d) AB is 63 mm, BC is 38 mm, AC is 81 mm.

4 Amanda, Beth and Carla are standing on the school field.
- Amanda is 45 metres from Beth,
- Beth is 20 metres away from Carla, and
- Amanda is 35 metres away from Carla.

Using a scale of 1 cm : 10 metres, construct a triangle to show their positions.

Section 15 — Perimeter, Area, Volume and Pythagoras

Perimeter of Composite Shapes

The perimeter is the total distance around the outside of a shape.
It can be found by adding the lengths of all the sides together.

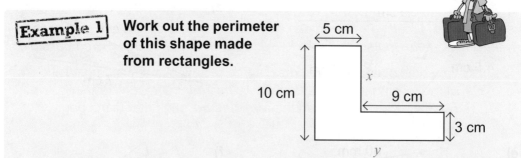

| **Example 1** | Work out the perimeter of this shape made from rectangles. |

1. First find the missing side lengths.
$x = 10 \text{ cm} - 3 \text{ cm} = 7 \text{ cm}$
$y = 5 \text{ cm} + 9 \text{ cm} = 14 \text{ cm}$

2. Add all the side lengths together to find the perimeter of the shape.
$P = 5 + 7 + 9 + 3 + 14 + 10 = \mathbf{48 \text{ cm}}$

Exercise 1

The diagrams in this exercise are **not** drawn accurately.

1   Find the perimeter of each of these shapes made from rectangles.

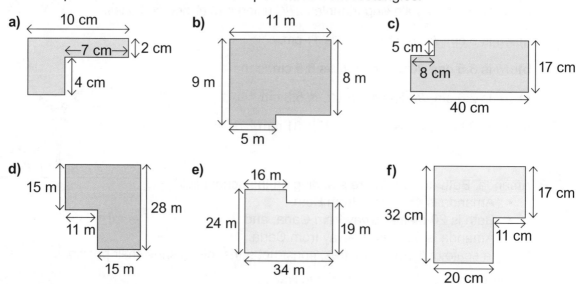

2 Find the length of fence required to go around each of these playgrounds.

a)

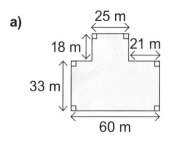

b)

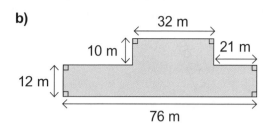

Investigate — Perimeter and Area

Farmer Ed is making a sheep pen. He has 20 pieces of fence. Each piece of fence is 1 metre long. He wants to make a pen with the largest area possible.

a) On some squared paper, draw some rectangular sheep pens using all of the fencing, using the edge of 1 square to represent 1 metre.
For each one, write down the area and the perimeter of the pen.

b) Which rectangle has the largest area?

c) Draw some pens made from more than one rectangle. Calculate the area for each one. How do the areas of these pens compare with the areas of similar rectangular pens that you drew in **a)**?

d) Ed thinks that the largest sheep pen he can make using all of the fencing has an area of 25 m². What shape is this sheep pen?

e) Do you think Ed is right or wrong?
Investigate the areas of some different shapes to see.

Circumference of Circles

The <u>diameter</u> of a <u>circle</u> is the length across the circle, going through the centre.

The <u>radius</u> is the distance from the centre to the edge of the circle.

The diameter of a circle is always twice as long as the radius:

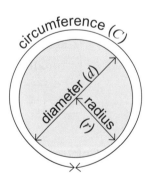

Diameter (*d*) = 2 × Radius (*r*)   or   *d* = 2*r*

The <u>circumference</u> (*C*) is the perimeter of the circle — i.e. the distance around the outside.
The circumference of a circle can be found using the formula:

Circumference (*C*) = π × Diameter (*d*)   or   *C* = π*d* = 2π*r*

This symbol (called "<u>pi</u>") stands for the number 3.14159265...
There's a button for it on your calculator.

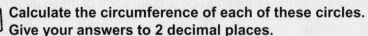

Example 2 Calculate the circumference of each of these circles. Give your answers to 2 decimal places.

a)

15 cm

1. The diameter of the circle is 15 cm.
   To find the circumference (C), use the formula: $C = \pi d$

2. Substitute in the value for d to find C. $C = \pi \times 15$

   $C = \textbf{47.12 cm}$

b)

6 cm

1. The radius of the circle is 6 cm.
   To find the diameter, multiply the radius by 2. $2r = d$

   $2 \times 6 = 12$ cm

2. Find the circumference (C) using the formula: $C = \pi d$

3. Substitute in the value for d to find C. $C = \pi \times 12$

   $C = \textbf{37.70 cm}$

Exercise 2

For this exercise, give your answers to 2 decimal places.

1 Calculate the circumference of each of the following circles.

a)

4 cm

b)

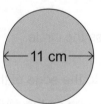

11 cm

c)

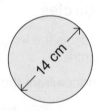

14 cm

d)

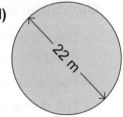

22 m

2 Calculate the circumference of each of the following circles.

a)

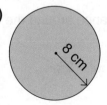

8 cm

b)

5 m

c)

9 mm

d)

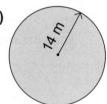

14 m

3 Calculate the circumferences of these circles.

a)
10 m

b)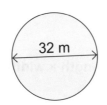
32 m

c)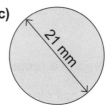
21 mm

d)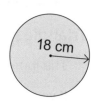
18 cm

4 Find the circumference of each of these circles with the diameter (*d*) or radius (*r*) given.

a) *d* = 7 cm   b) *d* = 13 m   c) *d* = 17 mm   d) *d* = 24 cm

e) *r* = 3 cm   f) *r* = 1 m   g) *r* = 16 cm   h) *r* = 15 mm

5 Find the circumferences of the following circles.

a) A circle with a diameter of 22 mm.   b) A circle with a radius of 4.5 cm.

c) A circle with a diameter of 14.5 m.   d) A circle with a diameter of 33 mm.

e) A circle with a radius of 11.5 cm.   f) A circle with a diameter of 12.5 mm.

6 Find the circumferences of the following.

a) A circular coin with a diameter of 27.3 mm.

b) A circular running track with a radius of 63.6 m.

c) A circular plate with a radius of 17.5 cm.

d) A circular mirror with a diameter of 15.7 cm.

7 Find the perimeter of each of these shapes.

a)
3 cm

b)
7 cm

c)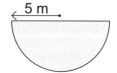
5 m

d)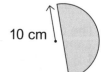
10 cm

e)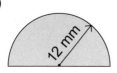
12 mm

f)
8 m

g)
6 mm

h)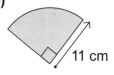
11 cm

15.2 Area

Triangles

The <u>formula</u> for the <u>area</u> of a rectangle is **length × width**.

If you cut a rectangle in half along its diagonal, you get two triangles that are the same size.

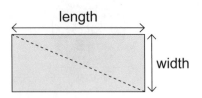
length
width

So the area of one of these triangle is half of the area of the rectangle.

The formula for the area of a triangle is: $\text{Area} = \dfrac{\textbf{base} \times \textbf{height}}{2}$ or $A = \dfrac{1}{2}bh$

The base is the length of the rectangle and the height is the width of the rectangle.

The height of the triangle in this formula is the <u>perpendicular</u> height, not the sloping height. The base and height of a triangle are always at <u>right angles</u> to each other.

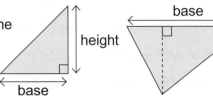
height
base
base
height

Example 1 Calculate the area of this triangle.

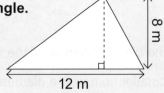
8 m
12 m

1. The base of the triangle is 12 m.
   The height of the triangle is 8 m.

2. Put these numbers into the formula to work out the area.

$$\text{Area} = \frac{\text{base} \times \text{height}}{2}$$

$$= \frac{12 \times 8}{2}$$

3. Remember to include units in your answer.
   Area is measured in square units.

$$= 48 \text{ m}^2$$

Exercise 1

The diagrams in this exercise are **not** drawn accurately.

1 Find the area of each of these triangles.

a)
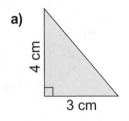
4 cm
3 cm

b)
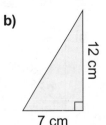
12 cm
7 cm

c)
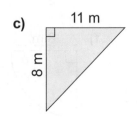
11 m
8 m

d)
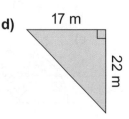
17 m
22 m

2 Find the area of each of these triangles.

a)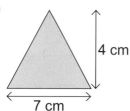
4 cm

7 cm

b)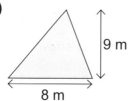
9 m

8 m

c)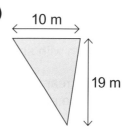
10 m

19 m

d)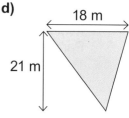
18 m

21 m

3 Find the area of each of these triangles, given their base (b) and height (h).

a) b = 12 cm, h = 18 cm

b) b = 17 m, h = 4 m

c) b = 13 cm, h = 22 cm

d) b = 29 mm, h = 14 mm

e) b = 9 cm, h = 30 cm

f) b = 27 mm, h = 12 mm

g) b = 31 cm, h = 20 cm

h) b = 33 m, h = 18 m

i) b = 24 mm, h = 13 mm

4 A triangular flag has the measurements shown in the diagram. What is the area of the flag?

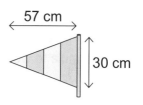
57 cm

30 cm

5 Carol's garden is 25 metres long and 11 metres wide. It is made up of a triangular patio and a triangular lawn with exactly the same dimensions, as shown. What area is covered by the patio?

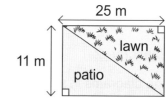
25 m

11 m

lawn

patio

6 A triangular sail is 4.5 metres tall and has a base of 2.1 metres. What is the area of the sail?

2.1 m

4.5 m

7 Find the area of each of these triangles.

a)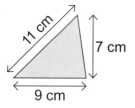
11 cm

7 cm

9 cm

b)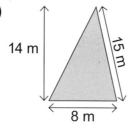
14 m

15 m

8 m

c)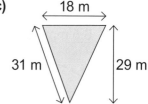
18 m

31 m

29 m

Parallelograms

Parallelograms have two pairs of parallel sides (opposite sides are the same length).
Parallel sides are shown with sets of matching arrows.

A parallelogram can be rearranged to make a rectangle with height h and base b. The area of this rectangle is $b \times h$.

So the area of a parallelogram is given by the formula: **$A = bh$**

Here, h is the perpendicular height, not the sloping height. It's measured at right angles to the base.

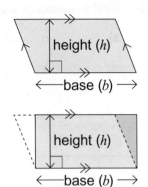

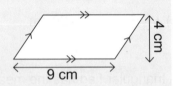

Example 2 Calculate the area of this parallelogram.

1. The base of the parallelogram is 9 cm.
   The height of the parallelogram is 4 cm.

2. Put these numbers into the formula to work out the area.

   $A = bh$
   $A = 9 \times 4$

3. Don't forget the units.

   $A = \textbf{36 cm}^2$

Exercise 2

The diagrams in this exercise are **not** drawn accurately.

1 Find the area of each parallelogram.

a)

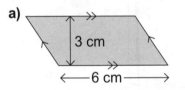

b)

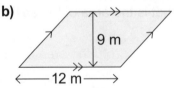

c)

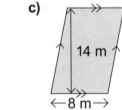

d)

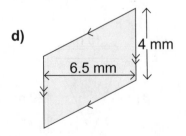

e)

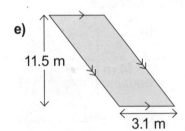

f)

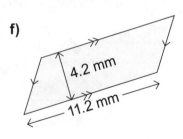

2 Work out the area of each of these parallelograms from the base (b) and height (h) given.

a) b = 16.1 cm, h = 11 cm

b) b = 9 mm, h = 17.2 mm

c) b = 3.7 cm, h = 15 cm

d) b = 10.3 m, h = 9 m

e) b = 17 cm, h = 18.9 cm

f) b = 31.2 cm, h = 7.8 cm

3 A school playground is the shape of a parallelogram.
It is 40.5 metres long and 21.5 metres wide.
What is the area of the playground?

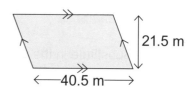

21.5 m

←—40.5 m—→

4 A field has sides with the dimensions shown
on the diagram. What is the area of the field?

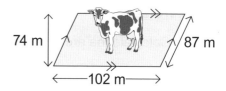

74 m

87 m

←—102 m—→

5 A toy is made up of two parallelograms
which have exactly the same dimensions.
Use the diagram to work out the area of the toy.

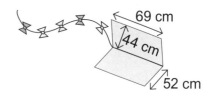

69 cm

44 cm

52 cm

Trapeziums

Trapeziums have one pair of parallel sides.

The area of a trapezium comes from the area of a parallelogram,
made up of two trapeziums with the same dimensions.

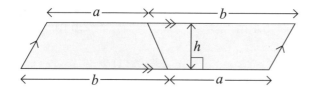

The area (A) of this parallelogram is:

$$A = (a + b) \times h$$

The area of one trapezium is equal to half of this.

$$A = \frac{1}{2}(a + b) \times h$$

a and b are the parallel sides, and h is the perpendicular height.

Example 3 Calculate the area of this trapezium.

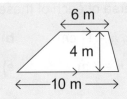

1. Write down the formula for the area of a trapezium.

$$A = \frac{1}{2}(a + b) \times h$$

2. Substitute in the values of a, b and h.

$$= \frac{1}{2}(6 + 10) \times 4$$

3. Give your answer with the correct units.

$$= \textbf{32 m}^2$$

Exercise 3

1 Calculate the areas of these trapeziums.

a)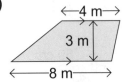

b)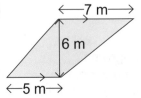

c)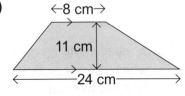

d)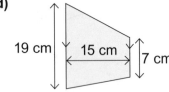

e)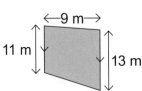

f)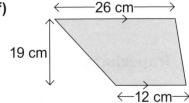

2 Find the area of:

a) the side of the house.

b) the side of the garage.

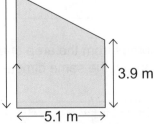

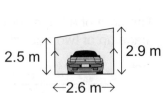

3 A trapezium-shaped paddling pool has a base with parallel sides of 1.9 metres and 2.1 metres, and a width of 1.4 m. What is the area of the base of the paddling pool?

4 A trapezium-shaped field has a width of 29.6 metres and parallel sides of 30.4 metres and 32.2 metres. What is the area of the field?

Circles

The area (A) of a circle is given by the formula: $A = \pi r^2$
where r is the radius.

Example 4 | **Find the area of these circles.**
Give your answers to 2 decimal places.

a)

5 cm

1. Write down the radius of the circle. | $r = 5$ cm

2. Substitute the value of r into the formula for A.
   Remember $r^2 = r \times r$
   | $A = \pi \times 5^2$
   $= \pi \times 25$
   $= 78.54$ cm^2

b)

18 cm

1. Use the diameter of the circle to find the radius. | $r = 18 \div 2$
   $r = 9$ cm

2. Substitute the value of r into the formula for A. | $A = \pi \times 9^2$
   $= \pi \times 81$
   $= 254.47$ cm^2

Exercise 4

For this exercise, give your answers to 2 decimal places.

1 Calculate the areas of the following circles.

a)

3 cm

b)

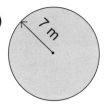

7 m

c)

4 mm

d)

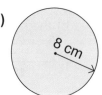

8 cm

2 Calculate the areas of the following circles.

a)

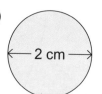

2 cm

b)

6 m

c)

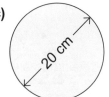

20 cm

d)

22 mm

3 Work out the areas of the following circles.

a)
11 mm

b)
15 cm

c)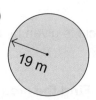
19 m

d)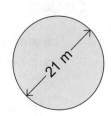
21 m

4 Find the areas of these circles with the diameter (d) or radius (r).

a) r = 2 mm   **b)** r = 6 cm   **c)** r = 10 m   **d)** r = 12 m

e) d = 10 cm   **f)** d = 4 cm   **g)** d = 12 mm   **h)** d = 16 m

i) d = 15 m   **j)** r = 14 mm   **k)** d = 19 cm   **l)** r = 23 cm

5 Find the areas of the following:

a) A circular pool with a radius of 11.3 metres.

b) A circular frisbee with a diameter of 27.4 centimetres.

c) The surface of a circular trampoline with a diameter of 4.8 metres.

6 Find the area of each of these semicircles.

a)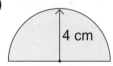
4 cm

b)
6 m

c)
11 mm

d)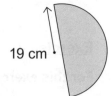
19 cm

e)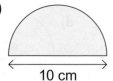
10 cm

f)
14 mm

g)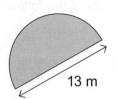
13 m

h)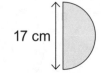
17 cm

7 Find the area of each of these quarter-circles.

a)
4 m

b)
5 mm

c)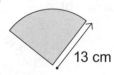
13 cm

d)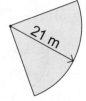
21 m

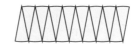
Composite Shapes

A composite shape is a shape made up of two or more simple shapes.
To work out the area of a composite shape, you work out the areas of the
simple shapes, then add the areas together.

Example 5 **Work out the area of this shape.**
Give your answer to 2 decimal places.

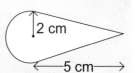

1. This shape is made up of a semicircle with
   radius 2 cm, and a triangle with a height of 5 cm
   and a base of double the radius, 2 × 2 = 4 cm.

2. Work out the area of a circle   Area of circle = πr^2
   with $r = 2$ using the formula: $= \pi \times 2^2$
                                                          $= 12.56...$ cm^2

3. Halve the answer to find the area   Area of semicircle = $12.56... \div 2$
   of half of a circle. $= 6.28...$ cm^2

4. Work out the area of the triangle   Area of triangle = $\dfrac{b \times h}{2}$
   using the formula:
                                                       $= \dfrac{4 \times 5}{2}$

                                                       $= 10$ cm^2

5. Add the two areas together to   Total area = $10 + 6.28...$
   find the overall area of the shape. $= \mathbf{16.28}$ **cm²**

Exercise 5

The diagrams in this exercise are **not** drawn accurately.

1 Calculate the areas of these shapes.

a)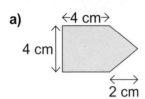

b)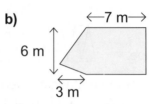

c)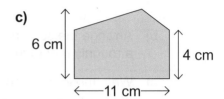

2 Calculate the areas of these shapes.

a)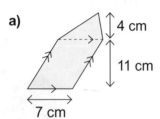

b)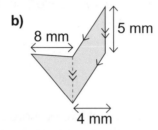

c)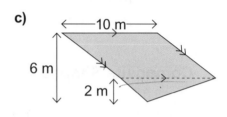

3 Calculate the areas of these shapes. Give your answers to 2 decimal places.

a)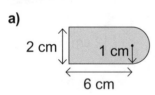

b)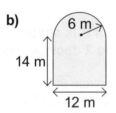

c)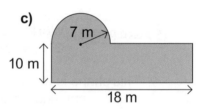

4 Calculate the areas of these shapes. Give your answers to 2 decimal places.

a)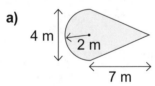

b)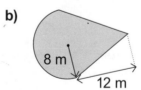

c)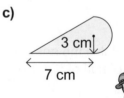

5 Calculate the areas of these shapes. Give your answers to 2 decimal places.

a)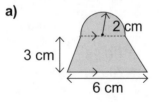

b)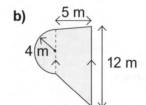

c)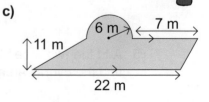

15.3 Volume

Cuboids

The formulas for the volume of a cube and a cuboid are:

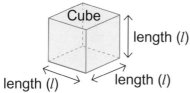

Volume = length³

$$V = l^3$$

Volume = length × width × height

$$V = l \times w \times h$$

Example 1 Work out the volume of the cuboid.

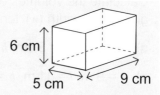

1. Write down the formula for the volume of a cuboid. $V = l \times w \times h$

2. Put the correct numbers into the formula and do the calculation. $V = 9 \times 5 \times 6$

3. The answer is a volume so the units will be 'cubed'. $V = \textbf{270 cm}^3$

Exercise 1

The diagrams in this exercise are **not** drawn accurately.

1 Calculate the volume of each of the following cubes.

a)
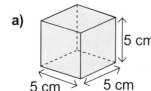
5 cm
5 cm 5 cm

b)
3 mm
3 mm 3 mm

c)
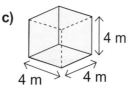
4 m
4 m 4 m

d)
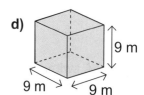
9 m
9 m 9 m

2 Calculate the volume of each of the following cubes.

a)
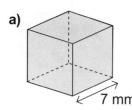
7 mm

b)
11 cm

c)
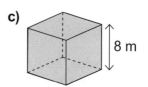
8 m

d)
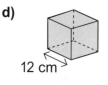
12 cm

3 Calculate the volumes of the following cuboids.

a)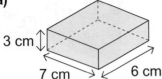

3 cm

7 cm   6 cm

b)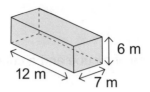

6 m

12 m   7 m

c)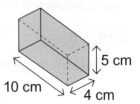

5 cm

10 cm   4 cm

d)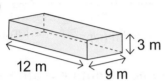

3 m

12 m   9 m

e)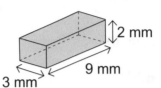

2 mm

9 mm

3 mm

f)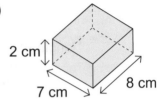

2 cm

7 cm   8 cm

4 Calculate the volumes of these cubes and cuboids, given their width (w), length (l) and height (h).

a) w = 5 cm, l = 5 cm, h = 11 cm

b) w = 12 mm, l = 12 mm, h = 11 mm

c) w = 9 m, l = 11 m, h = 7 m

d) w = 14 m, l = 10 m, h = 15 m

e) w = 3 cm, l = 14 cm, h = 18 cm

f) w = 13 mm, l = 13 mm, h = 13 mm

g) w = 16 cm, l = 5 cm, h = 9 cm

h) w = 12 m, l = 11 m, h = 6 m

5 A milk carton measures 11 cm × 11 cm × 24 cm. What volume of milk can the carton hold?

24 cm

11 cm   11 cm

6 A swimming pool is 25 metres long, 15 metres wide, and 2 metres deep. What is the volume of water the swimming pool can hold?

7 A matchbox is 62 mm long, 41 mm wide and 12 mm deep. What is the volume of the matchbox?

8 A shoebox is 20.5 cm wide, 29.8 cm long and 15.6 cm deep. What is the volume of the shoebox?

9 A bath can be modelled as a cuboid with dimensions 1.7 m × 0.8 m × 0.5 m.

a) What is the volume of the bath?

b) The bath is filled so that there is a depth
   of 0.2 m of water in the bottom of the bath.
   What volume of water is in the bath?

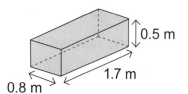

0.5 m

1.7 m

0.8 m

10 A sand pit can be modelled as a cuboid.
The sand pit is 120 cm long, 80 cm wide and 45 cm deep.

a) What is the volume of the sand pit?

b) The sand pit is filled so that the top of the sand is 10 cm away from the top of the pit.
   What volume of sand is in the sand pit?

Other Prisms

A prism is a 3D shape where the cross-section is the
same throughout the whole shape.

The volume of a prism is given by the following formula:

Volume = cross-sectional area × length

Cross-Sectional
Area

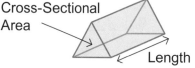

Length

| Example 2 | **Calculate the volume of this cylinder.**
Give your answer to 2 decimal places. |

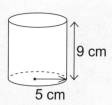

9 cm

5 cm

1. Start by working out the area of the cross-section,
   which is a circle.
   Use the formula for the area of a circle
   and substitute in the value for r.

   $A = \pi r^2$
   $A = \pi \times 5^2$
   $= \pi \times 25$
   $= 78.539...$ cm^2

2. Substitute the values for the cross-sectional area and
   the length into the formula for the volume of a prism.

   Volume = cross-sectional area × length   Volume = 78.539 × 9

   = **706.86 cm^3**

Exercise 2

The diagrams in this exercise are **not** drawn accurately.

1 Calculate the volumes of the following prisms from their lengths and cross-sectional areas.

   a) Area = 5 cm², length = 12 cm   **b)** Area = 9 m², length = 8 m

   c) Area = 14 mm², length = 6 mm   **d)** Area = 22 m², length = 5 m

   e) Area = 18 cm², length = 11 cm   **f)** Area = 19 mm², length = 21 mm

2 Calculate the volumes of the following prisms.

a) Area = 16 cm²

11 cm

b) Area = 23 m²

19 m

c) Area = 31 m²

20 m

d) Area = 52 cm²

16 cm

e) Area = 49 cm²

14 cm

f) Area = 28 mm²

14 mm

3 Calculate the volumes of the following prisms.

a)

4 cm

7 cm   10 cm

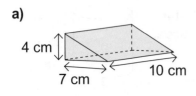

b)

18 m

11 m

8 m

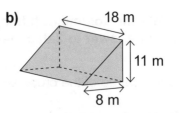

c) 6 m

16 m

7 m

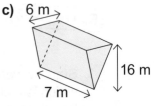

d)

11 cm

15 cm   9 cm

e)

11 mm

14 mm

28 mm

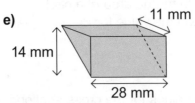

f)

12 m   30 m

14 m

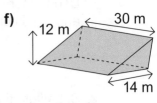

4 An attic is the shape of a triangular prism.
The height of the attic at its highest point is 2.2 metres
and the width of the attic is 5.7 metres.
The attic is 6.5 metres long.
What is the volume of the attic?

5 The following prisms have a trapezium-shaped cross-section.
Calculate the volume of each shape.

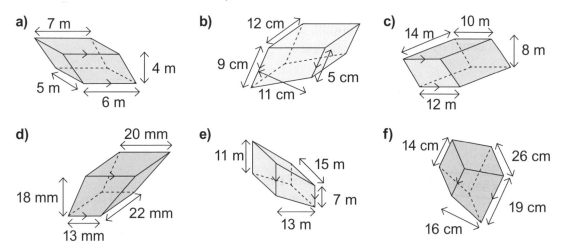

a) 7 m, 4 m, 5 m, 6 m

b) 12 cm, 9 cm, 5 cm, 11 cm

c) 10 m, 14 m, 8 m, 12 m

d) 20 mm, 18 mm, 22 mm, 13 mm

e) 11 m, 15 m, 7 m, 13 m

f) 14 cm, 26 cm, 19 cm, 16 cm

6 Calculate the volumes of the following cylinders. Give your answers to 2 decimal places.

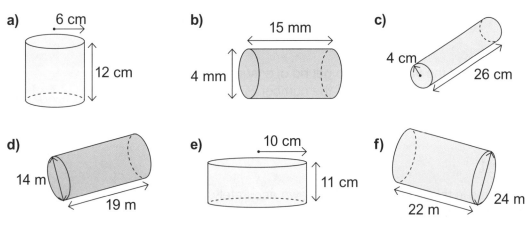

a) 6 cm, 12 cm

b) 15 mm, 4 mm

c) 4 cm, 26 cm

d) 14 m, 19 m

e) 10 cm, 11 cm

f) 22 m, 24 m

7 Mario keeps spaghetti in a cylinder-shaped jar.
The jar has a radius of 8.1 cm and a height of 20.8 cm.
What is the volume of the jar? Give your answer to 2 decimal places.

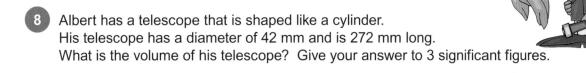

8 Albert has a telescope that is shaped like a cylinder.
His telescope has a diameter of 42 mm and is 272 mm long.
What is the volume of his telescope? Give your answer to 3 significant figures.

9 A cylindrical glass has a diameter of 6.8 cm and is 14.1 cm tall.
The glass is filled with water so that the water is 3.2 cm below the top of the glass.
What is the volume of water in the glass? Give your answer to 2 decimal places.

15.4 Pythagoras' Theorem

In a right-angled triangle, the lengths of the sides are connected by Pythagoras' Theorem:

$$h^2 = a^2 + b^2$$

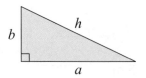

h is the hypotenuse — the longest side, opposite the right angle.
a and b are the shorter sides.

Example 1 **Find the length of the hypotenuse.**
Give your answer to 2 decimal places.

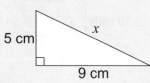

1. x is the hypotenuse.
   Substitute the values for a and b into the formula for Pythagoras' Theorem.

   $h^2 = a^2 + b^2$
   $x^2 = 5^2 + 9^2$
   $x^2 = 25 + 81$
   $x^2 = 106$

2. Find the value of x. To get rid of a 'square', take the square root of the number.

   $x = \sqrt{106}$
   $x = \mathbf{10.30 \ cm}$

Exercise 1

The diagrams in this exercise are **not** drawn accurately.
For this exercise, give your answers to 2 decimal places.

1 Calculate the length of the hypotenuse for each of the following triangles.

a)
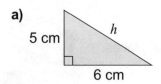

b)
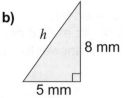

c)
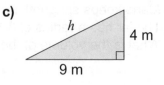

d)
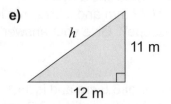

e)

f)
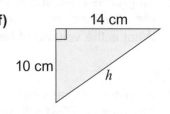

2 Work out the length of the ladder shown.

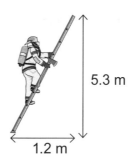

5.3 m

1.2 m

3 The size of a TV screen is found by measuring the length of the diagonal.
Find the size of a rectangular TV screen that is 67 cm wide and 48 cm tall.

4 Darius swims diagonally across a swimming pool with
a width of 25 metres and a length of 33 metres.
What distance does Darius swim?

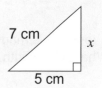

| Example 2 | **Find the length of the missing side, x.**
Give your answer to 2 decimal places. |

7 cm x

5 cm

1. x is one of the shorter sides.
   Substitute in the values of $h = 7$ cm and $b = 5$ cm
   into the formula for Pythagoras' theorem.

   $h^2 = a^2 + b^2$
   $7^2 = x^2 + 5^2$

2. Rearrange the equation so that x^2 is on its own.

   $x^2 = 7^2 - 5^2$
   $x^2 = 49 - 25$
   $x^2 = 24$

3. Solve to find x.

   $x = \sqrt{24}$
   $x = 4.90$ cm

Exercise 2

The diagrams in this exercise are **not** drawn accurately.
For this exercise, give your answers to 2 decimal places.

1 Calculate the lengths of the missing sides for the following triangles.

a)

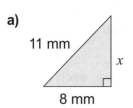

11 mm

x

8 mm

b)

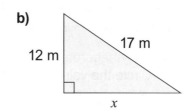

12 m   17 m

x

c)

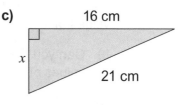

16 cm

x

21 cm

2 Calculate the lengths of the missing sides for the following triangles.

a)

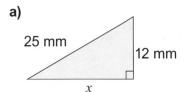

25 mm

12 mm

x

b)

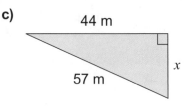

24 cm

31 cm

x

c)

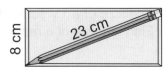

44 m

57 m

x

3 When placed diagonally, a pencil measuring 23 cm long fits exactly into a pencil tin that is 8 cm wide.
What is the length of the pencil tin?

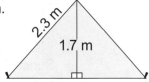

8 cm

23 cm

4 The bottom of a ladder is 1.3 metres away from the bottom of a wall and the top of the ladder is resting against the top of the wall.
If the ladder is 4.1 metres long, how high is the wall?

5 A tent flap is made from 2 identical right-angled triangles, as shown.
What is the width of the tent flap?

2.3 m

1.7 m

6 A boat has a triangular sail, as shown.
The sail has a width of 2.8 metres.
The length of each sloping side is 4.2 metres.
What is the height of the sail?

4.2 m   4.2 m

Section 16 — Transformations

16.1 Reflection

Reflection is a type of transformation. When an object is reflected in a line, its size, shape and distance from the line stay the same.

The line of reflection is called the mirror line — you need to know the equation of the mirror line to describe the reflection.

Example 1	**Reflect the shape $ABCD$ in the y-axis.** **Label the reflected points A_1, B_1, C_1 and D_1.** **Write down the coordinates of each point.**

1. The mirror line is the y-axis.

2. Reflect the shape one point at a time. Each reflected point should be the same distance from the mirror line as the original point. Label the reflection of point A with A_1, etc.

3. Write down the coordinates of each of the reflected points.

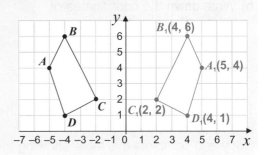

Exercise 1

1 Copy these diagrams, and reflect each shape in the y-axis.

a)

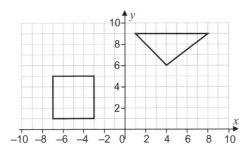

b)

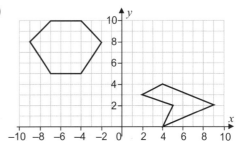

2 Copy these diagrams, and reflect each shape in the x-axis.

a)

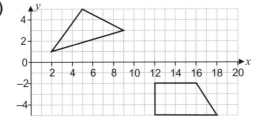

b)

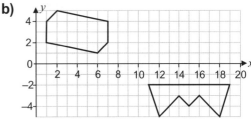

3 Copy this diagram.

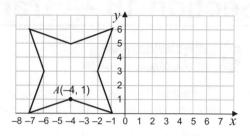

a) Reflect the shape in the y-axis.
Label the reflection of point A with A_1.

b) Write down the coordinates of the point A_1.

4 Copy this diagram.

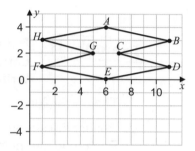

a) Reflect the shape in the x-axis.
Label the reflected points A_1, B_1, C_1, D_1, E_1, F_1, G_1 and H_1.

b) Write down the coordinates of
A_1, B_1, C_1, D_1, E_1, F_1, G_1 and H_1.

5 The quadrilateral $ABCD$ is reflected in the y-axis
to give the shape $A_1B_1C_1D_1$.
Copy and complete this table showing the
coordinates of the two shapes.

Shape	Reflected shape
$A(0, 4)$	$A_1(....., ...)$
$B(2, ...)$	$B_1(....., 6)$
$C(....., ...)$	$C_1(1, 7)$
$D(....., 4)$	$D_1(2, ...)$

Example 2	Reflect the shape $ABCDE$ in the line $x = 5$. Label the reflected points A_1, B_1, C_1, D_1 and E_1. Write down the coordinates of each point.

1. Draw the line $x = 5$. This is the vertical
   line passing through 5 on the x-axis.

2. Reflect the shape, one point at a time,
   using $x = 5$ as the mirror line.

3. Label the reflected points (the reflection
   of point A should be A_1, etc.) and
   write down their coordinates.

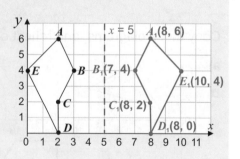

Exercise 2

1 Copy this diagram.

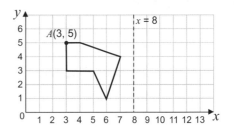

a) Reflect the shape in the line $x = 8$.
   Label the reflection of point A with A_1.

b) Write down the coordinates of the point A_1.

2 Copy this diagram.

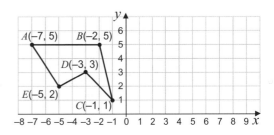

a) Draw the line $x = 1$.

b) Reflect the shape in the line $x = 1$.
   Label the reflected points A_1, B_1, C_1, D_1 and E_1.

c) Write down the coordinates of the
   points A_1, B_1, C_1, D_1 and E_1.

3 Copy this diagram.

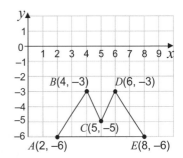

a) Draw the line $y = -2$.

b) Reflect the shape in the line $y = -2$.
   Label the reflected points A_1, B_1, C_1, D_1 and E_1.

c) Write down the coordinates of
   the points A_1, B_1, C_1, D_1 and E_1.

4 Copy this diagram and reflect the shapes
   in the line $y = x$.

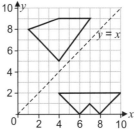

5 Use this diagram to give the equation of
   the mirror line that reflects:

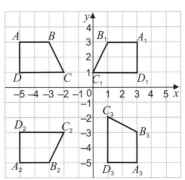

a) $ABCD$ onto $A_1B_1C_1D_1$

b) $ABCD$ onto $A_2B_2C_2D_2$

c) $ABCD$ onto $A_3B_3C_3D_3$

16.2 Rotation

When an object is rotated about a point, its size, shape and distance from the point of rotation all stay the same.

Rotations are described using three bits of information:

1) the centre of rotation   (the point it turns about)
2) the direction of rotation   (clockwise or anticlockwise)
3) the angle of rotation   (e.g. 90°, 180° or 270°)

clockwise   anticlockwise

Example 1

Rotate rectangle $ABCD$ 90° clockwise about the origin. Label the rotated shape $A_1B_1C_1D_1$ and give the coordinates of each point.

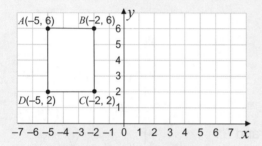

1. The origin is the point (0, 0) on the grid and 90° is a quarter turn.

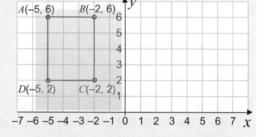

2. Draw over the shape on a piece of tracing paper.

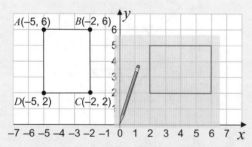

3. Place a pencil on the point (0, 0) and rotate the tracing paper 90° clockwise.

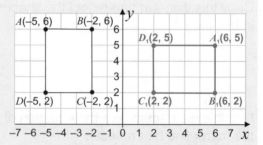

4. Draw the shape in its new position, label the corners and give their coordinates. Make sure the rotated point A is labelled with A_1, etc.

Exercise 1

1 Copy these diagrams, and rotate each shape 90° anticlockwise about the origin.

a)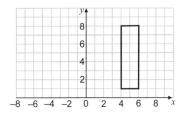

b)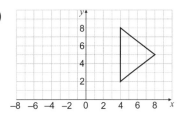

2 Copy these diagrams, and rotate each shape 180° about the origin.

a)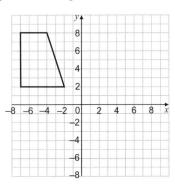

b)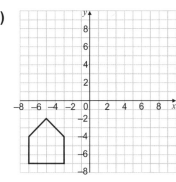

3 Copy these diagrams and rotate each shape 270° clockwise about the origin.
Label the rotated shape $A_1B_1C_1D_1E_1$ and write down the coordinates of each point.

a)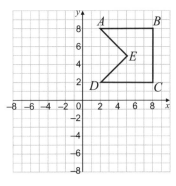

b)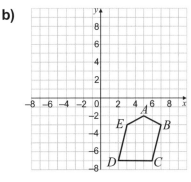

4 Copy this diagram.

Rotate the shape 90° anticlockwise about the point (1, 3).

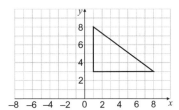

5 Copy this diagram.

a) Rotate shape A 90° clockwise about (1, 0).

b) Rotate shape B 270° anticlockwise about (−1, 0).

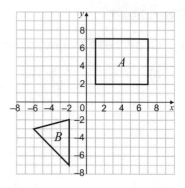

6 Copy this diagram and rotate shape $ABCDE$ 270° anticlockwise about (1, −1). Label the rotated shape $A_1B_1C_1D_1E_1$ and write down the coordinates of each point.

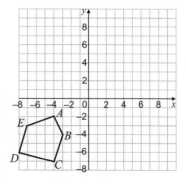

7 Copy this diagram.

a) Rotate shape $ABCDE$ 180° about (1, −1).

Label the rotated shape $A_1B_1C_1D_1E_1$ and write down the coordinates of each point.

b) Rotate shape $A_1B_1C_1D_1E_1$ 90° clockwise about (1, −3).

Label the rotated shape $A_2B_2C_2D_2E_2$ and write down the coordinates of each point.

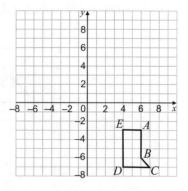

8 Fully describe the rotation that maps shape A onto shape B. You will need to give the angle, the direction and the centre of rotation.

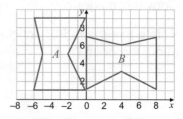

16.3 Translation

Translations describe the movement of a shape horizontally and vertically.

Translations are often described using vectors. The top number tells you the distance moved horizontally and the bottom number tells you the distance moved vertically.

$\begin{pmatrix} 7 \\ 3 \end{pmatrix}$ Move 7 right and 3 up.

$\begin{pmatrix} -2 \\ -3 \end{pmatrix}$ Move 2 left and 3 down.

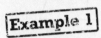 **Example 1** Translate shape A by the vector $\begin{pmatrix} 4 \\ -3 \end{pmatrix}$. Label the translated shape B.

1. The vector $\begin{pmatrix} 4 \\ -3 \end{pmatrix}$ means move the shape 4 to the right and 3 down.

2. Move each point in turn or move the whole shape at once.

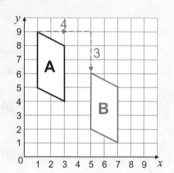

Exercise 1

1 Copy these diagrams and translate each shape by the vector $\begin{pmatrix} 2 \\ 4 \end{pmatrix}$.

a)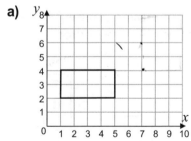

b)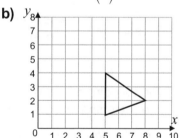

2 Copy these diagrams and translate each shape by the vector $\begin{pmatrix} 6 \\ -2 \end{pmatrix}$.

a)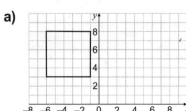

b)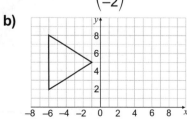

3 Copy these diagrams and translate each shape by the vector $\begin{pmatrix} -8 \\ -1 \end{pmatrix}$.

a)

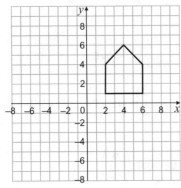

b)

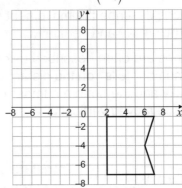

4 Copy this diagram. Translate shape E by the following vectors and label each translated shape.

a) $\begin{pmatrix} 3 \\ 4 \end{pmatrix}$ to give shape A

b) $\begin{pmatrix} -8 \\ 3 \end{pmatrix}$ to give shape B

c) $\begin{pmatrix} 2 \\ -9 \end{pmatrix}$ to give shape C

d) $\begin{pmatrix} -8 \\ -9 \end{pmatrix}$ to give shape D

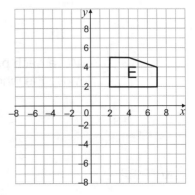

Example 2 Describe the translation that moves shape A onto shape B. Give your answer as a vector.

1. Pick a point on shape A and find the matching point on shape B.

2. Count how many squares horizontally and vertically the point has moved.

3. Write the translation as a vector.

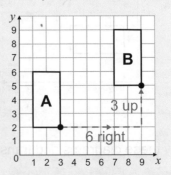

The shape has moved 6 squares right and 3 squares up so

the translation is described by the vector $\begin{pmatrix} 6 \\ 3 \end{pmatrix}$.

5 For each of these diagrams, give the translation vector that moves shape A onto shape B.

a)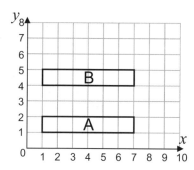

b)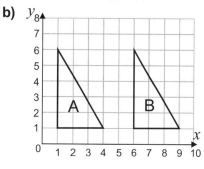

6 Use this diagram to give the vector that translates:

a) shape P onto shape Q

b) shape R onto shape S

c) shape T onto shape U

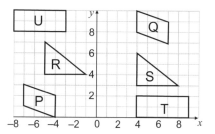

7 Use this diagram to give the translation vector that moves:

a) shape A onto shape B

b) shape B onto shape A

c) Compare your answers for **a)** and **b)**. What do you notice?

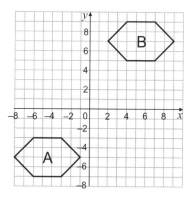

Investigate — Combinations of Transformations

a) Give a single transformation that moves shape A onto shape B. Is this the only one?

b) Give two transformations which combine to move shape A onto shape B. E.g. a reflection in the x-axis and then a reflection in the y-axis.

c) How many different combinations of transformations can you find to move shape A onto shape B?

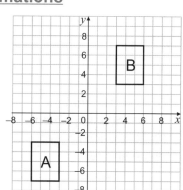

16.4 Enlargement

When an object is enlarged, its size changes but its shape stays the same.
Two objects that are the same shape but different sizes are <u>similar</u>.

<u>Enlargements</u> are described using
scale factors and centre of enlargements.

1) The <u>scale factor</u> tells you how much the lengths of the sides change.

2) The <u>centre of enlargement</u> tells you where the enlargement is measured from.

Example 1   **Enlarge this triangle by scale factor 3.**

1. Find the length of the sides for the shape you're enlarging.

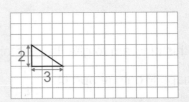

2. Multiply each side length by the scale factor to find the side lengths of the new shape.

The enlarged triangle will have:
- a base length of 3 × 3 = 9 squares
- a height of 2 × 3 = 6 squares.

3. Draw the enlarged shape using the dimensions you've found.

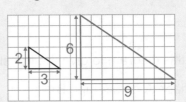

Example 2   **Enlarge this rectangle by scale factor 2 with centre of enlargement (0, 0).**

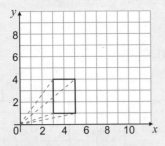
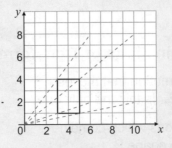
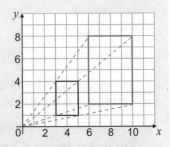

1. Draw a line from the centre of enlargement (0, 0) to each corner of the shape.

2. The scale factor is 2, so extend each line until it is 2 times as long as before.

3. Join up the ends of the extended lines to draw the enlarged shape.

Exercise 1

1 Copy these diagrams.
Enlarge each shape anywhere on the grid by the scale factor given.

a) scale factor 2

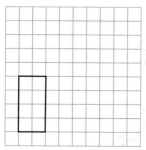

b) scale factor 3

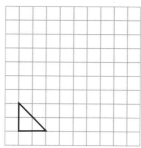

2 Copy these diagrams.
Enlarge each shape by the scale factor given, with centre of enlargement (0, 0).

a) scale factor 2

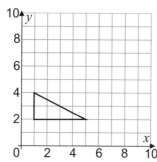

b) scale factor 3

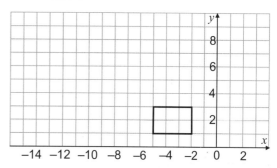

3 Copy these diagrams.
Enlarge all the shapes by the scale factor given, with centre of enlargement (0, 0).

a) scale factor 3

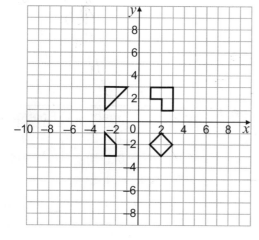

b) scale factor 2

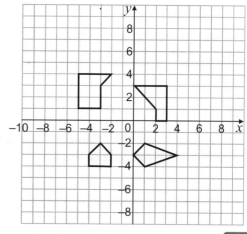

4 Copy these diagrams.
Enlarge each shape by scale factor 2 with centre of enlargement (1, 1).

a)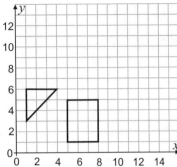

b)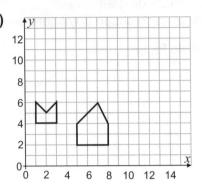

5 Copy these diagrams. Enlarge each shape by scale factor 3 with centre of enlargement P.

a)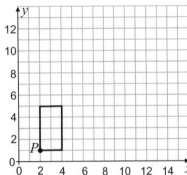

b)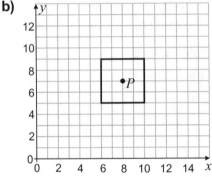

6 Copy this diagram.

a) Enlarge shape A by scale factor 2 with centre of enlargement (8, 2). Label this shape B.

b) Enlarge shape A by scale factor 2 with centre of enlargement (6, −6). Label this shape C.

c) Enlarge shape A by scale factor 3 with centre of enlargement (−1, −4). Label this shape D.

7 The square $ABCD$ is enlarged onto the square $A_1B_1C_1D_1$.

a) Copy and complete this table showing the coordinates of the two squares.

b) Use your table to find the scale factor and centre of enlargement.

Shape	Enlarged shape
$A(1, 2)$	$A_1(1, 6)$
$B(1, 5)$	$B_1(1, 15)$
$C(4, 5)$	$C_1(....., ...)$
$D(....., ...)$	$D_1(....., ...)$

Section 17 — Probability

17.1 The Probability Scale

Probability is about how likely it is that an event will happen.

The probability will be somewhere between impossible and certain.

You can put probabilities on a scale like this:

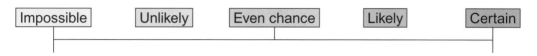

All probabilities can be written as a number between 0 (impossible) and 1 (certain).

So, using fractions, the probability scale looks like this:

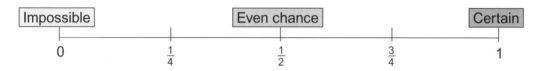

You can also write probabilities as decimals or percentages:

e.g. $\frac{1}{2}$, 0.5 and 50% are all different ways of writing 'even chance'.

Example 1   I spin a fair, six-sided spinner numbered 1-6.
This scale shows the probability of four possible events.
Match each description to the correct event.

The spinner lands on an even number.

There is an equal chance of getting an even or odd number.   This describes Event B.

The spinner lands on a number that is 4 or less.

Four out of six numbers are 4 or less, so this is fairly likely.   This describes Event C.

The spinner lands on a number between 1 and 6.

All the numbers are between 1 and 6, so this is certain.   This describes Event D.

The spinner lands on 6.

There's one 6 out of six numbers so this is quite unlikely.   This describes Event A.

Exercise 1

1   A card is picked at random from a shuffled pack of 52 playing cards.

This probability scale shows the probability of four possible events.
Match each description to the correct event.

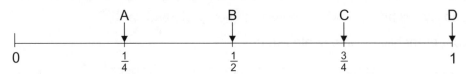

a) Picking either a red card or a black card.   **b)** Picking a card which is a club.

c) Picking a black card.   **d)** Picking a card which isn't a diamond.

2   This probability scale shows the probability of four events — A, B, C and D.
Match each description to the correct event.

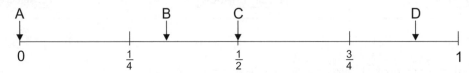

a) The next person to be born in this country being a boy.

b) Tossing a coin and getting neither heads nor tails.

c) Rolling a 1 or a 2 on a fair six-sided dice.

d) Getting green when you spin a fair spinner with 9 green sections and one red section.

3   Draw a probability scale from 0 to 1. Mark on the probability of these events:

a) Rolling a fair, eight-sided dice and getting a 1, 2 or 3.

b) Rolling a fair, four-sided dice and getting a 4 or less.

c) Tossing a coin and getting heads.

4   **a)** Match each letter on this scale to the correct probability.

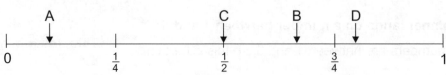

i) 0.5   **ii)** 10%   **iii)** $\frac{2}{3}$ **iv)** 0.8

b) Suggest an event for each of A - D.

17.2 Probability Experiments

Estimating Probabilities

You can estimate probabilities using the results of an experiment or what you know has already happened. Your estimate is called an experimental probability (or a relative frequency). Work out experimental probability using this formula:

$$\text{Experimental probability} = \frac{\text{Number of times the result has happened}}{\text{Number of times the experiment has been carried out}}$$

Example 1

A biased dice is rolled 100 times. The results are in the table.

Score	1	2	3	4	5	6
Frequency	14	13	26	23	13	11

Estimate the probability of rolling a 4 with this dice.

1. Find the number of times 4 was rolled.   4 was rolled 23 times.

2. Divide by the total number of rolls.   So probability = $\dfrac{23}{100}$

($\dfrac{23}{100}$ is equivalent to **23%** or **0.23**.)

Exercise 1

1   Tim wants to estimate the probability that a drawing pin lands with its point up when it's dropped. He drops the pin 50 times. It lands with its point up 17 times. Estimate the probability, as a percentage, that the drawing pin lands:

   a) with its point up   **b)** with its point down.

2   A spinner with four numbered sections is spun 100 times. The results are shown in the table.

   Find the relative frequency of each number. Give your answers as decimals.

Number	1	2	3	4
Frequency	49	34	8	9

3   Abigail rolls a dice and records the number that it lands on each time. Her results are shown in the table.

Number	1	2	3	4	5	6
Frequency	26	21	18	31	19	15

Find the relative frequency of each number. Give your answers as fractions.

Expected Frequency

You can <u>estimate</u> the number of times an event will happen by working out its <u>expected frequency</u>.

Expected frequency of an event = probability of the event × number of trials

Here, '<u>trial</u>' just means an action that could lead to the event happening — for example, a toss of a coin or a roll of a dice.

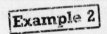 **Example 2** | **The probability that a biased dice lands on 6 is 0.4. How many times would you expect to roll a 6 if you rolled the dice 40 times?**

Multiply the probability of rolling a 6 by the number of rolls. $0.4 \times 40 = \textbf{16}$

Exercise 2

1 The probability that a biased dice lands on 5 is 0.6.
How many times would you expect the dice to land on 5 if it's rolled:

a) 10 times?   **b)** 60 times?   **c)** 100 times?   **d)** 1000 times?

2 A fair, six-sided dice is rolled 180 times. How many times would you expect to roll:

a) a 2?   **b)** a 5?   **c)** an odd number?   **d)** higher than 2?

3 This spinner has 3 equal sections.
How many times would you expect to spin 'penguin' in:

a) 90 spins?   **b)** 150 spins?   **c)** 540 spins?

4 70% of the people who buy bread from a bakery buy brown bread. If 30 people buy bread from the bakery tomorrow, how many of them would you expect to buy brown bread?

Fair or Biased?

Things like dice are <u>fair</u> if they have the same chance of landing on each side, otherwise we say they're <u>biased</u>. You can do an experiment to check for bias.

If you rolled a <u>fair</u> six-sided dice 100 times, you'd expect it to land on 6 about $\frac{1}{6}$ of the time (about 17 times). But if $\frac{1}{2}$ of the rolls (50) were 6, you'd say the dice was <u>biased</u>.

Example 3   Naveena thinks her dice is biased. She rolls it 50 times and records the results shown in the table.

Work out the relative frequencies of each score.

Score	1	2	3	4	5	6
Frequency	10	2	8	8	12	10

1. For each score, work out frequency ÷ total number of rolls.

2. Write the probabilities as decimals so they're easier to compare.

1: $\dfrac{10}{50} = 0.2$ 4: $\dfrac{8}{50} = 0.16$

2: $\dfrac{2}{50} = 0.04$ 5: $\dfrac{12}{50} = 0.24$

3: $\dfrac{8}{50} = 0.16$ 6: $\dfrac{10}{50} = 0.2$

Do you think the dice is fair or biased? Explain your answer.

Compare the relative frequencies to the theoretical probability of $\dfrac{1}{6} = 0.17$ for each score.

The relative frequency of a score of 2 is very different from the theoretical probability, so the experiment suggests that the dice is **biased**.

Exercise 3

1   This table shows the results when a four-sided dice is rolled 100 times.

    a) Work out the relative frequencies of the four numbers as decimals.

    b) Write down the theoretical probability of getting each of the numbers, assuming the dice is fair.

Number	1	2	3	4
Frequency	25	19	20	36

    c) Explain whether you think the dice is fair or biased.

2   An eight-sided dice numbered 1-8 is rolled 160 times. The number 2 comes up 36 times.

    a) How many times would you expect 2 to come up in 160 rolls if the dice is fair?

    b) Use your answer to part **a)** to explain whether you think the dice is fair or biased.

Investigate — Probability Experiments

a) Toss a coin 20 times and record all the outcomes. Work out the experimental probabilities of it landing on heads and tails.

b) Now toss the coin another 30 times and repeat the calculations for all 50 outcomes.

c) Try tossing the coin more and more times and repeating the calculations. What happens to the probability of the coin landing on heads the more times you toss it?

17.3 Theoretical Probabilities

Calculating Probabilities

You can work out the probability of an event happening using this formula:

$$\text{Probability of an event} = \frac{\text{Number of ways event can happen}}{\text{Total number of possible outcomes}}$$

You can only use this formula if each possible outcome is equally likely to happen —
e.g. rolling a dice or picking a ball at random from a bag containing balls of the same size.

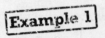 **Example 1** | A bag contains 5 yellow counters, 6 black counters and 4 white counters. One counter is picked at random. What is the probability that the counter is black?

1. Find the total number of possible outcomes.

   Total number of counters = 5 + 6 + 4 = 15

2. Find the number of ways the event 'pick black' can happen.

   There are 6 black counters

3. Put the numbers into the formula and simplify.

   $$\text{Probability of picking black} = \frac{\text{number of ways of picking black}}{\text{total number of counters}}$$

   $$= \frac{6}{15} = \frac{2}{5}$$

Exercise 1

For this exercise, give your answers as fractions in their simplest form, unless told otherwise.

1   A peg is picked at random from a bag containing 3 red pegs, 6 blue pegs and 1 green peg.

   a) What is the total number of possible outcomes?

   b) How many ways can the event 'picking blue' happen?

   c) Find the probability that a peg picked at random will be blue.

2   a) What is the total number of possible outcomes on this fair spinner?

   b) What is the probability of spinning:

   i) a 3?   ii) a 2?   iii) an even number?

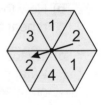

3 A box of chocolates contains 2 milk chocolates, 7 plain chocolates and 3 white chocolates. Find the probability that a chocolate picked at random will be a white chocolate. Give your answer as a fraction, a decimal and a percentage.

4 A fair, six-sided dice is rolled once.

a) Find the probability of rolling a 1.

b) How many ways can the event 'rolling a number greater than 3' happen?

c) Find the probability of rolling a number greater than 3.

5 A standard pack of playing cards is shuffled and one card is selected at random. Find the probability of selecting:

a) a king   **b)** a black card   **c)** a diamond

6 A box contains ten cards numbered 1-10. One card is picked without looking. Find the probability, as a decimal, that the card is:

a) a 2

b) a 4 or 6

c) a prime number

d) a number greater than 10

e) a multiple of 3

7 A school sells 400 raffle tickets for a raffle where the first prize is a hamper. Priya buys 5 tickets. Find the probability that she wins the hamper as a percentage.

8 Karl has six cards, numbered between 1 and 9. Four of his cards are:

| 1 | 4 | 2 | 3 |

If he picks one of his six cards at random, the probability that he picks an even number is $\frac{1}{2}$ and the probability that he picks a 2 is $\frac{1}{3}$.

Write down the possible numbers that could be on the other two cards.

For any event, there are only two possibilities — it either happens or doesn't happen.

So the probability of an event happening and the probability of the same event not happening always add up to 1. This means that:

Probability an event doesn't happen = 1 – (Probability the same event does happen)

Example 2 **The probability that Gemma passes her Maths test is 0.8.**
Find the probability that she doesn't pass her Maths test.

Gemma either passes or doesn't pass her Maths test, so:

Probability Gemma doesn't pass = 1 – (Probability Gemma does pass)
= 1 – 0.8
= **0.2**

Exercise 2

1 Ben travels to work by train each day.

a) The probability that he catches his train is 0.9.
What is the probability that he does not catch his train?

b) The probability that the train is late is 0.2. Find the probability that the train is not late.

2 The probability that a badminton player wins his game is 85%.
Find the probability that he doesn't win his game.

3 The probability that it will rain today is 0.66. What is the probability that it won't rain today?

4 There are 100 pupils in Year 9. 65 pupils are girls and 40 pupils wear glasses.
Giving your answers as decimals, find the probability that a randomly selected pupil:

a) is a boy **b)** doesn't wear glasses

5 A bag contains 7 red balls, 2 green balls, 3 yellow balls and 8 blue balls.
Find the probability, as a fraction, that a ball picked at random is:

a) not red **b)** not yellow **c)** not blue or yellow

6 A bag contains blue, gold and silver counters. The probability of picking a counter that is not blue is 0.6. The probability of picking a counter that is not silver is 0.8. Work out how many counters of each colour there are, given that there are 10 in total.

Sample Spaces

A <u>sample space diagram</u> can be used to list all the possible <u>outcomes</u> when two <u>trials</u> are combined. This is just a table with the outcomes of one trial down the side and the outcomes of the second trial along the top.

The sample space diagram for tossing two coins looks like this:

		Second coin	
		Heads	Tails
First coin	Heads	HH	HT
	Tails	TH	TT

Example 3 **Two fair spinners are spun and their scores added together. Spinner A is divided into three sections numbered 1-3 and spinner B is divided into three sections numbered 4-6.**

a) Draw a sample space diagram to show all the possible outcomes.

1. Draw a table with the outcomes from spinner A down the side and the outcomes from spinner B along the top.

2. Fill in each box by adding together the numbers from the left-hand column and the top row.

		Spinner B		
		4	5	6
Spinner A	1	5	6	7
	2	6	7	8
	3	7	8	9

b) Find the total number of possible outcomes.

Count the number of boxes in the table.   There are **9** possible outcomes.

Exercise 3

1   A coin is tossed and a fair four-sided spinner numbered 1-4 is spun.
Copy and complete the sample space diagram to show all the possible outcomes.

		Spinner			
		1	2	3	4
Coin	Heads	H1		H3	
	Tails				T4

2   A spinner with three equal sections of red, orange and green is spun twice.
Copy and complete the sample space diagram to show all the possible outcomes.

	Red	Orange	Green
Red			RG
Orange	OR		
Green			

3 Bags A and B each contain four numbered counters. A counter is taken from each bag and the numbers added together.

a) Copy and complete the sample space diagram to show all the possible outcomes.

b) Find the total number of possible outcomes.

		4	6	8
1	3			
			8	
				11
4		8		

4 Two fair six-sided dice are rolled and the scores multiplied.

a) Copy and complete the sample space diagram to show all the possible outcomes.

b) Find the total number of possible outcomes.

	1	2	3	4	5	6
1						
2			6			
3						
4						
5		10			25	
6						

Example 4

The sample space diagram shows all the possible outcomes of spinning two fair, three-sided spinners numbered 1-3 and adding the scores. Find the probability of scoring a total of:

	1	2	3
1	2	3	4
2	3	4	5
3	4	5	6

a) 3

1. There are 9 possible outcomes in total, and two of these are 3.

   Total number of possible outcomes = 9
   Number of ways of scoring 3 = 2

2. Work out the probability using the formula.

   $$\text{Probability} = \frac{\text{number of ways of scoring 3}}{\text{total number of outcomes}}$$

   $$= \frac{2}{9}$$

b) 5 or more

1. There are three outcomes that are 5 or more.

   Number of ways of scoring 5 or more = 3

2. Again, use the formula.

   $$\text{Probability} = \frac{\text{number of ways of scoring 5 or more}}{\text{total number of outcomes}}$$

   $$= \frac{3}{9} = \frac{1}{3}$$

Exercise 4

1 The sample space diagram shows all the possible outcomes when a fair four-sided spinner numbered 1-4 and a fair three-sided spinner numbered 1-3 are spun and the scores added together. Find the probability that the total score is:

	1	2	3
1	2	3	4
2	3	4	5
3	4	5	6
4	5	6	7

a) 4   **b)** 6 or more   **c)** an odd number

2 A coin is tossed and a fair six-sided dice is rolled.

a) Draw a sample space diagram to show all the possible outcomes.

b) Find the probability of getting:

    i) a 5 and heads   **ii)** a number less than 3 and tails

3 Two fair, six-sided dice are rolled and their scores added together.

a) Draw a sample space diagram to show all the possible outcomes.

b) Find the probability of scoring a total of:

    i) 7   **ii)** 11 or more   **iii)** less than 4

c) Find the most and least likely total scores.

4 Callum and Kerry play a game by rolling a red dice and a blue dice.

> The red dice is numbered 1, 2, 4, 4, 6 and 6.
> The blue dice is numbered 1, 2, 3, 4, 4 and 6.

Callum wins if the number on the red dice is bigger than the number on the blue dice, otherwise Kerry wins. Work out who is more likely to win the game and explain your answer. Use a sample space diagram if you need to.

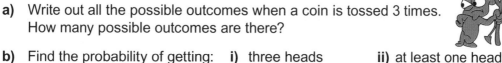

Investigate — Listing Outcomes

a) Write out all the possible outcomes when a coin is tossed 3 times. How many possible outcomes are there?

b) Find the probability of getting: **i)** three heads   **ii)** at least one head

c) Investigate the total number of possible outcomes when a coin is tossed four times. Can you find a rule for finding the number of possible outcomes for any number of coin tosses?

17.4 Sets

Sets

A set is a collection of items or numbers. Sets are shown by curly brackets { }. The things in a set are called elements. Here are some examples of sets:

A = {odd numbers}, B = {days of the week}, C = {apples, pears, oranges}, D = {1, 2, 3, 4}

n(A) means 'the number of elements in set A'.

ξ is the universal set — the group of things that the elements of a set are selected from.

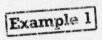 **Example 1** ξ = {whole numbers from 1-20}, A = {even numbers} and B = {prime numbers}. List the elements of each set.

1. For the universal set, just list all the numbers from 1 to 20.

   ξ = {1, 2, 3, 4, 5, 6, 7, 8, 9, 10, 11, 12, 13, 14, 15, 16, 17, 18, 19, 20}

2. Set A is the even numbers, but they must be taken from the universal set, so it's just the even numbers up to 20.

   A = {2, 4, 6, 8, 10, 12, 14, 16, 18, 20}

3. Similarly, set B is prime numbers up to 20.

   B = {2, 3, 5, 7, 11, 13, 17, 19}

Exercise 1

1 For each of the following sets: **i)** list the elements of the set
   ii) find n(set).

   a) A = {colours of the rainbow}   **b)** B = {days of the weekend}

   c) C = {standard UK coins}   **d)** D = {months of the year that start with J}

2 For each of the following sets: **i)** list the elements of the set
   ii) find n(set).

   a) A = {factors of 20}   **b)** B = {multiples of 3 up to 30}

   c) C = {square numbers up to 100}   **d)** D = {prime numbers between 20 and 40}

3 List the elements of the following sets, given that ξ = {whole numbers from 1-10}.

   a) A = {odd numbers}   **b)** B = {factors of 8}

   c) C = {prime numbers}   **d)** D = {multiples of 3}

4   List the elements of the following sets, given that ξ = {whole numbers from 30-50}.

   a) A = {square numbers}

   b) B = {multiples of 7}

   c) C = {factors of 30}

   d) D = {prime numbers}

5   ξ = {whole numbers from 1-20}, A = {1, 2, 3, 4, 6, 12}, B = {6, 12, 18} and C = {1}.
Write down possible descriptions of each of sets A, B and C.

6   ξ = {whole numbers from 1-25}, A = {even numbers} and B = {factors of 18}.

   a) Write out the elements of set A.

   b) Write out the elements of set B.

   c) C = {elements of either A or B}. Write out the elements of set C and find n(C).

   d) D = {elements of both A and B}. Write out the elements of set D and find n(D).

Venn Diagrams

Venn diagrams are used to display sets and to show when they overlap.

Each set is represented by a circle, and the universal set is a rectangle that goes round the outside of the circles.

If there are elements that belong to more than one set, the circles overlap and these elements go in the overlap, which is called the intersection.

Venn diagrams can either show the actual elements, or just the number of elements that belong in each bit of the diagram.

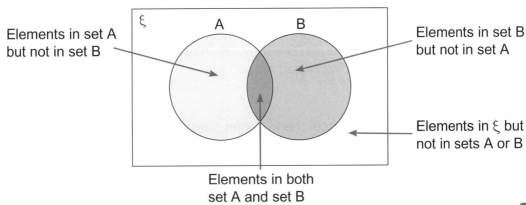

Elements in set A but not in set B

Elements in set B but not in set A

Elements in ξ but not in sets A or B

Elements in both set A and set B

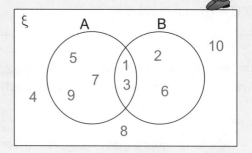

Example 2 ξ = {whole numbers from 1-10}, A = {odd numbers}
and B = {factors of 6}.
Show this information on a Venn diagram.

1. Write out sets A and B:
   A = {1, 3, 5, 7, 9}
   B = {1, 2, 3, 6}

2. 1 and 3 are in both sets, so they go
   in the overlap. The other elements
   of A and B go in the circles for A
   and B, but not in the overlap.

3. The elements of ξ that aren't in A
   or B go outside the circles
   (but inside the rectangle).

Exercise 2

1 Copy and complete the Venn diagram
    to show the following sets:
    ξ = {whole numbers from 1-12}
    A = {1, 3, 5, 7, 9}
    B = {1, 2, 3, 4, 6, 12}

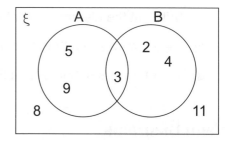

2 ξ = {a standard pack of playing cards}, A = {red cards} and B = {kings}.
    On a copy of the Venn diagram,

   a) write an S to show where the 10 of spades would go

   b) write an K to show where the king of hearts would go

   c) write an Q to show where the queen of diamonds
       would go

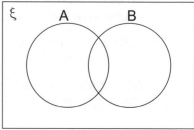

3 ξ = {Adam, Alice, Amy, Becky, Ben, Claire, Dave, Emma, Fiona, Greg},
    A = {names beginning with A} and B = {boys' names}.
    Show this information on a Venn diagram.

4 Use the Venn diagram to answer the following questions.

   a) Which elements appear in either set A or set B?

   b) Which elements appear in both set A and set B?

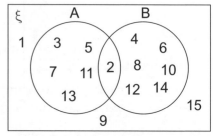

5   For ξ = {whole numbers from 1-12}, draw Venn diagrams to show the following sets:

  a) A = {2, 3, 4, 5}   B = {4, 8, 12}

  b) A = {1, 2, 3, 4, 5, 6}   B = {2, 4, 6, 8, 10, 12}

  c) A = {3, 6, 9, 12}   B = {8, 9, 10, 11, 12}

6   For ξ = {whole numbers from 1-15}, draw Venn diagrams to show the following sets:

  a) A = {odd numbers}   B = {multiples of 5}

  b) A = {factors of 8}   B = {factors of 10}

  c) A = {multiples of 3}   B = {multiples of 4}

7   ξ = {whole numbers from 1-25}, A = {even numbers} and B = {square numbers}.
Draw a Venn diagram to show the **number** of elements in each set.

8   ξ = {a standard pack of playing cards}, A = {diamonds} and B = {queens}.

  a) Draw a Venn diagram showing the **number** of elements in each set.

  b) Use your Venn diagram to answer the following questions.
  How many elements are there in:

  i) set A?   **ii)** either set A or set B?   **iii)** both set A and set B?

  iv) What is the probability that a randomly selected card will be the queen of diamonds?

  v) What is the probability that a randomly selected card
  will be either a diamond or a queen?

Investigate — Venn Diagrams

  ξ = {numbers from 1-15}, A = {odd numbers},
  B = {multiples of 3} and C = {square numbers}.

  a) Draw a Venn diagram to show sets A, B and C. You'll need three circles.

  b) Which elements go in the overlap of: **i)** A and B?   **ii)** A and C?

                                                   iii) B and C?   **iv)** A, B and C?

  c) Try and come up with three different sets where not all of the circles overlap.
  How many different Venn diagrams with three circles that overlap in different
  ways can you find?

Section 18 — Statistics

18.1 Bar Charts and Pictograms

Bar Charts

Bar charts (and bar-line charts) show how many items fall into different categories.
The number in each category is the frequency.

Example 1 **Will asked everyone in his class how they get to school.
The bar chart shows the results.**

a) What was the most popular transport?

Look for the tallest bar.   **Bus** was the most popular.

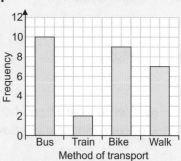

b) How many people did Will ask?

Add together the frequencies $10 + 2 + 9 + 7$
for each type of transport. $= 28$

c) What percentage of people walk to school?

1. Look at the 'Walk' bar. 7 people out of the total of 28 said 'walk'. Write this as a fraction.

$\dfrac{7}{28}$ of people walk

2. Divide the top number by the bottom number and multiply by 100.

$(7 \div 28) \times 100 = \mathbf{25\%}$

Exercise 1

1   Chris records how many cars are in a 4-space car park over 74 days. His results are in the frequency table. Copy the bar-line chart and use the frequency table to complete it.

Cars	Frequency
0	18
1	14
2	15
3	8
4	19

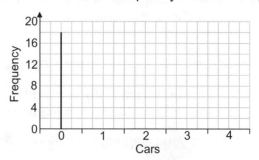

2   A cinema recorded the snacks that were bought one evening.
    The results are in the frequency table. Draw a bar chart to show this information.

Snack	Popcorn	Hotdog	Crisps	Chocolate	Fudge
Frequency	17	9	13	20	6

A dual bar chart shows the same categories for two different people or things.

Example 2 **Sophie and Dave recorded how many cups of tea they drank at work each day for a week. Their results are in the table.**

Day	Mon	Tues	Wed	Thur	Fri
Cups drunk by Dave	3	5	4	7	6
Cups drunk by Sophie	4	0	5	6	5

a) Draw a dual bar chart to show this data.

1. Each day will have two bars — one for Dave and one for Sophie.

2. Use different colours or shades for Dave and Sophie's bars, and include a key to show which is which.

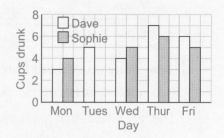

b) What fraction of the total cups of tea does Dave drink? Give your answer in its simplest form.

1. Calculate the total cups drunk by Dave and the total cups of tea drunk altogether.

$$3 + 5 + 4 + 7 + 6 = 25$$
$$25 + 4 + 5 + 6 + 5 = 45$$

2. Write these numbers as a fraction, with Dave's total as the numerator. Simplify the fraction as much as possible.

$$\frac{25}{45} = \frac{5}{9}$$

3 This dual bar chart shows the number of miles cycled by Tim and Stuart on four days.

a) Who cycled more miles on Friday?

b) How many miles did Tim cycle on Sunday?

c) How many more miles did Stuart cycle than Tim on Saturday?

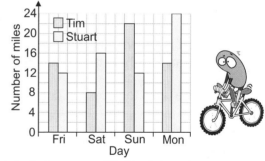

d) Tim claims that he cycled the most miles in total. Is he correct? Explain your answer.

4 The table shows the test scores of the boys and girls in a class.

Marks	0-10	11-20	21-30	31-40	41-50
Girls	0	4	6	7	8
Boys	1	2	9	7	6

a) Draw a dual bar chart to show this information. Use different coloured bars for 'boys' and 'girls'.

b) What percentage of boys scored 21 marks or more?

c) What does the graph tell you about the boys' scores compared with the girls'?

Pictograms

Pictograms show frequency using symbols or pictures instead of bars.
They always have a key to tell you what each symbol represents.

Example 3 **The pictogram shows how many apples Pete ate in 2 weeks.**

Week 1	🍎🍎🍎🍎🍎
Week 2	🍎🍎🍎

Key: 🍎 = 2 apples

a) How many apples did Pete eat in Week 1?

1. Count the symbols in the row for Week 1.   5.5 apple symbols

2. The key shows that each symbol represents 2 apples,
   so use this to find how many he ate.   5.5 × 2 = **11 apples**

b) Pete ate 7 apples in Week 3. Add this to a new row on the pictogram.

1. Work out how many symbols you   7 ÷ 2 = 3.5
   need to draw.
                                     So 3.5 symbols are needed.

2. Add a new row to the pictogram.

Week 3	🍎🍎🍎

Exercise 2

1   This table shows how many t-shirts
Ghassan bought in three months.

Month	Jan	Feb	Mar
Number of t-shirts	8	7	4

Use the table to copy and complete the pictogram.

Jan	
Feb	
Mar	

Key:  = 2 t-shirts

2   The number of new members in a club were recorded over four months.
The results are in this frequency table.

Month	September	October	November	December
Number of members	10	13	12	7

Draw a pictogram to show the results. Represent 2 club members using the symbol: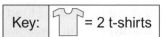

3 A class was asked to name their favourite sport. 12 people said tennis, 18 people said football, 9 people said rugby and 3 people said athletics. Copy and complete the pictogram to show this information.

Tennis	⊗ ⊗
Football	
Rugby	
Athletics	

Key: | ⊗ = 6 people |

4 The local cinema asked a group of people how many films they had watched in the last month. The results are shown in this pictogram.

0	◯
1	◯◯◯◯◯◯◖
2	◯◯◯
3	◯◯◯◯◯
4	◯◯◯
5	◯◯
Over 5	◖

Key: | ◯ = 10 people |

a) How many people had watched 1 film?

b) How many had watched 3 films or fewer?

c) How many had watched 4 films or more?

d) What fraction of the people had watched 3 films?

5 This bar chart shows the number of bags of different colours that Jess owns.

a) Draw a pictogram to represent this data. Use the symbol 👜 to represent 2 bags.

b) How many bags does Jess own in total?

c) How many of her bags are black or green?

d) What percentage of her bags are black?

6 This pictogram shows the number of parcels that were delivered to the people in a street one month.

a) Ralph received 2 more parcels than Paulo. Use this information to complete the key.

Key: ⊞ = ... parcels

b) Who received 8 parcels fewer than Jacob?

c) Who received $\frac{1}{5}$ of the total parcels?

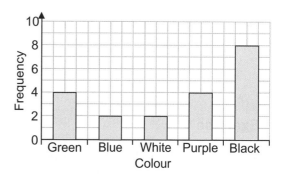

Sasha	⊞
Jacob	⊞ ⊞ ⊞ ▫
Ralph	⊞ ⊞
Josie	⊞ ▫
Helen	⊞
Paulo	⊞ ⬒

d) What percentage of the parcels went to either Sasha or Helen?

18.2 Pie Charts

Interpreting Pie Charts

In a pie chart, the size of the angle of each sector represents frequency.

Example 1 A student carries out a survey to find out which sport 120 students prefer to play. This pie chart shows the results.

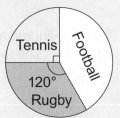

a) What is the most popular sport?

The most popular sport is the one with the biggest angle on the pie chart.

Football

b) What fraction of students prefer tennis?

1. Find the angle that represents tennis.   The angle for 'Tennis' is 90°

2. Write a fraction with this angle as the top and 360° as the bottom, then simplify.

Fraction who prefer tennis $= \dfrac{90°}{360°} = \dfrac{1}{4}$

c) How many students prefer rugby?

1. Find the fraction who prefer rugby using the angle, as before.

Fraction who prefer rugby $= \dfrac{120°}{360°} = \dfrac{1}{3}$

2. Then multiply this fraction by the total number of students.

$\dfrac{1}{3} \times 120 = (1 \times 120) \div 3 = \mathbf{40\ students}$

Exercise 1

1 This pie chart shows the proportions of students in a class who go to different after-school clubs.

What is the most popular after-school club?

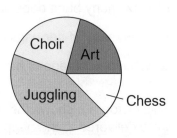

2 This pie chart shows the results of a survey about people's favourite ice cream flavour.

a) What is the least popular flavour?

b) Which flavour is more popular — vanilla or strawberry?

c) What fraction of people prefer mint?

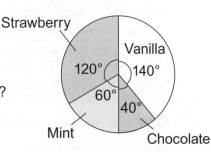

3 This pie chart shows the proportions of Ryan's class that have different pets. No one in his class has more than one pet.

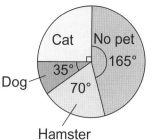

a) What is the most common pet?

b) Which pet is half as common as a hamster?

c) What fraction of the class doesn't have a pet? Give your answer in its simplest form.

d) Can you tell from the pie chart how many people in Ryan's class have a cat? Explain your answer.

4 Heather asks 600 people about their favourite sandwich filling. This pie chart shows the results.

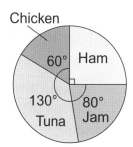

a) Which was the most popular sandwich filling?

b) What percentage of the people said ham was their favourite sandwich filling?

c) How many people said chicken was their favourite?

5 Katie asks 720 people what their favourite type of music is. She draws a pie chart of her results.

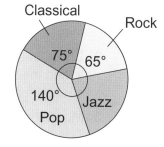

a) What fraction of the people picked classical music?

b) How many of the people chose pop music?

c) How many of them chose jazz music?

6 Marco asks 180 people to choose their favourite type of cake. The results are shown in this pie chart.

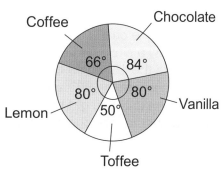

a) What fraction of people chose coffee or chocolate cake as their favourite?

b) How many people chose lemon or vanilla cake as their favourite?

c) How many people chose a cake **other than** toffee as their favourite?

7 James carries out a survey in a city. He asks people, "What is your favourite type of restaurant?" and draws a pie chart of his results.

a) 320 people chose Italian. Using this information, work out how many people chose:

   i) Chinese,

   ii) Thai.

b) What percentage of people chose either Mexican or Thai? Give your answer to the nearest whole number.

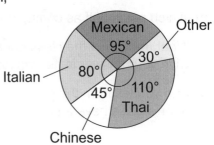

Constructing Pie Charts

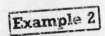 **Jill asks everyone in Year 8 their favourite colour. The frequency table shows her results.**

Colour	Red	Green	Blue	Pink
Frequency	8	16	28	8

Draw a pie chart to show this data.

1. Calculate the total frequency — this is the number of people in Year 8.

Total Frequency = 8 + 16 + 28 + 8
= 60

2. Divide 360° by the total frequency to find the number of degrees needed for each person.

Each person represented by:
360° ÷ 60 = 6°

3. Multiply each frequency by the number of degrees for each person. This tells you the angle you'll need in the pie chart for each colour.

Colour	Red	Green	Blue	Pink
Frequency	8	16	28	8
Angle	8 × 6° = 48°	16 × 6° = 96°	28 × 6° = 168°	8 × 6° = 48°

4. Draw the pie chart:
First draw a circle, then draw a start line from the centre. Measure the 48° angle from here and draw another line. Then measure the 96° angle from this line, and so on until you get back to the start line. Remember to label the sectors on the chart.

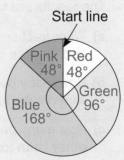

Exercise 2

1 Boris recorded the colours of all the cars at a car show. The results are shown in this frequency table.

Colour	Frequency
Black	6
Blue	18
Red	25
Other	11

    a) Find the total number of cars at the car show.

    b) Find how many degrees represent each car.

    c) Copy and complete this table to find the angle for each colour.

Colour	Frequency	Angle
Black	6	6 × ...... = 36°
Blue	18	18 × ...... = ...
Red	25	
Other	11	

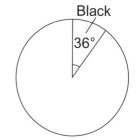

    d) Copy and complete the pie chart to show this data.

2 A library surveyed some of its members to find out their favourite type of book. Their results are shown in this table.

    a) Find the total number of people the library asked.

    b) Find how many degrees represent each person.

    c) Calculate the angle for each type of book.

    d) Draw a pie chart showing the results.

Type of Book	Frequency
Crime	18
Adventure	24
Thriller	22
Sci-fi	26

3 Ollie carried out a survey to find out how many pets the pupils in his year group have.

He recorded his data in this table:

Number of Pets	Frequency
0	46
1	42
2	20
3 or more	12

    a) Find the total frequency.

    b) Calculate the angle for each number of pets.

    c) Draw a pie chart showing the data.

4 Hasan recorded the instruments that students at his school play.
This table shows the results. Draw a pie chart showing the data.

Instrument	Frequency
Flute	17
Piano	16
Recorder	25
Violin	14
Guitar	18

5 Charlotte carried out a survey to find out which country people would prefer to visit.
15 people said America, 25 people said France, 17 people said Greece
and 23 people said Spain. Draw a pie chart showing Charlotte's results.

6 Alec asked 90 people to pick their favourite flowers from a choice of roses, tulips or lilies.
One third of the people said roses. Of the rest, twice as many people said tulips as lilies.
Draw a pie chart showing Alec's results.

Investigate — Misleading Graphs

*Scott surveys 100 people and asks "Do you have a mobile phone —
yes or no?" Only 36 people agree to answer the question.*

a) Look at these two graphs that show Scott's results.

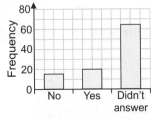 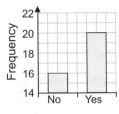

Why could the second graph be misleading?

b) Pie charts can also be misleading. Draw two different pie charts to
show Scott's results. Could either of them be misleading? Why?

c) Can you think of some more ways that someone might draw a graph
or chart so that the information it gives is misleading?

d) Why might people want to draw misleading graphs and charts?

18.3 Scatter Graphs

Correlation

A <u>scatter graph</u> shows two things plotted against each other.

Scatter graphs can be used to show whether two things are related to each other.

If the points on a scatter graph lie close to a straight line, the data shows <u>correlation</u> — the two things are related.

A <u>positive correlation</u> means that as one thing increases the other thing increases too.

A <u>negative correlation</u> means that as one thing increases, the other thing decreases.

If the points are all spread out, the data has <u>no correlation</u> — the two things aren't related.

Example 1 **For each of these scatter graphs, decide if it shows positive, negative or no correlation, and what that correlation means.**

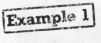
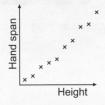

The points lie close to a straight line, and as x increases, so does y.

Positive correlation — people who are taller generally have bigger hands.

The points lie close to a straight line, and as x increases, y decreases.

Negative correlation — when daily rainfall is higher, less suncream is sold.

The points are all spread out — there's no pattern here.

No correlation — there is no relation between someone's height and their test score.

Exercise 1

1 For each of these scatter graphs, say if they show positive, negative or no correlation.

a)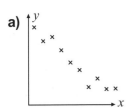

b)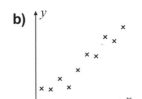

c)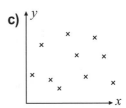

2 For each of these scatter graphs, say if they show positive, negative or no correlation, and explain what that correlation means.

a)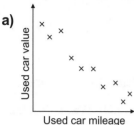

b)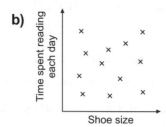

c)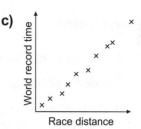

3 What correlation would you expect between each of these pairs of variables? Explain your answers.

a) Shoe size and glove size.

b) Outside temperature and visitors to a theme park.

c) Daily rainfall and sales of newspapers.

d) Score on a maths test and score on a science test.

e) Hours watching TV per evening and hours doing homework per evening.

Plotting Scatter Graphs

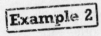 Jeremy wants to know if there is a link between a person's height and their shoe size. He measures the height and shoe size of 8 people, and records the results in the table shown.

Draw a scatter graph to show the data.

Height (cm)	165	159	173	186	176	172	181	169
Shoe Size	6	5	8	10	8	7	9	6

1. Draw a grid with 'Height' on the horizontal (x) axis and 'Shoe Size' on the vertical (y) axis.

2. Plot the values from the table just like you would plot x- and y-coordinates.

3. Don't join up the points on a scatter graph.

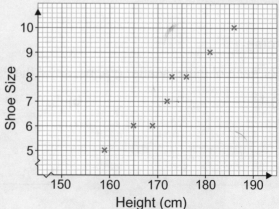

Exercise 2

1 A lemonade stall records the temperature outside and the number of glasses of lemonade sold over a period of 7 days. The results are shown on the scatter graph.

a) What was the highest temperature recorded?

b) What was the lowest number of glasses sold?

c) The lemonade stall needs to sell more than 7 glasses a day to make a profit. On how many days did it make a profit?

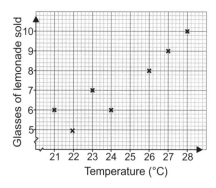

2 A group of youngsters were asked how many baby teeth they still had. The results are shown in the table.

Age (years)	5	6	8	7	9	7	10	6
Baby Teeth	19	18	12	13	6	15	4	20

Copy the grid shown and plot the points from the table.

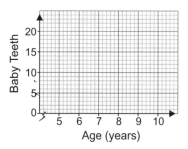

3 This table shows the number of tickets sold each day in the 10 days before the start of a local music festival.

Days Until Festival	1	2	3	4	5	6	7	8	9	10
Number of Tickets Sold	17	18	18	15	16	15	14	15	13	12

a) Copy the grid and plot the points from the table.

b) Does the scatter graph show positive, negative or no correlation?

c) Explain in words what this means.

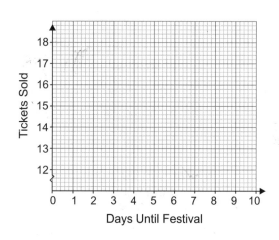

4 For each of these tables:

    i) Plot the data on a scatter graph.

    ii) Describe the correlation, if any, which the graph shows.

    iii) Explain in words what the correlation means.

a)

Depth of snow (inches)	6	4	1	8	3	4	2	9	5
Sledges sold	5	3	2	10	3	5	1	12	7

b)

Supporters at a football match	2500	3500	5000	4500	3000	6000	4000	3500
Number of pies sold	1300	1900	2500	2200	1600	3100	2300	2000

c)

Daily rainfall (mm)	11	15	0	6	2	3	10	8
Bars of chocolate sold	7	20	14	6	8	19	3	17

d)

Height of mountain (m)	400	800	740	1000	660	700	940	500
Temperature at summit (°C)	15.6	11.8	12.4	9.6	13.6	13.0	10.2	14.4

Investigate — Correlation and Cause

a) The scatter graph shows the correlation between the number of shark attacks and ice cream sales. Which of the following statements are true, which are false, and which can you not be sure about?

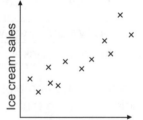

    i) As ice cream sales rise, so do the number of shark attacks.

    ii) An increase in shark attacks causes more people to buy ice creams.

    iii) An increase in ice cream sales causes more shark attacks.

    iv) The chance of a shark attack is lower when ice cream sales are high.

b) Can you think of something that might cause **both** ice cream sales **and** the number of shark attacks to increase?

c) Try to think of other situations where two things show correlation, but neither is caused by the other. E.g. Sales of Christmas puddings and sales of gloves.

Lines of Best Fit

If a <u>scatter graph</u> shows <u>correlation</u>, then you can draw a <u>line of best fit</u>.
This is a straight line which lies as close as possible to as many points as possible.

Example 3 | The scatter graph shows the marks scored by pupils in a maths test and in a science test.

a) **Draw a line of best fit for the data.**

Draw a line that lies as close to the group of points as possible. It doesn't have to actually touch any of the points.

b) **Jimmy scored 34 on his science test, but missed the maths test. Use the scatter graph to predict the score he would have achieved.**

Follow the grid up from 34 on the 'Science' axis until you reach the line of best fit, then follow the grid across to find the mark on the 'Maths' axis.

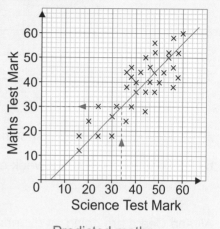

Predicted maths mark for Jimmy = **30**

Exercise 3

1 Which of these diagrams **A-D** shows a correctly-drawn line of best fit for the scatter graph?

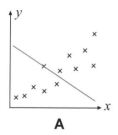

A

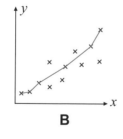

B

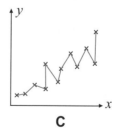

C

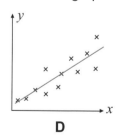

D

2 Decide if each of the following is a well-drawn line of best fit. Explain your answers.

a)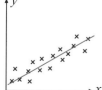

b)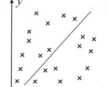

c)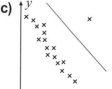

3 In an experiment, people were asked how many hours a week they spent exercising, and their BMI (body mass index) was recorded. The results are shown on the scatter graph. A line of best fit has been drawn.

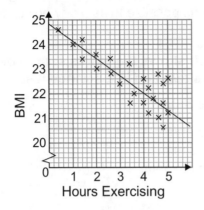

a) Describe the correlation shown by the scatter graph.

b) Frank spends 4 hours a week exercising. Use the line of best fit to predict his BMI.

4 Ali and Ceara are doing an experiment to find out how long different potatoes take to bake perfectly. Their results are shown in this table:

Potato weight (g)	150	180	250	200	330	280	220
Cooking time (min)	30	40	70	45	110	85	55

a) Copy this grid and use it to plot the points from the table:

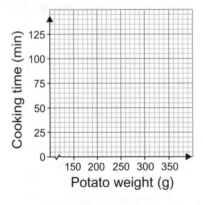

b) Draw a line of best fit for the data.

c) Use your line of best fit to estimate how long a 300 g potato will take to bake.

18.4 Averages and Range

Mode and Range

An average is a single number that represents a whole load of data.
The mode (or modal value) is a type of average. It is the most common value.
Sometimes a data set will have more than one mode, or no mode at all.

The range is a measure of how spread out a set of data is — it is the difference between the highest and lowest numbers in a list. To find the range you subtract the lowest value from the highest value.

Example 1 | Harry's scores in his last eight maths tests are:
79%   84%   75%   79%   71%   91%   89% 93%

a) What is his modal score?

1. It helps to put the numbers in order first.   71%   75%   79%   79%
                                               84%   89%   91%   93%

2. The mode is the most common score.   Mode = **79%**

b) What is the range of his scores?

Subtract the lowest number (71%) from the   Range = 93% − 71% = **22%**
highest number (93%) to find the range.

Exercise 1

1 Which number is the most common number in this list? 8 9 7 7 6 8 7

2 **a)** Put these numbers in order, from lowest to highest: 5 2 3 8 1 2

   b) Find the range of the list of numbers.

3 Find the mode and range for this list of numbers: 6 2 4 0 6 1

4 For each of these lists of numbers, find: **i)** the mode   **ii)** the range

   a) 8, 7, 9, 8, 7, 2, 7   **b)** 17, 23, 28, 19, 23, 18, 29

   c) 10, 1, 8, 7, 1, 9, 4, 6   **d)** 10, 11, 11, 10, 11, 10, 11, 11

   e) 46, 48, 40, 52, 59, 52, 56, 41, 57   **f)** 84, 46, 51, 55, 72, 46, 51, 57, 46, 83

   g) 98, 93, 91, 94, 81, 85, 94, 92, 91   **h)** 183, 123, 124, 105, 165, 127, 192, 104

5 This list shows the number of matches in ten different boxes:

64, 62, 69, 67, 70, 65, 61, 67, 63, 71

a) What is the modal number of matches in a box?

b) What is the range of the number of matches in a box?

6 The list shows the price of the same book in six different shops. Find the modal price.

£6.99, £7.49, £6.49, £7.49, £5.99, £4.99.

7 Phil records the number of people on the school bus each day one week. His results are:

35, 32, 36, 30, 32

a) What is the range of the number of people on the bus over the week?

b) What is the modal number of people on the bus?

8 Six cyclists record the total number of miles they cycle in a year.

Cyclist	Alf	Kareem	Rachael	Rob	Jo	Brad
Distance (miles)	646	834	912	896	646	1026

a) What is the range of their distances? **b)** What is their modal distance?

9 These are the maximum temperatures each day for a week in Norway:

−1 °C, −5 °C, −3 °C, −1 °C, 2 °C, −2 °C, −1 °C

a) What is the range of the temperatures? **b)** What is the modal temperature?

10 For each of these lists of numbers, find: **i)** the mode **ii)** the range

a) −6, −8, −3, −2, −2, −3, −3, −7, −6 **b)** 2.2, 2.3, 2.1, 2.5, 2.9, 2.7, 2.1, 2.3, 2.1, 2.8

c) 8, −7, −11, 7, −11, 12, −6, 5 **d)** −4.3, −5.9, 1.8, −2.7, −5.9, 2.7, −1.6, 3.7

11 Lindsey thinks of four numbers. The mode of the numbers is 7 and the range is 5. The smallest number is 4. What are the numbers that she thought of?

Median

The <u>median</u> is another type of average. It is the middle value in a list of numbers written in order.

Example 2   **Adam records the maximum temperature each day for a week. The results are:**
4 °C   3 °C   4 °C   5 °C   2 °C   1 °C   7 °C

1. First put the numbers in order.

    1   2   3   4   4   5   7

2. Then find the middle number in the list.

So the median is **4 °C**.

Example 3   **Gemma records the number of goals she scores at six netball matches: 6   14   8   11   9   12**

1. Put the numbers in order.

    6   8   9   11   12   14

2. The middle is between two numbers — 9 and 11.

median

3. The median is halfway between these two numbers. Add them together and divide by 2 to find the median.

(9 + 11) ÷ 2 = 20 ÷ 2 = 10

So the median is **10 goals**.

Exercise 2

1   What is the median of these numbers?

      5   7   8   9   9   11   12

2   **a)** Put this list of numbers in order:

      11   10   14   19   16   15   9

b) Write down the median.

3   Find the median for each of these lists of numbers:

   a) 13, 17, 14, 11, 19   **b)** 42, 39, 47, 45, 37

   c) 9, 35, 2, 18, 20   **d)** 5, 15, 7, 12, 8, 9, 6

   e) 1, 2, 1, 1, 3, 2, 2   **f)** 27, 33, 9, 17, 30, 22, 14

   g) 99, 76, 84, 91, 86, 72, 29   **h)** 106, 118, 105, 103, 115, 109, 102, 113, 100

4 a) Put this list of numbers in order: 8   12   11   6   5   6

b) Write down the middle two numbers from your list.

c) Find the median of the list of numbers.

5 Find the median for each of these lists of numbers:

a) 16, 14, 12, 11

b) 2, 6, 2, 9

c) 5, 7, 8, 4, 9, 1

d) 14, 18, 16, 21, 24, 15

e) 20, 90, 50, 40, 10, 70, 30, 80

f) 72, 68, 54, 49, 52, 70, 74, 48

6 These are the ages of seven players on a football team: 22, 20, 23, 19, 24, 22, 18
What is the median age?

7 The number of books sold in a book shop over six days are: 96, 108, 98, 84, 102, 96
What is the median number of books sold?

8 These are the ticket prices for six different train journeys: £32, £8, £16, £24, £28, £14
What is the median price of a ticket?

9 Find the median for each of these lists of numbers:

a) 5.7, 4.8, 6.3, 2.3, 4.9

b) 1.5, 7.8, 4.6, 4.2, 2.8, 4.9, 3.6, 5.2

10 a) Put these numbers in order, from lowest to highest: 2   5   −1   −7   −3

b) Find the median of the list of numbers.

11 Find the median for each of these lists of numbers:

a) −8, 1, −4, −2, −1

b) −8, −12, −7, −6, −3

c) −4, −1, −3, −5, 2, 5

12 Six students take a test. The marks, out of 15, that five students achieved
are 5, 12, 13, 8 and 10. Find a possible mark for the sixth student if:

a) the median mark is 11

b) the median mark is 9.5

Calculating the Mean

The <u>mean</u> is a type of <u>average</u>. You find the mean by adding all the numbers in a list together and then dividing by how many numbers there are.

> **Example 4** **Tom records how many goals he scores each month for six months. His results are: 6   9   7   9   12   8**
>
> **Work out the mean number of goals Tom scores.**
>
> 1. First add the numbers together. $6 + 9 + 7 + 9 + 12 + 8 = 51$
>
> 2. There are 6 numbers in the list, so divide by 6. $51 \div 6 = \textbf{8.5 goals}$
>
> 3. Tom can't actually score 8.5 goals — often the mean you calculate won't be a number in the list.

Exercise 3

1   **a)** Add together the numbers in this list: 5   4   7   3   6

   b) Find the mean of the five numbers.

2   Find the mean for each of these lists of numbers:

   a) 8, 5, 9, 2   **b)** 5, 3, 7, 1

   c) 8, 7, 11, 6   **d)** 14, 9, 13, 12

   e) 15, 11, 21, 13   **f)** 12, 10, 14, 8, 16

   g) 16, 19, 21, 13, 21   **h)** 20, 24, 23, 22, 27, 28

   i) 20, 60, 30, 70, 80, 35, 55   **j)** 23, 27, 27, 18, 24, 25, 22, 18

3   Find the mean for each of these lists of numbers:

   a) 6, 7, 5, 8   **b)** 9, 12, 7, 10

   c) 8, 9, 7, 8, 7   **d)** 20, 24, 23, 19, 27

   e) 32, 34, 28, 31, 24   **f)** 64, 61, 65, 57, 47, 52, 56, 50

   g) 3, 4, 3, 4, 3, 4, 5, 3, 3, 4   **h)** 54, 64, 45, 54, 57, 59, 62, 63, 61, 58

4   The price of a bottle of lemonade in three different shops is 86p, 99p and 79p.
What is the mean price?

5   These are the ages of a group of friends: 19, 26, 24, 22, 29
What is the mean age?

6   Sara buys six potatoes. They weigh: 125 g, 147 g, 198 g, 134 g, 142 g and 154 g.
What is the mean weight?

7   These are the daily temperatures of a swimming pool over a week:

28 °C, 30 °C, 29 °C, 31 °C, 28 °C, 30 °C, 30 °C

What is the mean daily temperature? Round your answer to the nearest whole number.

8   Jasmine is knitting a scarf. She writes down the length of scarf that she knits
each day: 15 cm, 19 cm, 28 cm, 21 cm, 17 cm

a) What is the mean length of knitting she does each day?

b) She knits another 14 cm of the scarf the next day.
What is the new mean length of scarf she knits?

9   Find the mean for each of these lists of numbers:

a) −3, −5, −7, −1   **b)** −8, −10, −7, −11   **c)** 3, 4, −12, −7

d) 8.4, 7.6, 5.8, 6.8   **e)** 11.5, 12.3, 10.4, 14.2   **f)** 22.1, 24.4, 27.3, 20.6

10 Work out the mean of these temperatures: −1.2 °C, −3.4 °C, 2.8 °C, −4.5 °C, 1.3 °C

> ## Investigate — Working Backwards from the Mean
>
> *The mean of a list of five numbers is 6.*
>
> **a)** List some combinations of values for these 5 numbers.
>
> **b)** How many possible combinations do you think there are?
> What else would you need to know in order to be able to
> say for sure what the five numbers are?

Outliers

An <u>outlier</u> is a value that is a lot higher or lower than the other values in a set of data.

Outliers can affect the mean and range more than the mode and median. So, before you do any calculations with your data, it's a good idea to check for outliers.

> **Example 5** **These are the heights of everyone in a swimming class:**
>
>   109 cm   107 cm   175 cm   112 cm   113 cm   108 cm   111 cm   109 cm
>
> **a) Find the outlier in the data.**
>
> | Look for a number that is much higher or lower than the others. | **175 cm** is a lot higher than the rest of the data — it'll be the teacher's height. |
>
> **b) Find the range, median and mean of the heights, with and without the outlier.**
>
> 1. For the range, subtract the lowest value from the highest value.
>
>   With outlier: 175 – 107 = **68 cm**
>   Without outlier: 113 – 107 = **6 cm**
>
> 2. For the median, put the values in order, and find the middle value.
>
>   Values in order:
>   107, 108, 109, 109, 111, 112, 113, 175
>
>   Middle value with outlier
>   = (111 + 109) ÷ 2 = **110 cm**
>   Middle value without outlier = **109 cm**
>
> 3. For the mean, add up all of the values and divide by the number of values.
>
>   With outlier = 944 ÷ 8 = **118 cm**
>   Without outlier = 769 ÷ 7 = **110 cm**

Exercise 4

1 Find the outlier in this set of data: 3, 6, 1, 2, 4, 5, 3, 18, 4, 5, 2, 6

2 For the data below, find: **i)** the median   **ii)** the range

   a) without the outlier,   **b)** with the outlier.

            32   38   29   26   33   12   30   28   25

3 The following list is a record of the miles that some people cycled over a week:
      120 miles   135 miles   256 miles   111 miles   129 miles   118 miles   126 miles

   Find the mean of the data: **a)** with the outlier,   **b)** without the outlier.

   Round each answer to the nearest whole number.

18.5 Averages and Range from Tables

Mode and Range

Frequency tables are a better way to record data than lists if you've got a lot of data.

For example, 30 people were asked to rate their local park on a scale of 1 to 5.
Here are their answers in a list:

3 2 2 3 1 4 5 1 1 2 5 5 1 3 3
4 2 2 2 4 1 1 1 4 3 1 2 1 1 3

It's hard to make sense of this data at a glance.
Here are their answers in a frequency table:

Score	1	2	3	4	5
Frequency	10	7	6	4	3

You can now see straight away that most people gave the park a low score.

 Example 1 The frequency table shows the number of cars owned by a group of people.

Number of cars	0	1	2	3
Frequency	6	10	2	1

a) Find the modal number of cars.
This is the number with the highest frequency.

Modal number of cars owned = **1 car**

b) What is the range of the number of cars owned?

Range = largest value – smallest value
= 3 – 0 = **3 cars**

Exercise 1

1 This frequency table shows the number of siblings the students in a class have.

Number of siblings	0	1	2	3	4
Frequency	5	11	4	1	1

What is the modal number of siblings?

2 This frequency table shows the number of biscuits the people in a company eat one day:

Number of biscuits	2	3	4	5	6	7
Frequency	4	7	3	2	1	1

a) What was the modal number of biscuits eaten that day?

b) Work out the range of the data.

Median

To find the <u>median</u>, imagine all of the data in the table written out in order. The median will be halfway through the list of data.

Example 2	The frequency table shows the number of books read in a month by a group of people.

What is the median number of books read?

Number of books	0	1	2	3
Frequency	2	9	5	4

1. The frequencies tell you that the list of all the individual data values would be:
   0, 0, 1, 1, 1, 1, 1, 1, 1, 1, 1, 2, 2, 2, 2, 2, 3, 3, 3, 3

2. There are 20 values, so the median is halfway between the 10th and the 11th values. These are both 1.

   $$\text{Median} = \frac{1 + 1}{2} = \textbf{1 book}$$

3. To find the median position in the table, add the frequencies across the table.

   The 11th position (2 + 9) is at the end of the '1' group. So the median position (between the 10th and 11th) is also in the '1' group.

Exercise 2

1 This frequency table shows the number of pairs of trainers owned by 21 of Phil's friends:

Number of pairs of trainers	1	2	3	4
Frequency	5	11	4	1

a) What is the position of the median friend?

b) Work out the number of pairs of trainers the median friend owns.

2 Kamal recorded the temperature every day on his holiday:

Temperature (°C)	20	21	22	23	24	25
Frequency	2	3	3	4	2	1

What was the median temperature on Kamal's holiday?

3 Gary asked the members of a swimming team how many times they train each week. Work out the median of the data from this frequency table:

Number of times	1	2	3	4	5	6	7
Frequency	1	3	6	4	2	1	1

Mean

You can use frequency tables to find the <u>mean</u> of a set of data, but you have to do a bit of extra calculation first.

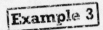 **Example 3**

This is a frequency table showing the number of people in each house on a street.

Find the mean number of people in each house.

People	Frequency
1	7
2	12
3	13
4	8

1. Add an extra row and an extra column to the table.

2. In the extra column, multiply the number of people by the frequency.

3. In the extra row, add up all the numbers in the frequency column to find the **total number of houses**...

People	Freq.	People × Freq.
1	7	1 × 7 = 7
2	12	2 × 12 = 24
3	13	3 × 13 = 39
4	8	4 × 8 = 32
Total	40	102

4. ...and add up all the numbers in the 'People × Frequency' column to find the **total number of people**.

5. Divide the total number of people by the total number of houses to find the mean.

$$\text{Mean} = \frac{\text{Total number of people}}{\text{Total number of houses}}$$

$$= 102 \div 40 = \textbf{2.55 people}$$

Exercise 3

1   This table shows the number of words remembered correctly in a memory test.

Words remembered	Frequency	Words × Frequency
7	2	7 × 2 = 14
8	3	8 × 3 = 24
9	6	9 × 6 = ...
10	2	
11	2	
12	1	
Total		

a) Copy and complete the table.

b) Use the table to find the mean number of words remembered.
   Give your answer to the nearest whole number.

2 This table shows the number of glasses of lemonade drunk by people at a party.

a) Copy the table and add a 'Glasses × Frequency' column and a 'Total' row.

b) Complete the table by filling in the column and row you've added.

Glasses	Frequency
1	3
2	7
3	3
4	1

c) Use your table to find the mean number of glasses of lemonade drunk by the people at the party. Give your answer to the nearest whole number.

3 Florence is taking part in a bird-spotting survey. She records the number of blackbirds she sees each day, and puts the results into a frequency table.

Use the table to find the mean number of blackbirds seen by Florence each day.
Give your answer to the nearest whole number.

No. of blackbirds seen each day	Frequency
0	7
1	6
2	4
3	5
4	3

4 A car salesroom advertises on the local radio station. The table shows the number of cars sold for the 20 days before and after the advert was played.

a) Find the mean number of cars sold per day **before** the advert.

b) Find the mean number of cars sold per day **after** the advert.

No. of cars sold per day	Frequency before advert	Frequency after advert
0	6	3
1	7	6
2	4	6
3	2	3
4	1	2

c) Do you think the advert was successful? Explain your answer.

Investigate — Grouped Frequency Tables

Frequency tables can show data grouped together.

The marks in a class maths test were:
34, 49 ,40, 29, 7, 19, 46, 24, 34, 42, 37, 18, 41, 39, 43

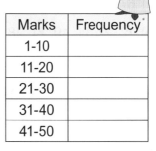

a) Copy the grouped frequency table, and fill it in to show the frequencies of the maths test scores.

b) What might you do to find the mean, median, mode and range from the table?

c) Will the averages and range be more or less reliable from the table than from the list? Explain why.

Marks	Frequency
1-10	
11-20	
21-30	
31-40	
41-50	

18.6 Comparing Distributions

Stem and Leaf Diagrams

Stem and leaf diagrams are similar to bar charts,
but the bars are made out of the actual data.
A stem and leaf diagram always needs a key to explain how to read it.

Example 1   **These are the ages of some people at a concert:**
23, 49, 58, 59, 44, 30, 25, 44, 56, 20, 51, 38, 49, 47
Put this data into a stem and leaf diagram.

1. You can group the ages according to their first digit.
   Write down the 'stems' — the first digit of the ages.

   ```
   2 |
   3 |
   4 |
   5 |
   ```

2. Next make a 'leaf' for each data value by
   adding the second digit to the correct stem.
   So the first '3' next to the '2' stem represents 23.

   ```
   2 | 3 5 0
   3 | 0 8
   4 | 9 4 4 9 7
   5 | 8 9 6 1
   ```

3. Order the leaves in each row from smallest to largest.

   ```
   2 | 0 3 5
   3 | 0 8
   4 | 4 4 7 9 9
   5 | 1 6 8 9
   ```

4. Include a key to explain what one
   stem and leaf pair represents.

   ```
   2 | 0 means 20
   ```

Exercise 1

1   Use the following sets of data to make ordered stem and leaf diagrams, including keys.

a) 67, 31, 53, 49, 62, 42, 39, 40, 52, 59, 32, 66

b) 12, 27, 11, 49, 21, 38, 27, 48, 24, 29, 14, 14

c) 92, 91, 86, 70, 96, 84, 71, 69, 86, 87, 94, 89

d) 73, 56, 69, 49, 53, 62, 70, 82, 73, 63, 74, 81

e) 2.1, 3.8, 2.4, 1.5, 3.2, 0.7, 2.5, 3.6, 3.1, 0.4, 2.6, 3.5

f) 7.1, 6.2, 9.9, 8.4, 7.7, 8.5, 7.3, 6.5, 5.4, 8.6, 7.8, 8.0

2 Jeremy counts the number of vehicles that
drive past his house every day for 22 days.
Use the data to make an ordered stem and leaf diagram.

| 45 | 43 | 55 | 37 | 58 | 29 | 20 | 31 | 47 | 43 | 61 |
| 56 | 61 | 33 | 48 | 62 | 54 | 51 | 53 | 48 | 32 | 47 |

3 The times taken for 16 children to run a race are recorded in seconds.

| 11.4 | 15.6 | 12.9 | 14.3 | 12.6 | 11.5 | 10.8 | 14.9 |
| 15.4 | 11.8 | 12.0 | 15.7 | 13.7 | 13.8 | 12.8 | 14.2 |

a) Use the data to make an ordered stem and leaf diagram.

b) The teacher says, "over half the children beat last year's record of 12 seconds".
   Is he correct? Explain your answer.

Example 2	**This stem and leaf diagram shows the**	4	1 6 8
	number of cupcakes sold by a bakery	5	2 4 4 8 9
	each day for 21 days. Use it to find:	6	1 2 5 7 7 7 9 9
		7	0 0 4 5 6

| 4 | 1 means 41 cupcakes |

a) the mode

1. Look for the number that is repeated
   most often in one of the rows.
   Here there are three 7's in the third row.   Mode = 6|7

2. Use the key to work out what this represents.   **= 67 cupcakes**

b) the median

1. Work out the position of the median.
   There are 21 values, so...   Median = 11th value

2. Count along the leaves to find the 11th value,   Median = 6|5
   starting with the first row.   **= 65 cupcakes**

c) the range

Find the range by subtracting the   Range = 76 – 41
smallest value from the largest.   **= 35 cupcakes**

Exercise 2

1 For each of these stem and leaf diagrams, find:
    i) the mode of the data   **ii)** the median of the data   **iii)** the range of the data

a)
```
4 | 3 7
5 | 2 5 6
6 | 0 0 1 4 5 5 9
7 | 2 2 3 4 6 6 6 7 9
```
| 4 | 3 means 43 |

b)
```
10 | 1 3 3 3 4 5 7 9
11 | 2 2 6 6 6
12 | 5 6 7 7 8
13 | 5
```
| 10 | 1 means 101 |

c)
```
0 | 1 7 8
1 | 3 4 5 5 9
2 | 0 2 4 5 7 7 8 9
3 | 1 1 1 4 6 6 9
```
| 0 | 1 means 0.1 |

2 The stem and leaf diagram shows the height jumped, in centimetres, by 23 children in a high-jump competition.

a) Find the mode of the data.

b) Find the median of the data.

c) Find the range of the data.

```
 7 | 8 8 9
 8 | 1 1 2 6 6
 9 | 5 5 5 6 7 8 9 9 9
10 | 2 3 5 7 7 9
```
| 7 | 8 means 78 cm |

3 The data listed is the rainfall, in millimetres, each day in Barrowton over 20 days.

26	41	8	32	49	52	48	42	14	15
25	26	31	32	42	41	32	22	43	46

a) Use the data to draw an ordered stem and leaf diagram.

b) Find the mode of the data.

c) Find the median of the data.

d) Find the range of the data.

4 The times taken for 20 children to complete an obstacle course are recorded in seconds.

10.9	11.9	12.8	13.9	13.2	12.3	12.5	11.4	13.8	15.5
14.7	10.5	11.3	15.5	12.9	11.8	16.3	13.7	12.4	13.3

a) Use the data to draw an ordered stem and leaf diagram.

b) For the data, find: **i)** the mode   **ii)** the median   **iii)** the range

c) Do you think the mode or the median represents the data better? Explain your answer.

Back-to-back stem and leaf diagrams can be used to compare
two sets of data, plotted as two sets of leaves with a shared stem.
One set of data is plotted, as usual, on the right, with the other
plotted "backwards" on the left.

> **Example 3** Two classes of 14 pupils, Class A and Class B, both
> took the same test. The pupils' results were recorded.
>
> **Class A: 18, 33, 29, 31, 39, 28, 22, 41, 37, 11, 12, 31, 19, 42**
> **Class B: 43, 42, 29, 22, 38, 41, 38, 12, 39, 32, 50, 48, 42, 44**

**a) Use the data to make an ordered
back-to-back stem and leaf diagram.**

1. Identify the 'stems' for both sets of data
and write them down as one stem.

1
2
3
4
5

2. Build the 'leaves' for both sets of data off
the same stem. Put one set of data on
the right-hand side of the stem, and the
other set on the left-hand side.

Class A		Class B
9 2 1 8	1	2
2 8 9	2	9 2
1 7 9 1 3	3	8 8 9 2
2 1	4	3 2 1 8 2 4
	5	0

3. Order the 'leaves' so the smallest values
are closest to the stem.
Remember to add a key.

Class A		Class B
9 8 2 1	1	2
9 8 2	2	2 9
9 7 3 1 1	3	2 8 8 9
2 1	4	1 2 2 3 4 8
	5	0

> 8 | 1 for Class A means 18
> 1 | 2 for Class B means 12

**b) Describe the shape of the diagram.
What conclusions can you draw from this?**

Look at the shapes of the two sides of the diagram
and describe how they're different.

Class A had more scores in the first three rows,
while Class B had more scores in the last 2 rows.
Class B also had the highest score, and Class A had the lowest score.
This means that Class B generally did better in the test than Class A.

Exercise 3

1 Use the following data to complete the back-to-back stem and leaf diagram.
Give your answer as an ordered diagram with a key.

Girls: 19, 24, 8, 20, 23, 14, 29, 38, 3, 33, 23, 22, 17, 23, 27

Boys: 48, 45, 47, 35, 28, 49, 21, 37, 41, 44, 38, 40, 46, 27, 31

Girls		Boys
8	0	
4 9	1	
3 0 4	2	8
	3	5
	4	8 5 7

2 Robert and Edward are playing a game.
They play 20 rounds and record the number
of points they score in each round.
They present their scores in an ordered
back-to-back stem and leaf diagram.
Describe the shape of the diagram.
What conclusions can you draw from this?

Robert		Edward
8 9 9 5	0	
6 3	1	2 4 6 8 8
8 8 8 7 6	2	7 8 8 9 9 9
9 4 2 1	3	5 5 7 7 8 8 9 9
8 7 3 2 0	4	0

5 | 0	for Robert means 5
1 | 2	for Edward means 12

3 The following data shows the amounts that the pupils in two classes
spend in their school tuck shop on one day.

Class 3: 20p, 37p, 45p, 10p, 35p, 22p, 17p, 38p, 12p, 23p, 19p, 39p, 26p, 28p, 11p

Class 4: 40p, 51p, 37p, 18p, 38p, 49p, 35p, 39p, 55p, 5p, 44p, 56p, 47p, 32p, 21p

a) Use the data to make an ordered back-to-back stem and leaf diagram with a key.

b) Describe the shape of the diagram. What conclusions can you draw from this?

4 The temperature in two towns, Coleighton and Budford, is
measured every day for 2 weeks. The data is recorded in °C.

Coleighton: 14.7, 15.3, 14.9, 12.8, 13.2, 14.6, 15.8, 16.3, 15.2, 14.9, 16.8, 16.9, 16.2, 15.8

Budford: 11.2, 13.6, 11.7, 11.4, 13.2, 17.0, 11.8, 12.3, 13.7, 12.1, 11.5, 14.2, 13.2, 12.0

a) Use the data to make an ordered back-to-back stem and leaf diagram with a key.

b) Find the median and range of temperatures for each town.

c) Compare the temperatures of each town.

Comparing Distributions

Averages, such as the mean, median and mode, can be used to compare sets of data.

The range can be used to compare the spread of two or more sets of data.

A large range means that there is a larger variation of values in a data set.
It can sometimes indicate an outlier.

Example 4 | **Use the following information to draw some conclusions about the heights of the girls and boys in Class 1.**

The boys in Class 1 have: a mean height of 175.3 cm.
a median height of 177 cm.
a range of 33 cm.

The girls in Class 1 have: a mean height of 155.1 cm.
a median height of 147 cm.
a range of 53 cm.

1. Compare the mean heights.

The mean height for the boys is larger than the mean height for the girls.
This means that, in general, the **boys are taller than the girls**.

2. Compare the median heights.

The median height for the boys is larger than the median height for the girls.
This again suggests that the **boys are taller than the girls**.

3. Compare the range of heights.

The range of boys' heights is smaller than the range of girls' heights.
This means that the **boys' heights are more consistent**.
The girls' range is very large, which suggests that there is
an **outlier** in the data. The outlier is probably larger than the rest
of the data as it makes the mean height greater than the median height.

Exercise 4

1 The median shoe size of boys in a class is 7, but for the girls the median is 5.
What does this tell you about the boys' shoe sizes compared with the girls'?

2 The temperature in Chillton and Toaston are measured every day for one month.
The mean temperature in Chillton is 17 °C and the mean temperature in Toaston is 29 °C.
What conclusion can you draw from the mean values?

3 Two teams took part in a table tennis competition. They recorded how many points each team member scored. The range of points for the red team is 16 points. The range of points for the blue team is 3 points. What conclusion can you draw from this?

4 Alice weighs 20 dogs and 20 cats.
The mean weight for the dogs is 32 kg and the mean weight for the cats is 4 kg.
The range in weights for the dogs is 45 kg and the range in weight for the cats is 0.5 kg.
State **two** conclusions that you can draw from this information.

5 A ferry company is comparing the number of passengers carried per day on two of its routes. Route 1 carries a median of 36 passengers per day with a range of 12.
Route 2 carries a median of 56 passengers with a range of 51.
State **two** conclusions that you can draw from this information.

6 Two classes sit an exam. Their marks are recorded as a percentage.
Class X had a mean score of 80%, a median score of 76% and a range of 12%.
Class Y had a mean score of 72%, a median score of 74% and a range of 14%.
State **two** conclusions that you can draw from this information.

7 An audience watched two films and gave each film a score between 1 and 100.
Film 1 had a mean score of 75, a median score of 76 and a range of 22.
Film 2 had a mean score of 49, a median score of 63 and a range of 51.
State **three** conclusions that you can draw from this information.

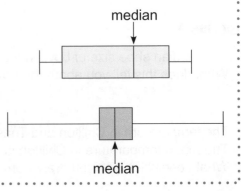

Investigate — Comparing Spreads

'Box plots' are a way of showing where the middle 50% of values lie in a data set. The longer the 'box', the more spread out these values are. The boxes have 'whiskers' that extend to the lowest and highest values of the data set.

Look at these two box plots:

a) What real life data could they represent?

b) What conclusions could you draw from the box plots if they represented:

  i) the ages of two groups of people?

  ii) the test scores of two classes?

median

median

Glossary

2D Shapes

Flat shapes with 2 dimensions.

3D Shapes

Solid shapes with length, width and height.

Addition

Finding the sum when two or more numbers are combined.

Alternate Angles

A pair of equal angles found in a 'Z' shape within two parallel lines.

Angle Bisector

A straight line that cuts an angle exactly in half.

Approximation

A number that is not exact because it has been rounded or estimated.

Area

The space inside a 2D shape.

Average

A measure of the most typical value in a set of data. Mean, median and mode are types of average.

Back-to-back Stem and Leaf Diagram

A stem and leaf diagram where two data sets are plotted on the same 'stem'.

Bar Chart

A chart where the height of the bars shows the frequency of each category.

Bar-line Chart

A chart where the height of the lines shows the frequency of each category.

Base

In a power, this is the number or letter which is multiplied by itself.

Biased

Where something, e.g. a dice or a spinner, is more likely to land on one or more of its sides than others.

BODMAS

An acronym to describe the order that operations should be done in a calculation containing multiple operations.

Brackets

Symbols, such as ( ), [ ] or { }, used to group things together.

Calculator

A device used to do mathematical operations.

Cancelling Down

Dividing every number in a fraction or ratio by the same number to reduce it to a simpler form.

Centre of Enlargement

The point where an enlargement is measured from.

Centre of Rotation

The point an object turns about in a rotation.

Certain

Will definitely happen.

Circle

A round 2D shape with a constant distance between the centre and the edge, known as the radius.

Circumference

The distance around the outside of a circle (its perimeter).

Coefficient

A number placed before a variable in an expression.

Common Denominator

Fractions have a common denominator when their denominators are the same.

Common Factor

A number that divides exactly into two or more different numbers.

Common Multiple

A number that appears in the times table of two or more different numbers.

Composite Shape

A shape made up of two or more simple shapes.

Cone

A 3D shape made from a circular base and a pointed curved surface.

Congruent

The same shape and size. Congruent shapes have all sides and angles the same.

Construction

A drawing of a line, angle or shape using a ruler, protractor and compass.

Conversion Factor

The number you multiply or divide by to convert between different units.

Coordinates

A pair of numbers (x, y) that describe the position of a point on a grid or set of axes, e.g. (2, 3).

Correlation

The relationship between two variables, usually shown by the points on a scatter graph. Correlation can be either positive or negative.

Corresponding Angles

A pair of equal angles found in matching corners where a line crosses two parallel lines.

Cross-Section

The shape you get when you cut through a 3D shape, parallel to the end surface.

Cube (power)

A number or letter raised to the power of 3.

Cube (shape)

A 3D shape with 6 identical square faces.

Cube Root

The inverse of raising a number to the power of 3.

Cuboid

A 3D shape with 3 pairs of matching rectangular faces.

Cylinder

A 3D shape with 2 circular faces joined by a curved surface.

Decimal

A number where tenths, hundredths and thousandths, etc. are written after a decimal point.

Decimal Place

The position of a digit to the right of the decimal point.

Decimal Point

A dot placed to the right of the units column in a decimal number.

Decrease

If something decreases, it gets smaller.

Denominator

The bottom number of a fraction.

Diameter

The length across a circle, going through the centre.

Direct Proportion

When the ratio between two things stays the same. If you increase one thing, the other increases at the same rate.

Distance

How far an object has travelled.

Division

The act of sharing a number into equal parts.

Dual Bar Chart

A type of bar chart where two sets of data are plotted for each category.

Edge

Where two faces meet in a 3D shape.

Element

A single value or item in a set.

Enlargement

Changing an object's size but keeping the shape the same.

Equation

An algebraic statement made up of two expressions separated by an equals sign. E.g. $y = 2x + 3$.

Equilateral Triangle

A triangle with three equal sides and three equal angles of 60°.

Estimate

A less accurate value of a number, often the solution to a calculation where rounded numbers have been used instead of the actual values.

Estimating

Roughly calculating the answer or outcome of something. You can estimate probabilities using the results of an experiment or what you know has already happened.

Even Chance

When something is just as likely to happen as not happen. The probability is $\frac{1}{2}$.

Event

A result that matches one or more possible outcomes of a trial. E.g. rolling an even number on a dice.

Expand

Multiply out brackets to remove them from an expression.

Expected Frequency

How many times you'd expect an event to happen during a certain number of trials.

Experimental Probability

An estimate of how likely something is to happen based on the results of an experiment. It's also called a relative frequency.

Expression

A collection of terms made up of numbers and letters, separated by + or − signs.

F

Face

A surface of a 3D shape.

Factor

A number that divides exactly into another number.

Factorise

Rewrite an expression by putting in brackets with a factor on the outside.

Fair

Where something, e.g. a dice or a spinner, is equally likely to land on all of its sides.

Formula

A rule for working something out, often written using an algebraic expression.

Fraction

A part of a whole, written as one number on top of another.

Frequency

How many items are in a category.

Frequency Table

A table showing how many times each value in a set of data occurs.

G

Gradient

The steepness of a line — a measure of how much it slopes.

H

Highest Common Factor (HCF)

The highest number that can be divided exactly into a set of numbers.

Horizontal

A flat line with a gradient of zero.

Hour

A unit of time. There are 60 minutes in 1 hour, and 24 hours in a day.

Hypotenuse

The longest side of a right-angled triangle, opposite the right angle.

I

Imperial Units

A standard set of (non-metric) units for measuring, including inches, feet, yards, ounces, pounds, stones, pints and gallons.

Impossible

Has no chance of happening.

Improper Fraction

A fraction where the numerator is greater than the denominator. These are also called top-heavy fractions.

Increase

If something increases, it gets larger.

Interior Angle

An angle inside a polygon.

Intersecting Lines

Lines that cross at a point.

Intersection

The overlap on a Venn diagram, which contains elements that belong to more than one set.

Inverse

The opposite operation. E.g. subtraction is the inverse of addition.

Isosceles Triangle

A triangle with two equal sides and two equal angles.

K

Key

An instruction for reading a diagram or graph.

Kite

A quadrilateral with two pairs of equal sides and one pair of equal angles.

L

Like Terms

Terms that contain the same letters (raised to the same powers).

Line of Best Fit

A line drawn on a scatter graph which passes as close to as many of the plotted points as possible, and shows the correlation of the variables.

Line of Symmetry

A mirror line where you can fold a shape so that both halves match up exactly.

Line Segment

A straight line between two points.

Lowest Common Multiple (LCM)

The smallest number that's in the times table of a group of numbers.

Map

An accurate drawing showing large distances on a smaller scale.

Mean

The average of a set of data, found by adding up all of the values and dividing by the number of values.

Median

The middle value when you put a set of data in size order.

Metric Units

A standard set of units for measuring, including mm, cm, m, km, g, kg, tonnes, ml and litres.

Minute

A unit of time. There are 60 seconds in 1 minute, and 60 minutes in 1 hour.

Mirror Line

The line that a shape or object is reflected in, or a line of symmetry through a shape.

Mixed Number

A number made up of a whole number part and a fraction part.

Mode (or Modal Value)

The most common value in a set of data.

Modelling

Using an equation or a graph to represent a real-life situation.

Multiple

A value in a number's times table.

Multiplication

The act of multiplying numbers together.

Multiplier

Used to describe the decimal equivalent of a percentage, which you multiply a value by to find a percentage of it.

Negative

Any number less than zero.

Negative Correlation

As one variable plotted on a scatter graph increases, the other decreases.

No Correlation

The points plotted on a scatter graph are spread out and show no relation.

Numerator

The top number of a fraction.

Operation

Something you do to one or more numbers, such as add, subtract, multiply or divide.

Order of Rotational Symmetry

The number of positions, in one full turn, you can rotate a shape into so that it looks the same.

Origin

The point with coordinates (0, 0) on a graph. It's where the axes cross.

Outcome

A possible result of a probability trial.

Outlier

A value in a set of data that is much higher or much lower than the rest of the data.

Parallel Lines

Lines that are always the same distance apart and never meet.

Parallelogram

A quadrilateral with two pairs of equal sides (opposite sides are equal and parallel) and two pairs of equal angles.

Percentage

'Per cent' means 'out of 100'. Percentage shows an amount as a number out of 100.

Percentage Change

The amount a value increases or decreases by, given as a percentage of the original value.

Perimeter

The total distance around the outside of a shape.

Perpendicular Lines

Two lines which cross at right angles.

Perpendicular Bisector

A straight line that cuts another line in half and is at right angles to it.

Pi

The number 3.14159265..., written using the Greek letter π.

Pictogram

A type of chart where frequency is represented by symbols or pictures.

Pie Chart

A chart where the angles of each sector are proportional to the frequency of each category.

Polygon

An enclosed shape whose sides are all straight.

Positive

Any number greater than zero.

Positive Correlation

As one variable plotted on a scatter graph increases, so does the other.

Power

A way of showing that a number or letter (the base) is being multiplied by itself a certain number of times. The power tells you how many of the base to multiply together.

Power of 10

10 raised to the power of any whole number.

Prime Factor

A factor of a number that is a prime number.

Prime Number

A number that has no factors except itself and 1.

Prism

A 3D shape which is the same shape and size all the way through.

Probability

How likely it is that something will happen.

Probability Scale

A scale from 0 to 1 that can be used to show how likely it is that something will happen.

Product

The result when two things are multiplied together.

Proportion

How two numbers relate to each other.

Pythagoras' Theorem

A formula linking the lengths of the sides of a right-angled triangle. Pythagoras' theorem states that $h^2 = a^2 + b^2$, where h is the hypotenuse and a and b are the shorter sides.

Quadrant

A quarter of a grid.

Quadratic Equation

An equation which contains an x^2 term, but no higher powers of x.

Quadrilateral

A four-sided shape.

Radius

The distance from the centre to the edge of a circle.

Range

The difference between the highest value and the lowest value in a set of data.

Ratio

The amount of one thing compared to another, written e.g. $2:1$.

Rearrange

To make a different letter or number the subject of a formula.

Reciprocal

You can find the reciprocal of a fraction by swapping the places of the numerator and denominator.

Rectangle

A quadrilateral with two pairs of equal sides and four right angles (90°).

Reflection

A transformation where a shape is flipped in a mirror line. OR A mirror image of another shape, with every point the same distance from the mirror line as in the original shape.

Regular Polygon

A polygon with all sides of equal length and angles that are all equal.

Regular Tetrahedron

A 3D shape whose 4 faces are identical equilateral triangles.

Relative Frequency

Another term for an experimental probability. It's an estimate of how likely something is to happen based on the results of an experiment.

Rhombus

A quadrilateral with four equal sides (opposite sides are parallel) and two pairs of equal angles.

Right Angle

An angle of 90°.

Right-angled Triangle

A triangle with one angle of 90°.

Root

The inverse of a power.

Rotation

Turning an object, either clockwise or anticlockwise, through a given angle at a given point.

Rounding

Approximating a number to one which is easier to work with (e.g. has fewer decimal places or is a multiple of 10, 100 etc.)

S

Sample Space Diagram

A table showing all the possible outcomes from a combination of two or more trials.

Scale

The numbers on a map or plan that show how actual distances will be represented on the map.

Scale Factor

The amount each length increases by in an enlargement.

Scalene Triangle

A triangle in which all three sides and all three angles are different.

Scatter Graph

A graph showing two things plotted against each other. The plotted points are never joined with a line, but the graph may show a line of best fit.

Second

A unit of time. There are 60 seconds in 1 minute.

Sector

A slice of a pie chart.

Sequence

A pattern of numbers or shapes that follow a certain rule.

Set

A collection of items or numbers, shown using curly brackets {}.

Significant Figures

The first non-zero digits in a number.

Similar

When two objects have the same shape but different sizes.

Simple Interest

A type of interest where the same percentage of the original amount is added on at regular intervals.

Simplify

Make something simpler, e.g. by dividing by common factors or collecting like terms.

Speed

How fast an object is travelling.

Sphere

A round 3D shape which looks like a snooker ball.

Square (shape)

A quadrilateral with four equal sides and four right angles (90°).

Square (power)

A number or letter raised to the power of 2.

Square-based Pyramid

A 3D shape which has a square base and 4 triangular faces meeting at a point.

Square Root

The inverse of raising a number to the power of 2.

Standard Form

A method of writing numbers as multiples of powers of ten — it's useful for very large or very small numbers.

Steepness

A measure of the slope of a line — also called the gradient. A steeper line has a bigger slope.

Stem and Leaf Diagram

A diagram that groups together values in a set of data that start with the same number.

Straight Line Graph

A graph where all the points lie on a straight line. The coordinates fit equations of the form $y = mx + c$.

Subject

The letter on its own on the left-hand side of a formula.

Subtraction

Finding the difference between two numbers.

Symmetry

A shape has (line) symmetry if you can draw on a mirror line where one side of the shape is the exact reflection of the other.

T

Term (of an expression)

Each of the 'bits' in an expression, separated by plus or minus signs is called a term. A term can be numbers, letters or both.

Term (of a sequence)

A number or pattern in a sequence.

Time

How long something takes.

Times Table

Counting up in steps of a number.

Transformation

Changing the size, orientation or position of an object.

Translation

Changing the position of an object by sliding it horizontally and vertically.

Trapezium

A quadrilateral with one pair of parallel sides.

Trial

An action in a probability experiment that will end in an outcome — for example, tossing a coin or picking out a card.

Triangle

A three-sided shape.

Triangular Prism

A 3D shape which has 2 triangular faces and 3 rectangular faces.

Universal Set

The group of things from which the elements in a set are selected.

Variable

An unknown quantity, usually shown by a letter. Variables can take different values.

Vector

Mathematical notation for describing how far a shape moves left or right and up or down.

Venn Diagram

A way of displaying sets, using a circle to represent each set.

Vertex (Vertices)

A corner of a shape.

Vertical

A line going straight up and down.

Vertically Opposite Angles

Opposite angles around the point where two lines intersect. Vertically opposite angles are equal.

Volume

The amount of space that a 3D shape takes up.

x-axis

The horizontal axis of a graph.

y-axis

The vertical axis of a graph.

y-intercept

The point at which a graph crosses the y-axis.

Index

T

U

V

X

Y

M2NN31